Mind and Philosophers

Mind and Philosophers

by John Lachs

VANDERBILT UNIVERSITY PRESS
Nashville, Tennessee
1987

Published in 1987 by Vanderbilt University Press
Printed in the United States of America

The author and publisher make grateful acknowledgment to the editors of the following periodicals for permission to reprint those articles in this collection that first appeared in their publications:

"Angel, Animal, Machine: Models for Man" first appeared in *The Southern Journal of Philosophy* (Vol. V, No. 4, 1967, pp. 221-27).
"The Impotent Mind" first appeared in *The Review of Metaphysics* (Vol. XVII, 1963, pp. 187-99).
"Epiphenomenalism and the Notion of Cause" first appeared in *The Journal of Philosophy* (Vol. LX, 1963, pp. 141-46).
"Meaning and the Impotence Hypothesis" first appeared in *The Review of Metaphysics* (Vol. XXXII, 1979, pp. 515-29).
"Two Concepts of God" first appeared in *The Harvard Theological Review*. (Vol. LIX, 1966, pp.227-40). Copyright © 1966 by the President and Fellows of Harvard College. Reprinted by permission.
"Santayana's Philosophy of Mind" first appeared in *The Monist* (Vol. XLVIII, 1964, pp. 419-40). Copyright © 1964, THE MONIST, La Salle, Illinois 61301.
"The Proofs of Realism" first appeared in *The Monist* (Vol. LI, 1967, pp. 284-304). Copyright © 1967, THE MONIST, La Salle, Illinois 61301.
"Santayana's Moral Philosophy" first appeared in *The Journal of Philosophy* (Vol. LXI, 1964, pp. 44-61).
"Belief, Confidence and Faith" first appeared in *The Southern Journal of Philosophy* (Vol. X, No. 2, 1972, pp. 277-85).
"Peirce, Santayana and the Large Facts" first appeared in *Transactions of the Charles S. Peirce Society* (Vol. XVI, 1980, pp.3-13).
"Hume on Belief" first appeared in *The Review of Metaphysics* (Vol. XXX, 1976, pp. 3-18).
"Fichte's Idealism" first appeared in *American Philosophical Quarterly* (Vol. IX, 1972, pp. 311-18).
"Pre-Socratic Categories in Fichte" first appeared in *Idealistic Studies* (Vol. VI, 1976, pp. 160-68).
John Lachs, "The Omnicolored Sky: Baylis on Perception" from FACT, VALUE, AND PER-CEPTION. Paul Welsh, editor. Pages 139-150. Copyright © 1975 *Duke University Press*.
"Self-Identity Without a Self" first appeared in *The Review of Metaphysics* (Vol. XVIII, 1965, pp. 548-65).

Library of Congress Cataloging-in-Publication Data

Lachs, John.
  Mind and philosophers.

  1. Philosophy.   2. Mind and body.   I. Title.
B29.L26 1987   128   87-2076
ISBN 0-8265-1222-4

Other Books by John Lachs

Animal Faith and Spiritual Life: Unpublished and Uncollected Works of George Santayana with Critical Essays on His Thought

Marxist Philosophy: A Bibliographical Guide

The Science of Knowledge by J. G. Fichte (translation and introduction with Peter Heath)

Physical Order and Moral Liberty: Previously Unpublished Essays of George Santayana (edited with an introduction with Shirley M. Lachs)

The Ties of Time (poems)

Intermediate Man

The Human Search (with Charles E. Scott)

Contents

Introduction

Philosophy is both a profession and a vocation. As a profession, it devotes itself to the education of students and the study of specialized, technically complex, and often arcane problems. As a vocation, it remains what it has always been, a tenacious search for answers to some of life's most difficult questions. The weakness of professional philosophy is its tendency to lose sight of the human problems it ought to resolve. Philosophy as an earnest search for meaning in life, on the other hand, tends to fail for lack of conceptual sophistication.

The essays collected in this volume and written between 1959 and 1980 clearly belong to professional philosophy in both tone and context. Yet their ultimate aim is to explore larger problems and to set the groundwork for dealing with them. For the focus of attention throughout is human nature, not so much in the details of its structure or its social and moral manifestations as in its most general features and constituents. What sort of beings we are is the issue at the center of the most difficult problems in ethics, epistemology, and metaphysics, and how mind and body are related is the question at the very core of all inquiries into human nature.

Accordingly, a number of these essays are directed at exploring and defending a particular view of the mind-body relation. Materialism appears to me to be the theory "to beat." Though vastly implausible to anyone attentive to the subjective life, it is becoming ever more attractive because of the theoretical advances and the practical results of science. The notion of an independent mind has lost whatever allure it may have held in earlier days. The special promise of epiphenomenalism, the theory I favor, is that it combines the insight of the physical dependence of consciousness with the palpable truth of its irreducible subjectivity. Of the rich variety of mind-body views, only epiphenomenalism can allow free rein to objective physical science without relegating immediacy, the internal life, and the phenomenal world to the status of virtual illusion.

Although the view that consciousness is an impotent by-product of physical events has been known, and attacked, since Plato's day, the first four essays in this volume, focusing directly on this theory, constitute the most thorough exploration and most extensive defense of it to date. It is a hypothesis without the monistic elegance of some of its rivals and has been assailed variously as yielding too much, and too little, to materialism. Yet it seems to me the most plausible of the available mind-body options, a view much more successfully ignored than refuted in the history of thought.

Attention to epiphenomenalism naturally leads to interest in George Santayana, the only major philosopher who has wholeheartedly embraced it. Santayana has also had his share of neglect. His *The Life of Reason* was celebrated as an important work of rationalist humanism, but his later, mature ontology was dismissed for reasons as various and incompatible as being too naturalistic and too Platonistic. In fact, in a remarkably clearheaded yet sweeping synthesis, he attempted to fulfill the promise of epiphenomenalism by combining a materialist account of the physical world with an exquisitely accurate phenomenological analysis of consciousness. This is the Santayana the four essays on him reprinted here (Chapters VI–IX) explore; together they constitute the most detailed and systematic study of his ontology available today.

My interest in materialism reveals the motive for my studies of J. G. Fichte, as well. It has once again become respectable, even fashionable, to read Hegel. But Hegel's voraciously dialectical idealism does not present a sharp contrast to the claims of the materialist; Fichte's less sophisticated (or sophistical?) version does. My attempt in the two essays here (Chapters XII and XIII) is to state clearly and to evaluate the bold but obscure ideas of this watershed figure. The initial attractiveness and ultimate failure of these notions is not tantamount to, but paradigmatic of, the collapse of idealist programs.

Although concern with human nature and attention to the mind-body problem are relatively common among philosophers, the reader will note that my choice of theories and thinkers for consideration and my cognitive strategy are by no means customary or fashionable. Analytic training and a native bent have given me a keen appreciation for clarity of thought and caution in judgment. At the same time, a love of the immediately actual, of sensation and the imaginary, has kept me a friend of appearances. In spite of this, however, the interests canvassed here were determined neither by the analytic programs dominant at the time of the earlier essays nor by the hermeneutical concerns popular today.

I look for enlightenment somewhere between these waves of fashion, in the land where most of traditional metaphysics falls. The classical formulations of philosophical problems strike me as helpful and easily adapted to the current conditions of life. Their language enables us to engage in a dialogue across the ages with some of the finest minds of the human race. In philosophy, unlike in science, the latest is rarely the best; without contact with the greats of the past, we produce thin gruel. My strategy is, accordingly, to seek instruction wherever I can find it. If in this process some unjustly neglected philosophers are brought back into notice, the benefit may well be public as well as personal and private.

Those who look for the novel may gain some satisfaction from what I say in defense of such unpopular views as epiphenomenalism, about Santayana and Santayana's relation to Peirce, concerning Hume, and, by no means least, about the idea of God. Novelty and ultimate truth aside, my intention was to make these essays clear and their language accessible beyond a narrow circle of specialists. Most important of all, I hope that the abstract nature of the subject matter will not obscure their relevance to current trends in the world and to the pressing concerns of our daily lives.

CHAPTER 1

Angel, Animal, Machine:
Models for Man

G EORGE SANTAYANA once said that philosophical systems, like good dishes or like women, have their characteristic odors. If the special traits of a philosophy are best determined by the scent of it, its special odor is most readily revealed by what it says about the nature of man. In recent years we have had the great good fortune to smell the clean sea air of materialism. The joy of smelling the ocean after centuries of incense and decades of the positivistic chemistry lab is so great that many of us feel a permanent commitment to the robust though simple odor of salt air. Such commitment is understandable—it was the battle against superstition and the smell of death that made Lucretius a materialist—but it may be time to recall that the ocean wind does not carry the subtlest scents and that no man can acknowledge the sea alone.

One of the philosophically most exciting controversies today concerns the relation of men to machines. The questions of whether men are machines, whether machines can think, and what men can do that machines cannot duplicate are widely discussed in philosophical journals and in books. These questions are, of course, not recent. Descartes asked similar questions in the seventeenth century and came to the conclusion that animals were machines, as were men on the physical side of their nature. De la Mettrie in the eighteenth century and T. H. Huxley in the nineteenth both decided that men were machines, although their notions of what a machine was differed substantially. On first hearing, the question, Are men machines? conveys an ominous impression. Many of us are afraid that if the correct answer turns out to be affirmative, it will be tantamount to the discovery that we really consist of gears, radio tubes, and baling wire. The picture we get is that of humanoid monsters, and we instinctively reject the thought that a careful autopsy might show to the world that we were but ingenious toys made of metal and plastic.

This, of course, is but the nervous person's reaction to a question misunderstood. The reason it has been supposed that human beings are machines is neither to humiliate them nor to discover their manufacturer. There is no expectation of finding that we are really assembled out of inanimate components instead of being produced by the usual, well-known method. The significance of asking the question is entirely different. What we are interested in is whether it is possible to gain some insight into the nature of man by using as our model a complex inanimate object. If the model of the machine turns out to be a profitable one, it will not establish that machines should be given a place as a species in the animal kingdom nor that man should be considered a clever artifact. The most we can expect the machine model to do is to tend to substantiate the suspicion we have long had that humans are continuous in their nature not only with apes and other animals, but also with the totality of the inanimate world.

In Western philosophical tradition, there have been at least three major models for the nature of man. The angel model construed man's essence as consisting of a soul of supernatural origin, moral potentiality, and immortal destiny. Advocates of the animal model saw humans as natural beings continuous with the beasts, although endowed with reason, language, and a social life that no other animal could hope to imitate. Finally, the machine model provides an interpretation of man as of the same substance with the entirety of the physical world. According to this view, we manifest no trait or mechanism that is uniquely ours. Whatever any person can do can be duplicated by inanimate mechanisms carefully designed. The historically predominant view of humans for at least the past two thousand years has been the dualistic one that construes them partly on the animal model and partly on the angel model. Our bodies are the bodies of beasts; our minds are angels custom-made by God with free will to err, through the ample use of which we reject our better nature and make ourselves prisoners of the flesh.

This dualistic theory of man sufficed in one form or another for all philosophical, religious, and literary purposes for millennia. In the past 150 years, its adequacy has been brought into serious question. As a result of advances in the physical and the biological sciences, we have had increasing evidence that the postulation of an immaterial soul is unnecessary in order to account for any aspect of human behavior. There is little scientific enlightenment to be gained from the angel model; it is, therefore, easy to suppose that this model has no cognitive usefulness. If we can account for more and more of human behavior on the basis of supposing that humans are animals only, or that they are machines, it is reasonable to suppose that before long biology, psychology, and cybernetics will be able to give an explanation of every aspect of human life without any reference to an imperceptible and immaterial mind. And if we do not need the hypothesis of a soul to account for human behavior, there can be no possible justification for supposing that such entities exist.

This line of reasoning gained currency during the 1920s, and it now appears to be the predominant view in what has been called "the philosophy of mind." The twentieth century has seen a series of attempts to develop materialistic or behavioristic philosophies of man. Such monistic attempts have been substantially aided by the fact that there is tacit in science a world view that is clearly monistic and, in a significant sense of the word, materialistic.

I cannot conceal my conviction that materialism is inadequate both as a theory of the nature of man and as a theory of the nature of reality. However, it is at least a plausible theory today: it is plausible in a sense in which interactionism is no longer plausible. If materialistic monism can be shown to be inadequate, it will not be on behalf of some view that claims the coexistence of two operative principles of human nature. We must give full credence to the scientist who maintains that an ideally adequate theory of human behavior need have no reference to any but physical entities, and that it need not utilize any concepts that cannot be tied to the observation of spatiotemporal events. In view of the evidence available to us today and in view of existing scientific trends, only two major theories of human nature are at all plausible: the first is monistic materialism, the second is dualistic epiphenomenalism. Theories maintaining the interaction or the mere parallel but otherwise unrelated development of minds and bodies are not viable alternatives today.

By materialism, I mean the theory that only matter and its modifications are real. According to this view, each human being is but a portion of the natural world: each consists of nothing but matter of an unusually high organizational level. Human thinking is an activity of the brain, and every form of human behavior can be explained by reference to what may be discovered concerning the structure and constituents of man's organs along with the laws governing their operation. By "matter," the materialist, of course, does not mean anything like the extended substance of Descartes or the hard pelletlike particles of nineteenth-century physics. Instead, he might attempt to give an account of the nature of matter in terms of spatiotemporal "action patterns," as did Professor Donald Williams of Harvard University. Alternatively, he may mean by it no more than the unitary, spatial, and temporal field of action in which all changes occur and in which transformations are, in principle, always traceable.

Epiphenomenalism, or what is sometimes called "the impotence hypothesis," is a theory that consists of two propositions. It maintains that every mental event has its origin in physical processes and that no mental event brings anything into existence. The important thing about this theory is that it does not deny the existence of minds. It denies only that minds have physical power. Although it is different from anything we find in the body, human consciousness should not be regarded as an entity that exists independently of a highly developed nervous system. It is not a supernatural being imprisoned in the flesh. It consists of a string of mental events, each momentary and evanescent. These pearls are strung on the continuous thread of physical life in the animal brain. They are the resultants or concomitants of physical process, but never its cause. They are the immaterial cognitive acts that constitute the fruition of animal life.

Since the epiphenomenalist construes the human mind as physically impotent, he is free to accept everything that science can tell us concerning the operation of the world. He has the advantage of the materialist in that he can view the physical universe as a single, self-governing, and self-sustaining system. This entire universe is open to scientific inquiry, and hence it is reasonable to suppose that the development of an adequate, biologically based psychology is only a matter of time. The insight of the unity of man and nature is, in this way, fully accepted. Man on the physical side is seen as continuous with the inanimate and the animal realms. However, the angel model is not fully abandoned in favor of the machine view. It is, we might say, stripped to fighting weight in order to retain whatever moral insight it might give into the nature of man. Humans are thus seen as compounds of conscious mind, which is a spectator of time and existence, and potent body, which is a self-sustaining organism in time and space. As T. H. Huxley, one of the early exponents of epiphenomenalism, put it, man is a "conscious automaton." Two models often used as aids to the imagination in conceiving this theory are those of the locomotive in relation to its smoke and the human being in relation to his or her shadow. The locomotive creates its smoke; it is not the smoke that makes the wheels of the locomotive go round. The person standing in sunlight creates a shadow; the shadow has no effect on the person. Similarly, the body creates consciousness, but the pure acts of awareness can have no influence over bodily motions. They cannot even ensure that any further acts of consciousness will be produced.

There are two major lines of attack against the impotence hypothesis. The first, from the side of materialism, brings into question the postulation of a consciousness that is nonphysical and hence not open to scientific measurement and inquiry. The second, from the side of interactionism, focuses on the question of why a mind, once it has been postulated, should be supposed to lack causal power. I shall deal with the second objection first. After I have dealt with it, I shall go on to show why I think that epiphenomenalism is to be preferred to the simple materialistic account of the nature of man.

Let me begin by admitting that the notion of an entity or an event that is causally impotent is an unusual one. However, it appears more unusual and more counterintuitive than it really is. There are many instances of causal impotence with which we are familiar, and which do not appear to us to be at all puzzling. The

feeling of pain that is the symptom of some psychosomatic disorder clearly has no causal influence over what our organism does
to remedy the disease. The colors certain chemical compounds
acquire are in no sense *causally* involved with the chemical properties of the compounds. They are the signs that certain properties are present; they are neither those properties nor the causes
of them. And if it is supposed that the mind is a causal force
because it appears to itself to be that, there are numerous models
in nature on the basis of which this appearance of power may be
explained. In our unsophisticated moments we do suppose, after
all, that lightning is the cause of thunder, even though there is the
best of scientific evidence that both lightning and thunder are
coeffects of an electrical disturbance.

If it were supposed that the mind is a substance or an entity in
the sense in which dualists in the tradition of Descartes speak of
substances and entities, it would be difficult to see how consciousness could be essentially, as distinct from merely temporarily or accidentally, impotent. However, there is little reason
for us to speak of the mind as a *thing*. If it is conceived as a series of
events, albeit events of a very special kind, there need be no
overwhelming difficulty in supposing that it lacks physical force.
What the dualist has to establish is that there are good experiential or theoretical reasons for maintaining the physical potency of
mind. Since we have no direct experience of the causal power of
consciousness—even our experience of volition does not give us
this—the interactionist has to base his arguments on our *beliefs* or
convictions that our minds are physically active. Common human
beliefs, however, do not constitute adequate grounds for maintaining any theory, much less one that new developments in
science make less probable each day.

The experiential grounds of interactionism are, therefore,
weak. The theoretical grounds for it are even weaker. If we can
have a theoretically adequate monism, we should certainly prefer
it to interactionism on the grounds of simplicity and elegance. We
should, therefore, give our assent to the interactionist's claims
only if it is clear that no theoretically adequate monism is possible. However, I do not wish to rest my case against interactionism
on considerations of simplicity and on shifting the burden of

proof to the Cartesian dualist. There are two very powerful arguments against any theory of the interaction of body and mind. The first is one to which I have already alluded. The more human operations we can explain without any reference to a nonphysical mind, the more probable it becomes that further operations, as yet scientifically unexplained, will be accounted for in due course. There appears to be no theoretical reason why every form of human behavior, including language, social life, and reasoning, could not be fully explained by physical science in the coming centuries.

The second argument serves to bolster this reasonable view of the potential adequacy of physical science to physical fact. Suppose that the Cartesian dualist is correct in interpreting the relation of mind to body as being one of mutual interaction. What reason would we then have for distinguishing mind from body? Admittedly, we would distinguish it from gross physical organs, and possibly even from the electrical activities of the brain. But if we take seriously the contemporary view of matter according to which whatever exists in the spatial and temporal field of activity is material, we must admit that a potent mind would have to be a part of the material world. It would, of course, be quite different from matter in its most obvious forms—about as different, let us say, from cars as supermarkets are from kinetic energy or coconut juice is from cosmic rays. But essentially, mind would, on this view, be material: it would belong in a single continuous field of action with everything else that acts. Its transformations would, in principle, be traceable. Its effects on common physical objects, and the effects of common physical objects on it, would be open to investigation by some conceivable science and could someday be reduced to laws. Someday, perhaps, we could even invent a special device, some artificial sense organ that would enable us to tune in on the world of minds, roughly in the way the radio enables us to tune in on a remarkable and at one time unsuspected realm of material waves.

The argument against interaction terminates in a dilemma. If mind has physical force, it is a material object in a wide but significant sense of this term. If, however, consciousness is discontinuous with physical nature, it can have no physical potency.

Either mind is immaterial and thus impotent, or it is an effective force and hence shares the materiality of its effects. I do not see how any interactionist can escape this dilemma. Its conclusiveness rests on the conception of matter I have indicated, and it leaves materialism and epiphenomenalism as the only plausible theories of human nature.

The one clear advantage of materialism over the impotence hypothesis is that of simplicity. Other things being equal, it is always better to choose the simpler, more economical view; and a monism is always simpler than a dualism. Materialism and epiphenomenalism are equally adequate in allowing full scope to science in the material world. Both maintain that we must turn to science in order to gain knowledge of physical reality in the macrocosm as well as in the microcosm of man. Both are naturalistic in the sense of maintaining that reality is a single system that operates in accordance with discoverable laws without the interference of any external agents. However, epiphenomenalism has three major advantages over the materialistic view. The first is the advantage of having a higher initial probability. We have two distinguishable kinds of experience: we perceive pipes and witness gallbladder operations, and we also experience anger and hope the future will be better than the past has been. Some of our experiences reveal to us a spatiotemporal world of changing objects; others give insight into our silent streams of feeling. The difference between external, observable events and internal, introspectible states clearly favors a dualistic view.

Professor Herbert Feigl of the University of Minnesota has argued for materialism in the following way. Admittedly, he says, sentences referring to mental events cannot be translated without loss of meaning into sentences that are only about physical events or tendencies. However, even though such sentences differ in meaning or connotation, they can agree in their referent. The phrase "Evening Star" differs in meaning from the phrase "Morning Star" even though both "Morning Star" and "Evening Star" refer to the same planet, namely, Venus. In a similar way, descriptions of certain physical events and descriptions of mental states are but different ways of describing the same thing. If this view is correct, descriptions in physical terms and descriptions in terms of consciousness differ only in what they say: what is being described in both cases is—the brain. The differences in description are due to differences in purpose and context; science, however, will eventually be able to show that both types of descriptions are descriptions of a single set of events.

My objection to this argument is twofold. First of all, it is highly probable that words that differ in their meaning also differ in their referent. This contributes to the initial probability of epiphenomenalism: an initial probability that can be counteracted only if we have considerable evidence that the referents of two different kinds of statements in fact coincide. Such evidence, if it could be had, could be amassed only by science. My second objection consists in reminding us that in this case science can, in fact, never provide adequate evidence for identity. Although identity can be clearly established in such cases as the Evening Star–Morning Star example, it cannot be done in the case of brain events and consciousness. Let us suppose that observation and calculation show that the orbit of the Evening Star can be correlated exactly with the orbit of the Morning Star. Is this by itself enough to identify the two heavenly bodies? A further principle is needed to establish identity: the principle that two bodies cannot occupy the same space at the same time. Without this principle, which appears to us to be obviously true, the most we could argue would be the perfect correspondence of the orbits of what may well be two planets: we could never legitimately infer that they are, in fact, a single entity.

Now my claim is that even if we were to find a brain event for every change in our consciousness, the most we could have would be a perfect correlation of the physical and the mental. In this context we can never have the additional principle that is requisite for asserting identity. The reason for this is that the identity principle involved must be either one of spatial identity or one of the identity of causal properties. It is agreed on all sides that conscious events are putatively nonspatial; the difference between the epiphenomenalist and the identity theorist on this count is simply that the former accepts the phenomenal nonspatiality of consciousness whereas the latter searches for some way in which the putatively nonspatial may be identified with what is located in physical space. It should be evident at once that the principle used in establishing the identity of things or sets of events on the basis of their spatial location cannot advance the cause of identifying spatial with putatively nonspatial events. As regards the second possible principle, we might begin by noting that the advocate of the impotent mind assigns no causal properties to consciousness at all. Since the mind makes no effective contribution to the economy of the person, the epiphenomenalist can readily admit the identity of a brain event with that brain event *plus* its accompanying conscious state, *as far as their causal properties are concerned*. The distinction between the mind and the body, however, in no way depends on their varied potentials. It rests, on Feigl's own admission, on the fact that the mind is putatively characterized by such features as privacy, intentionality, and nonspatiality, and we have considerable introspective and some analytic evidence to establish that fact. It follows from this that the identity of the causal properties of the brain with those of the brain-mind complex—an identity that the epiphenomenalist not only accepts but welcomes as a direct consequence of his view—in no way compels him to surrender the distinction between the physical and the mental.

I have argued against materialism that initial probability is on the side of the impotence hypothesis. Let me briefly mention the other two main advantages of this theory. One is that not only does epiphenomenalism account more naturally for the experienced duality of events, it is also virtually impossible for the materialist to explain how error and illusion and, most important of all, intentionality are possible. Intentionality is that peculiar property of mental events by which they can be *about* something other than themselves. Physical events simply are: they cannot be about anything. They cannot contain in themselves reference to something that does not exist and never will; but nothing is simpler than to think that Socrates smoked Camels or that Hades is located directly under the dean's office. It is intentionality that makes the truth or error of mental discourse possible, and I fail to see how brain events can in any sense be either true or false.

The final great advantage of epiphenomenalism is its ability to appropriate and use all the insights of the great dualistic tradition of Western thought while it loses none of the important lessons of monistic science. By maintaining the existence of a consciousness whose function is cognition and enjoyment, we can readily account for religious experience, mystical insight, and aesthetic appreciation. We can accept whatever is valid and significant in phenomenology, while we place it in the context of a naturalistic metaphysics. We can adopt the moral insights of Christianity without losing sight of the material foundations that undergird all feeling and value. A fully developed epiphenomenalist view of the nature of man may well succeed in reconciling the natural with the ideal and in unifying the world of inner feeling with external fact.

I have no desire to minimize the difficulties of the impotence hypothesis, and I certainly do not wish to give the impression that it is the solution to all philosophic ills. However, it does appear to me that this theory has received considerably less attention than it deserves. In supporting it, I have attempted to show that even if the machine model of the nature of man turns out to be the most profitable of all the models hitherto proposed, we need not suppose that it gives an insight into all of human nature. To put it simply, even if human beings are machines, they are not *only* machines. There is another component of human nature that, although it is the product of physical forces and lacks potency, is nevertheless the source of all meaning and value. A fully successful human life would aim at the actualization of this potential for contemplation, feeling, and enjoyment as much as it would strive to secure the physical goals of health, security, and equilibrium. By accepting the existence of the human mind, epiphenomenalism makes the development of a value system possible. By acknowledging the mind's dependence on the body, it fosters the modesty and sanity of the mind. By insisting on the spontaneous and fanciful character of the objects of the mind, it promotes the liberation of consciousness from the concerns of the body. The impotence hypothesis is no insult to the mind: on the contrary, it has the virtue of seeing in each of us not only organic intelligence to act in space but also an element of free imagination and disinterested thought. If materialism smells of simple salt air, epiphenomenalism retains a whiff of the great outdoors. Yet it combines with this the pungent odors of the painter's attic, where consciousness paints a colored image of the world.

CHAPTER 2

The Impotent Mind

MY TASK in this paper is to show that epiphenomenalism cannot be disposed of in a "conclusive fashion."[1] Epiphenomenalism is a theory that consists of two universal propositions: one about the origin of mental events and another about their causal efficacy. They are (1) every mental event has as its total cause one or a set of physical processes; and (2) no mental event is a total or a partial cause of any physical process. I leave the question of the precise distinction between the mental and the physical for another time. For our present purposes, it will suffice to say that by "physical process" I mean such events as the explosions of supernovae, the ionization of gases, and the firing of neurons, and by "mental event" I mean such occurrences as the thought of feasting ghosts, the remembrance of things past, and the lust for life. I presume that all of us are acquainted with some such events. The nature of the causal connection between physical processes and mental events is an issue I have explored in another place.[2] My only concern here will be with the validity of the claim that epiphenomenalism (or, as I shall also call it, "the impotence hypothesis") is a "thoughtless and incoherent theory."[3]

To show that this contention is unfounded, I shall examine six of the most popular arguments against the impotence hypothesis. Each of them has been considered conclusive against epiphenomenalism by one distinguished philosopher or another.

---

[1] A. C. Ewing, *The Fundamental Questions of Philosophy* (New York: Macmillan, 1951), 127.

[2] See "Epiphenomenalism and the Notion of Cause," pp. 29–34 below.

[3] A. E. Taylor, *Plato: The Man and His Work* (Cleveland and New York: Meridian Books, 1956), 198.

My strategy will be to separate the arguments into three major groups; I shall then state each as clearly as I can and attempt to assess their force impartially.

Professor Taylor contends that epiphenomenalism is "incompetent to take account of the obvious facts of mental life."[4] The claim is that our everyday experience acquaints us with numerous instances of the mind's action on the body, as well as of the body's action on the mind. I shall term this set of objections "the Counterintuitive Arguments" since their essence is the insistence that careful attention to the plain facts of experience is sufficient to prove the epiphenomenalist wrong.

There are three forms of the Counterintuitive Argument, each stressing the efficacy of a different type of conscious experience. The first is the argument from volition, the second is based on a consideration of some special forms of thought or purely cognitive experience, and the third takes as its point of departure certain acknowledged features of the emotive life.

The Counterintuitive Argument from Volition runs as follows. Volition is a consciousness of effort that often stands in a peculiarly intimate connection with subsequent physical (or mental) events. There is a high degree of correlation between conscious efforts directed at performing certain actions and the actual execution of those actions. The relationship is especially intimate in that not only are volition and action constantly conjoined, but the former is precisely the attempt to bring the latter into existence. Further, an essential part of any volition is envisaging its effect. It appears, therefore, that merely by reflecting on the nature of volition we can recognize that it is a cause, and that when we will something we have an actual experience of causal process. All of this is borne out by the fact that we ordinarily believe that certain bodily movements occur at certain times *because* certain conscious events had occurred at immediately antecedent times, that is, that mental events are causal factors in bringing about at least some bodily states.

Now I do not think anyone would have the audacity to deny that we do believe in the causal efficacy of volition. However,

4 *Ibid.*

possessing this belief proves nothing. The issue turns on what reasons we can give to support it. It seems that there are three distinct but interconnected reasons. First of all, in volition we seem to have firsthand experience of creative process; we seem actually to be observing the smooth passage involved in the conversion of a thought into reality. Second, it seems patent that the relation of volition to willed bodily event is intimate in the extreme since the volition forecasts the event and is "active" in the sense that it appears poised to bring it about. Finally, we have the overwhelming spectacle of effectuated will, the apparent harmony of will and nature. Our belief that the bond of volition with the willed bodily (or mental) state is authentic and indissoluble is enhanced not only by our appreciation of the intimate connection of the two and by the alleged experience of process, but also by the steady success of volition at fulfilling its promise.

If the claim that in volition we are immediately aware of causative process could be substantiated, the fate of epiphenomenalism would be sealed. However, there is nothing to be said for this dictum, and the remaining two considerations do not suffice to establish the truth of the belief in the efficacy of volitional consciousness. We are no more aware of causal process in volition than we are in observing the transmission of shove down a line of freight cars. When I decide to wriggle my nose, what I experience is the conscious effort to do just that with the appropriate kinesthetic (and possibly visual) sensations immediately following. The experience, as Hume pointed out long ago, is that of one event succeeding another, not that of the *production* of the later event by the earlier. If *per impossibile* we could actually observe the creative process, we would not be in the dark as to how it comes about that sometimes our will is done; as it is, with the method of birth concealed, we are left to delight in the occasional achievement.

But if we do not have immediate experience of the alleged creativity of consciousness, it is of no avail to insist on the intimate connection of volition and achievement: on the tendency of will to predict the future and the fact that it appears to be an "active" experience. The epiphenomenalist has a ready explanation. Volition gives the appearance of being a causal factor because it is the mental counterpart of a process in the physical organism that *is* a causal factor. Instead of being the necessary and sufficient condition of a certain action, consciousness of effort to bring it about is a concomitant of the necessary and sufficient condition; instead of being the cause of the physical effect, it is the coeffect of the physical cause, the mental "transcript" of a physiological state. It is the physical processes of the body that cause the occurrence and determine the content of conscious events. The harmony of volition and achievement will, then, no longer seem mysterious once we recall that the processes that give rise to a consciousness of effort are the same that initiate fulfillment of its promise.

One might urge that if epiphenomenalism were true all states of consciousness would be "passive" accompaniments of physiological processes. This would eliminate the distinction between active and passive forms of awareness, yet volition clearly appears to be an "active" experience. But this argument also has a fatal flaw. Accounting for the possibility of the distinction does not present any difficulty for the epiphenomenalist, for if there are passive (receptive) and active (outdirected) states of the organism, it is no secret why we have "passive" and "active" experiences. The organism is evidently passive with respect to external stimulation and active when outgoing process is centrally induced. It may, therefore, well be that the appearance of activity on the conscious level is due to the occurrence of movement and action within the animal. Volition throws lame sparks testifying that electric current is busily at work.

The epiphenomenalist's defense derives its strength from two quarters. First of all, it is clear that the premises of this form of the Counterintuitive Argument do not suffice to prove its conclusion. Second, facts that serve as the basis of this argument can as well be accounted for on the hypothesis of the impotence of consciousness. If epiphenomenalism were true, it would be reasonable to expect the kind of confusion about the efficacy of thought that is perhaps implicit in our everyday beliefs and that has been raised to the status of dogma by philosophers. The unsophisticated man easily confuses the conspicuous attendant of the cause with the cause; when the mainspring is hidden, what is really a part of the complex effect may itself be construed as the causal source. We still tend to believe that flashes of lightning cause thunder (instead of being its coeffects, since both the thunder and the lightning are brought about by the same electrical disturbance), and the early history of medicine is replete with cases where one of a set of symptoms is singled out as the unitary "cause" of the disease. The epiphenomenalist may well argue that the explanation of the miracle of effectuated will, the persistent harmony of will and nature, is not to be sought in some mind that mysteriously imposes its designs on the recalcitrant stuff of the world, but in a living animal that, struggling in the universal flux, for a brief moment overcomes the renitency of its surroundings and produces in the process an inner sense of its effort and passing dominance. Volition is a form of consciousness indicative of the fact that physical changes directed at the execution of some action are occurring or have just occurred.

Let me devote brief attention to the two remaining forms of the Counterintuitive Argument, the first from Cognition, the second from Emotion. The claim that cognitive experiences are physically efficacious is based on the following type of consideration. It is well known that the thought of ripe plums makes the mouth water, and recognition of a speeding car may, under suitable conditions, be a mental fact with radical issue in the realm of action. Now, the critic may urge, since experiences of this type are common and the intimate connection between mental event and physical outcome is admitted on all sides, the epiphenomenalist's claim that the mind is causally lame carries no conviction.

This argument is open to the same objections as the previous one. The "intimate" connection of mental event and physical outcome does not imply direct causal relatedness; we may even make a fair case for the view that the antecedent probability of such a direct causal tie is not appreciably greater than that of the rival hypothesis that their tie is indirect, running through a common physical source. The fact that thought is followed by appropriate physical change is by no means unambiguous evidence for the view that it was a causal factor in bringing about that change. To argue as though it were may well be to commit the fallacy of *post hoc ergo propter hoc*. At any rate, the claim that recognition as a mental fact has physical consequences is at best a hypothesis, and the fact that the common man tends to embrace it does not have the least tendency to show that it is a conclusively established one.

Exactly the same considerations apply to the Counterintuitive Argument from Emotion. The fact that fear is correlated with a wild pounding of the heart or rasping dry throat, or that anger tends to make a man breathe fast and even to cloud the eyes, is no evidence against epiphenomenalism. The sole fact that the Counterintuitive Arguments suffice to establish beyond all reasonable doubt is that epiphenomenalism is counterintuitive. However, I do not see why any exponent of the doctrine should consider this in the least alarming. The Copernican system of the universe is wildly counterintuitive, as are Freudian theories of subconscious motivation and any number of other respectable hypotheses. It is, of course, necessary to remind ourselves that it is no virtue for a theory to lack the recommendation of being in accord with the everyday intuitions of mankind. There have to be good reasons for preferring such counterintuitive hypotheses to their less counterintuitive rivals. But it is not my present purpose to consider the reasons *for* epiphenomenalism; I am concerned only with evaluating some of the arguments against it. And my conclusion is that none of the Counterintuitive Arguments comes even remotely near to refuting the impotence hypothesis. Moreover, the facts adduced against epiphenomenalism in these arguments can be readily and adequately explained on the hypothesis that epiphenomenalism is true. Finally, I must remark that the impotence hypothesis is by no means *completely* counterintuitive, for while it appears to run counter to a number of our common beliefs and experiences, certain other common experiences tend directly to confirm it.

The unifying character of the next group of arguments I shall consider is that each of them is based on a feature of "the natural history of consciousness."[5] I shall give them the name "Arguments from the Distribution of the Intensity of Consciousness," a phrase that combines the vice of being cumbersome with the virtue of descriptive accuracy. The deployment of awareness is

[5] William James, *The Principles of Psychology* (New York: Dover, 1950), 1:142.

such, it is argued, as would be reasonable to expect if it were efficacious. It seems to be present whenever intelligent actions are performed and absent whenever activity is restricted to an invariable, automatic level. Moreover, it is most intense when the need for intelligence is greatest and sinks to a minimum when truncated forms of discernment suffice for the performance of the action. I shall present two subsidiary forms of this argument. Although I intend to judge each on its own merits, I shall at once make a general comment. It appears that any force this type of argument may have is derived from its successful application of the Method of Concomitant Variation. The claim is that the intensity of consciousness varies concurrently with some such feature as the complexity or the urgency of the action to be performed. Now my remark is that even on the most charitable interpretation, even if—and this is by no means beyond doubt—a clear case can be made for such concomitance, the argument cannot prove the causal efficacy of consciousness. Mill's Fifth Canon of Induction states quite explicitly that a phenomenon that varies whenever another phenomenon does "is either a cause or an effect of [the latter], *or is connected with it through some fact of causation.*"[6] Mill goes on to point out with great acuteness that concomitant variation of two phenomena is no proof of the causal efficacy of either, since the same concomitance would be observed if they were "two different effects of a common cause."

The first form of the Argument from the Distribution of the Intensity of Consciousness is perhaps its most common one. We notice that we have to pay no attention at all to automatic actions such as the beating of the heart and little, if any, to habit-actuated ones. However, consciousness is agonizingly intense in situations where indecision is great or the complexity of some task excessive. A person caught in some inimical state will think furiously to find a way out, or will, at least, be acutely aware of the danger to which he is exposed. Since conscious consideration appears necessary for the resolution of the worst predicaments and the consummation of exacting performances, the causal

---

[6] John Stuart Mill, *A System of Logic* (London: Longmans, 1959), 263. My italics.

efficacy of at least some mental events cannot be reasonably denied.

Now even if there were such an invariable concomitance of intense consciousness with complex problem solving, it would, as I have suggested before, not prove the mind's efficacy. But not even this invariable concomitance can be established. For some of the most complex, nonhabitual performances are executed without the least thought. Trying to prevent falling on the back of my head once I have slipped on an icy hill involves a series of actions of staggering speed and complexity. But even if I had an hour to reflect, I could not think out what to do and how. If it be objected that this example prejudices the issue, for what is involved here is a set of automatic body adjustments, it may be well to remind the critic that it is by no means a unique case. Solutions of complex mathematical or philosophical problems "pop" into our heads, sometimes without effort. And sometimes the intensity of attention directed at solving a problem is directly proportional to the resultant frustration: the only way the required result can be reached is by diverting attention from the issue or by "sleeping on it." The correlation of intense consciousness with high-grade problem solving is too spotty to serve as the premise of any compelling argument.

The general form of the epiphenomenalist answer to counterarguments should, by now, be clear. When confronted with an apparent instance of effective consciousness, the epiphenomenalist characteristically moves to disjoin efficacy and awareness, assigning the former to the physical organism while the latter in its varied modes is left as the distinguishing mark of the mental. The significance of this procedure is that it reminds us that the efficacy of consciousness is not "given": it is not an indubitable fact of experience but a theory we frame to account for observed conjunctions. The weaker the evidence in favor of this theory, the more epiphenomenalism remains unrefuted. Incidentally, of course, this method of rejoinder also calls attention to the fact that epiphenomenalism is itself but a hypothesis. This is an issue about which a great deal should be said; nothing, however, will be said in this paper. Let me just remark, before I go on to the second form of the Argument from the Distribution of the Intensity of

Consciousness, that while its refutation or confirmation is by no means independent of the findings of physical science, epiphenomenalism itself is not a scientific hypothesis.

An examination of our everyday beliefs would probably turn up considerable public support for the view that pain functions as a biological deterrent to action. I will not touch an electric wire because of the excessively disagreeable sensation of shock, and one may even check one's tendency to be a glutton if only the memory of the previous night's dyspepsia is vivid enough. As is clear in the case of such experiences as toothaches, the more intense the pain, the more it functions as a signal to the organism to take remedial action. It is of the greatest moment for the welfare of the animal that pains be associated with function-impeding processes and pleasures with life-enhancing ones. An animal that would find suffocation irresistibly pleasurable and the consumption of food the source of excruciating and perdurable pains would not grow up to father broods of young. Hence, it is clear that pain is biologically important and causally effective, the argument contends. But it is also a form of consciousness. Certain conscious events thus seem indispensable links in at least some causal chains that result in overt bodily acts.

There is nothing to be said for this argument. Since pains are grounded in the body or in the action of some external object on the body, the claim that our acts of evasion and aversion, or our positive attempts at suppressing the source of irritation, are due even partly to the efficacy of the feeling of distress is pure hypothesis. Since it is on the same plane as the noxious object or the injured organ, it seems more likely that the physiological counterpart of the consciously undergone pain occasions the avoidance response than that this purely physical response is due to a feeling of helpless suffering. The Argument from Pain lacks even the apparent plausibility of the Argument from Volition, for suffering is the most passive, most infuriatingly impotent of experiences. If suffering were efficacious in mending the rent fabric of organs, it would be criminal to administer pain relievers; as it is, the natural tendency of the sick man is to sleep, that is, to "switch off" the mind altogether and let the body make whatever repairs it can. To reply here that the paradigm case of the efficacy of pain is to be looked for in the influence it exerts over intelligent choice and not in the circumstances surrounding its questionable role once bodily injury is sustained is of no avail. The reason is obvious. For the wisdom gathered from past pains to affect our choice, it must in the first place be remembered. But there is little reason to suspect that consciousness of pain is a necessary condition of the formation of a trace that will occasion our finding certain things or actions objectionable, and there is even less reason to suppose that the avoidance response is due to remembered pain rather than the activated trace. The same kind of argument applies to the supposed role of pain in bringing about avoidance habits. It may well be that if pain accompanies the joint occurrence of a kind of stimulus with a kind of behavior, the probability increases that the behavior will not occur the next time the stimulus occurs. But far from demonstrating the efficacy of pain, this only shows that under the circumstances either the pain or (what is more likely) its physiological counterpart was causally involved.

I shall now consider Pratt's interesting Argument from the Impossibility of Reasoning. The argument goes as follows. Reasoning in some sense involves the awareness of logical relations. Thus, it is permissible to affirm certain propositions as conclusions if certain other propositions have been affirmed as premises, and this only because the two sets of propositions stand in certain intimate logical connections. Awareness of some such logical connection is an indispensable co-cause of the mental act of affirming a proposition as conclusion on the basis of one or more propositions that serve as premises. If awareness of logical relations did not play a causal role in inference, no conclusion we reach could ever claim to be based on logic. Then if we happened to think logically, it would be merely "because the brain molecules shake down, so to speak, in a lucky fashion."[7] And the inevitable outcome of such an absurd view of inference would seem to be that even the best arguments its exponents can marshal to demonstrate its truth do not entitle them or anyone else to believe it. For belief in a theory is the outcome of physiological changes in

[7] J. B. Pratt, *Matter and Spirit* (New York: Macmillan, 1922), 20.

the brain and never of the awareness of good arguments for it. Thus if epiphenomenalism were true, logical inference would be impossible. And if logical inference is impossible, we cannot really *know* that epiphenomenalism is true, in the sense of "know" that implies the ability to give reasons on demand.

I shall restate the basic claim of this argument somewhat more precisely. By the statement that a person P inferred the proposition C from the propositions A and B, we mean at least (1) that the occurrence of C as a thought in P's mind was due to a total cause of which P's thought of A and P's thought of B were parts, and (2) that another cause factor leading to the occurrence of C in P's mind was P's belief that A and B jointly imply C. It is obvious that no claim is made to the effect that the original entertainment of A and B together with the awareness that A and B jointly imply C represent the total cause of the assertion of C. No proposition or set of propositions entails only one proposition; hence, implication is not sufficient to determine the direction of inference. However, even a proof that mental events are indispensable *parts* of complex causes would be enough to show the bankruptcy of the impotence hypothesis.

But the argument cannot even establish this. If consciousness of logical relations were a necessary condition of inference, we would not be justified in believing any of the results of the local DEC 10 or, for that matter, the Kalin-Burkhart Logical Truth Calculator. For surely these machines do not work by the apprehension of logical relations, although they do seem to manage quite well when it comes to tracing implications. If to do logic is to engage in a transformation game in accordance with rules, this is not a whit surprising. The rules specify with complete determinateness the logically permissible moves in any situation, and it is simple enough to construct a mechanical or electrical model for this. The "passage" from proposition to proposition could be represented by actual motion; lack of a circuit or a switch in the "off" position might serve to express in a material medium the absence of the logical relation of implication.

In order to work out the details, one has only to look at the blueprint of some recent logic machine. To say that a machine programmed to solve problems of the lower functional calculus is working in accordance with logic merely because "the molecules shake down . . . in a lucky fashion" is either to insist, quite correctly of course, that if the machine had broken down, it would not have performed properly or to remind us that we are dealing with "molecules," that is, physical entities here. So we are, but the fact that the brain is, among other things, a high-efficiency cybernetic calculator does not in any way imply that its operation in accordance with the physically coded rules of logical inference is a matter of "luck." If the brain is primed to function according to a system of rules isomorphic with the laws of logic, nothing could be more reasonable than that we should time and again have the conscious experience (brain produced) of inferential passage from thought to thought. Thus, the causal source of the "inference" of C from A and B need have as its constituent neither P's thought of A and his thought of B nor his conscious belief that A and B jointly entail C. If this is one of those comparatively rare occasions when the inference is fully explicit, the two thoughts and the belief will indeed occur, but both their occurrence and the passage from them to the conclusion C will be due to the steady whir of the calculator below. Obviously, the soundest test that a machine works in accordance with the logical rules of inference is its ability to come up with the right answer consistently, just as the ultimate proof that a certain machine can play chess is to be looked for in its adroitness at outmaneuvering opponent after opponent. If, after just having lost his game to the machine, a player were to insist that the rules of chess "had nothing to do" with the moves of his opponent because *it* can act only in accordance with the way its "molecules shake down," we would at once know the source of his distress. And perhaps we know it in the current case as well. It is not easy to cede unique possession of a skill that we think attests our supremacy.

The upshot of my argument is this. None of the six objections I have considered comes anywhere near to refuting epiphenomenalism. Other objections, which I did not think essential to include, are equally inconclusive. There is good reason to believe that "epiphenomenalism . . . is a thoughtless and incoherent theory" is a claim both thoughtless and incoherent. This, of course, does not mean that the impotence hypothesis has been or may be proved true. It means only that it is not a theory that may be discarded or disregarded in quite as cavalier a fashion as too many philosophers have too often done. The detailed assessment of the evidence for epiphenomenalism is a task still to be performed. The probable truth of the impotence hypothesis cannot be established without such detailed investigation of the arguments that make for as well as against it—an investigation that has to be carried out in the context of equally thorough examinations of rival mind-body theories.

CHAPTER 3

Epiphenomenalism and the Notion of Cause

THE COMPLEX of issues known as "the mind-body problem" has long exercised the ingenuity of contemporary philosophers. Spontaneous concern for the neoteric, however, has caused some of these thinkers to forget that the introduction of new approaches to a problem should always be coupled with a careful study of older, established theories. The case of epiphenomenalism is an exceptionally clear instance of such inattention or negligence. While epiphenomenalism is a major, historically recurrent[1] attempt to solve the mind-body problem, recent thinkers have devoted little effort to a systematic study of its logical structure. Such a study is, I feel, long overdue, and it is my purpose in this paper to initiate it. I shall do so by exhibiting one significant aspect of the "logic" of epiphenomenalism.

The heart of epiphenomenalism is the contention that the mind is not a substantive entity capable of molding its environment: it is, rather, a series of conscious acts or moments of consciousness. Each conscious act is causally dependent on processes in the nervous system of some living body. But no physical process or

---

[1] Plato (*Phaedo* 86ff.) attacked a view closely resembling epiphenomenalism. There is little doubt that Thomas Hobbes was an epiphenomenalist; see his *Elements of Philosophy concerning Body,* pt. IV, ch. 25, no. 3, in *The English Works of Thomas Hobbes* (London: John Bohn, 1839), 1: 391–92. T. H. Huxley expounded and defended the view in an article entitled "On the Hypothesis that Animals Are Automata and Its History," *Method and Results* (New York: Appleton, 1896), 199–250. To give just one more example, C. D. Broad in *The Mind and Its Place in Nature* (London: K. Paul, Trench, Trubner, 1925), 476, argues that if there is no independent evidence that minds ever exist apart from the body, epiphenomenalism "is to be preferred as involving the minimum of assumptions."

mental (or conscious) act is causally dependent on any mental act; minds are neither the total nor a partial cause of anything.

Loosely speaking, we can say that, on the epiphenomenalist's view, bodies affect minds but minds cannot affect bodies. This way of putting the matter, however, may lead to misunderstanding. Thus, Professor Broad is led to say that epiphenomenalism is a theory maintaining the one-sided action of body on mind.[2] This designation of the view is incorrect in a fundamental way. For the assertion that the body acts *on* the mind presupposes what the epiphenomenalist denies: the independent existence of minds. Since for the epiphenomenalist a mind is not a "thing" or an entity but a set of intimately related conscious acts and such conscious acts or consciou*sings* exist as the momentary effects of neural events, no neural event can bring about a *change* in consciousness. For the epiphenomenalist, bodily processes do not act on or modify the mind: they create it.

How are the mental acts that constitute a mind "created"? What meaning can be attached to the word "cause" in the sentence "Each mental act has as its total cause one or several brain processes"? Epiphenomenalists are conspicuously silent on these issues. The reason for their silence, however, is not hard to find. Epiphenomenalism is incompatible with each of the three major theories of the nature of causation. I propose to show that if anyone wishes to maintain that the relation of the mind to the body is epiphenomenal, he cannot also claim that it is an instance of the relation of causal *entailment* or that the generation of mental acts is the result of causal *activity*. I shall also show that, on the *regularity* view of causation, epiphenomenalism cannot even be stated as a distinct and recognizable theory.

The reason why exponents of epiphenomenalism cannot consistently subscribe to the activity view of causation is obvious. The activity view takes volition as the paradigm of causal efficacy. For the epiphenomenalist, however, an act of will is merely a symptom or an index of brain activity; it is a conscious event indicative of the fact that physical changes directed at the execution

2 Broad, *op. cit.*, 118.

of some action are occurring or have just occurred.[3] Will cannot serve the epiphenomenalist as the model for all causation since, along with all other mental phenomena, he must account it impotent.

There are at least two reasons why it is impossible to use the entailment view as a key to the transphysical "causation" involved in giving rise to an impotent mind. The first reason is the nature of the entailment model itself. Every proposition is entailed by, and entails, some others. Thus, given any proposition p, we can always find another proposition g such that either g alone or g in conjunction with $h, i, \ldots, n$ entails p. Moreover, given p, we can also find another proposition q such that either p alone or p in conjunction with $r, s, \ldots, z$ entails q. If the epiphenomenalist decides to explicate the causal relation between events on the analogy of the entailment relation obtaining between propositions, the unbroken chain of entailments commits him to a causal web without any blind alleys. The principle that every proposition is entailed by, and entails, some others has as its etiological counterpart the principle that every event has a cause and, in turn, *is a cause*. By the latter principle, there are no effects that are not also (at least) partial causes. Thus, if the entailment model is taken seriously, it becomes logically impossible to maintain that mental events are epiphenomenal, that is, that they are effectless effects.

Second, there is no logical difference between the kind of thing that may be a cause and the kind of thing that may be an effect. Anything that qualifies as the effect-term of the causal relation also qualifies, by general ontological type at least, as the cause-term. Anyone who is a child may, in due course, become a parent; the relation "being the cause of," like the relation "being the parent of" or "being the child of," takes both its constituent terms from the same general class.[4] Thus, any event of which we can correctly say that it was causally entailed by one or more other events is one about which we are also entitled to say that it, alone

---

[3] Huxley, *op. cit.*, 240, 244.

[4] For the sake of simplicity, I treat causation as a dyadic relation in this context.

or in conjunction with other events, may causally entail some future events. Now the epiphenomenalist insists that mental events qualify as the effect-terms of certain causal relations. Since effect-terms and cause-terms belong to the same ontological category, his claim that mental events, which are effects, can never be causes is entirely untenable.

Causal impotence is a sufficient reason for classifying mental events as belonging to an ontological category different from that of any possible member of the causal chain. By using the entailment view or, for that matter, the regularity view to explicate the nature of the body-dependence of mind, the epiphenomenalist leaves no room for the ontological commitments his theory necessitates. His view requires that the generation of mental events involves more than regularity of succession and something different from causal entailment. For not only do mental events belong in a unique causal order; the epiphenomenalist, by arguing the "impotence" of one type of event, at once commits himself to some theory about the "active" nature of other types.

It may be instructive to develop some of the distinctive features of epiphenomenalism in terms of the regularity view of causation. It is essential for the epiphenomenalist to maintain both of the following propositions: (1) given any event M_1 with characteristically mental properties, there is another event B_1 that displays in some determinate form the characteristic features of a nervous event and that may be said to be the cause of M_1 in the sense that M_1 follows B_1 and events like M_1 usually or always follow events like B_1; (2) further, any physical event B_2 is caused by some other physical event B_1 in the sense that B_1 precedes B_2 and events resembling B_1 usually or always precede events resembling B_2.

These two propositions appear to give the essence of the epiphenomenalist's claim. In fact, however, they give considerably more. If events like B_1 are regularly followed by events like B_2 as well as by events like M_1 (as is the case with all consciousness-generating central-nervous events) and if events of the type B_2 are regularly followed by events resembling M_2, there is every reason to say that events like M_2 are the effects of events like M_1. Since events like M_1 are concomitants of events resembling B_2, they regularly precede events like M_2. This is sufficient justification for calling the mental event M_1 a cause.[5] Thus, if brain processes have effects, the mental acts that accompany them also have effects. Since on this view uniformity of succession *is* causation, the supposition that certain occurrences may regularly be followed by events they have not caused is quite unintelligible.

The epiphenomenalist's stand is incompatible with the regularity view precisely because he must maintain that at least some instances of uniform sequence—such as acts of will followed by bodily movements—are not instances of causal connection. Further, any attempt to state epiphenomenalism in the terms of the regularity view is doomed to failure. The epiphenomenalist cannot deny that physical changes succeed certain mental acts, and on the regularity view, such constant conjunction is tantamount to causal connection. Thus, any "statement of epiphenomenalism" is at once revealed as being, in reality, a statement of interactionism. The regular-sequence theory of causation is insensitive to the differences between parallelism, epiphenomenalism, and interactionism, and as such it can be of no use whatever to the epiphenomenalist.

The manifest impossibility of rendering its view of the body-dependence of mind in terms of any of the three major theories of the nature of causation need not betoken the total collapse of epiphenomenalism. I shall propose one course of action open to the epiphenomenalist. It may not be his only possible escape, and in any case I shall not develop it beyond the stage of a mere suggestion. My suggestion is that, following Aristotle, the epiphenomenalist may interpret the mind as the form of the body. He could then construe the difference between mental act and physical change in terms of the distinction between activity (*energeia*) and process (*kinesis*).[6] The sum total of vital processes, latent as well as operative, of an organized body could then be said to be

---

[5] The same argument applies, *mutatis mutandis*, to the case of psychophysical causation.

[6] There are helpful treatments of this distinction in two works that have long suffered from neglect. See Sir Alexander Grant, *The Ethics of Aristotle* (New York: Arno Press, 1973); and F. C. S. Schiller, *Humanism* (London: Macmillan, 1912).

the "psyche" or soul of that body. If the psyche is the body's first actuality, consciousness may be interpreted as the psyche's un-hindered functioning. The living act of awareness is thus the body's second entelechy, or the soul in act. The relation of phys-iological process to mental act is that of the potential to the actual or that of the first entelechy to the second.

The attempt to uphold the inefficacy of consciousness will estop the epiphenomenalist from subscribing to the view that, at least in the case of living animals, formal or final "causes" may have a generative role. Since the biological organism has tradi-tionally served as a paradigm of the efficacy of the final cause, the rejection of it in this area may well lead the epiphenomenalist to a wholesale dismissal of teleological causation. If he admits no final causes, he will consider form or actuality to be impotent. The word "impotent" might serve as a clue here. To say that con-sciousness is impotent is to claim that it carries no potencies, has no power to bring anything into existence. And to be fully actual is precisely to be destitute of unactualized potentialities. Thus, "impotent" becomes a laudatory instead of a pejorative term, and the mind, in spite (or because) of its inefficacy, will be construed as possessing all the perfections of the fully actual.

This attempt to fit the emergence of epiphenomenal mind into a larger conceptual frame has never, to my knowledge, received the elaboration it deserves.[7] It is an attempt that is, no doubt, heavily burdened with its own difficulties. It has, however, the advantage of leaving room for the necessary ontological commit-ments of the epiphenomenalist. And by adopting the categories suggested, he can at least free himself of the egregious task of dealing with effectless effects. Thus if epiphenomenalism is at all defensible, the attempt to defend it had best be made in the context of some such conceptual scheme.[8]

[7] George Santayana appears to have maintained this general view of the relation of "psyche" to consciousness, but he never worked out the theory in detail. See his *Scepticism and Animal Faith* (New York: Dover, 1955), 217; also his *The Realm of Spirit* (New York: Charles Scribner's Sons, 1940), 94.

[8] I wish to express my thanks to Professor Frank A. MacDonald of the College of William and Mary for his helpful suggestions and criticism.

CHAPTER 4

Meaning and the Impotence Hypothesis

(with Michael P. Hodges)

E PIPHENOMENALISM is a theory of the relation of mind to body that has been more frequently attacked than maintained throughout the history of philosophy. Its earliest reported advocate appears to have been Simmias in Plato's *Phaedo* with his harmony theory of mind. The most recent defense is probably that of Keith Campbell in his book *Body and Mind* (1970). Between the two, such thinkers as T. H. Huxley, Bradley, James, Broad, and Santayana have found the view worth serious attention. Recently, interest in epiphenomenalism has benefited from increased attention to materialism. Advocates of various forms of materialism find it important to dispose of the view because it shares with materialism the central strength of founding its claims on the autonomy of physiology as the science of the operations of the human body. Unfortunately, this interest is often confined to a cursory rejection of the position and seldom, if ever, extends to a serious attempt to articulate it with care.

Epiphenomenalism consists of three claims: (1) mental events are irreducibly distinct from physical events; (2) each mental event is dependent both for its existence and for its properties on physical events; and (3) no mental event exerts any causal influence either on other mental events or on physical events. The first claim identifies epiphenomenalism as a dualistic theory, which is a source of both strength and weakness. The second and third claims taken together assert the complete dependence of the mental on the physical and thus amount to commitment to the autonomy of physical operations. The mental, while conceded an ontologically irreducible status, is said to be causally impotent. The physical is identified as its indispensable causal ground. At the same time, whatever occurs within the human body is asserted to be fully explicable by reference to antecedent physical events and the laws that relate them. It is his commitment to the autonomy of the physical that allows the epiphenomenalist to welcome the findings of modern science. At the same time, this autonomy of the physical and the consequent potential adequacy of science to physical fact are not thought to compel surrender of a dualist ontology.

The major strength of epiphenomenalism is that it provides room for two apparently conflicting sets of our intuitions. It is clearly dualistic, taking seriously the apparent difference between the mental and the physical. But it also gives science its due by leaving the field open for its in-principle unrestricted capacity to explain physical events in terms of physical theory. In this way, it serves as a middle ground between Cartesian interactionism and modern materialism.

Although epiphenomenalism is a dualistic theory, there is no reason why it must be understood in a classical Cartesian context. Descartes's dualism was one of substances. The mind-body relation was thought by him to be one between an individual substance—mind—and a mode of material substance—a body. Insofar as the notion of substance is at all clear, the epiphenomenalist must specifically deny that mind is a substance. The essence of the impotence hypothesis is the rejection of any independent or enduring status for consciousness.

Some philosophers find the concept of substance so unclear as to make any proposition in which it functions suspect. Accordingly, they prefer to avoid the notion when attempting to articulate the mind-body relation. Instead, their discussions proceed in terms of a dualism of properties or of predicates. This is perfectly acceptable to the impotence theorist: all the major classical mind-body alternatives, including epiphenomenalism, are clearly statable in these terms.

Though the impotence hypothesis has some obvious and powerful advantages, it has also been the subject of a wide variety of criticisms. The most often repeated one is the counterintuitiveness of the position. Our experience is supposed to provide us with abundant examples of the operation of the mental on the physical. After all, does not the thought of the cookies in the jar cause me to get up and go to the kitchen?

Certainly epiphenomenalism is counterintuitive in the sense that if it is true, some of our entrenched beliefs are false. But it is unclear just why this should dispose of the theory out of hand. In any case, various systematic attempts have been made to deal with these by-now standard objections to epiphenomenalism, and there is little advantage in repeating them here.[1] However, a new line of objection, focusing on the notion of meaning, has emerged in recent discussions. This objection is at once interesting and powerful. It is interesting because in recent philosophical discussions a great deal of attention has been paid to semantic notions: the objection provides the epiphenomenalist with an opportunity to develop his position in this area. It is powerful because, if correct, it shows epiphenomenalism to be incoherent.

Unfortunately, the situation with this new objection is rather unusual. Although various philosophers have hinted at, suggested, and referred to it, we cannot find anyone who has explicitly stated it in print. It is said to have been frequently discussed, but it is rare to see even a substantial reference to it in the literature. Perhaps the closest thing to a published formulation of it is in Paul Meehl's "The Complete Autocerebroscopist" in *Mind, Matter and Method* (1966). There he suggests a principle that, if true, would reduce epiphenomenalism to incoherence. In the context of discussing the counterintuitive character of any position that denies causal efficacy to the mental, he says,

> The fascinating question whether, and how, a genuine semantic tie " 'red' means red" could exist for a knower, lacking any causal (raw feel $\rightarrow$ tokening) tie, I shall not attempt to treat here.[2]

[1] See "The Impotent Mind," pp. 16–28 above.

[2] Paul Meehl, "The Complete Autocerebroscopist," in *Mind, Matter and Method*, ed. Paul Feyerabend and Grover Maxwell (Minneapolis: University of Minnesota Press, 1966), 143.

In a footnote he adds that Wilfrid Sellars brought home to him the full force of this as an objection to epiphenomenalism. Correspondence with Meehl, Sellars, and Feigl indicates that at least Feigl and Sellars still find what we shall call the "semantic tie principle" (STP) plausible and devastating against epiphenomenalism.[3]

Although this principle has not been formulated with great precision or defended, it does contain the germ of a powerful objection against epiphenomenalism.[4] What STP appears to assert is that for a term to refer to a phenomenal quality, the term must occur in tokenings that are causally connected with occurrences of that phenomenal quality. The idea is that the meaning of at least such terms as "red," of which no discursive definition is possible, is inextricably tied to the actual production of the relevant sounds or written marks, and the presence of the corresponding sense qualities must be at least sometimes among the causes of these tokenings. If the occurrence of the raw feel never figures as a cause of the tokening behaviors in which the term designating it occurs, then "red" could not come to mean red.[5] If it were true that a semantic tie between "red" and the phenomenal quality red could exist only if the occurrence of the quality were at least a part cause of tokenings in which the term

[3] It may be thought that no one actually holds STP. This, however, is false. In correspondence, both Feigl and Sellars indicate that they do in fact subscribe to some form of the principle. Feigl, for example, says that there is a causal link between brain activity that is cross-categorically identical with subjective experience and the tokenings of qualia-predicates. "In pure semantics," he writes, "this causal tie is deliberately ignored (abstracted from) but, of course, it is indispensable for an account of the learning and the use of language." (Letter to Hodges and Lachs, June 14, 1973.)

Our suspicion is that those who doubt that anyone holds STP do so precisely because upon careful formulation (as we attempt in this paper) it loses a great deal of its plausibility. This, however, is not an unusual feature of philosophical views and constitutes an important reason why STP deserves careful scrutiny. So long as it is not brought into sharp focus, it can lurk as the apparently invincible foundation of important philosophical moves; the moment it is dragged into the light of day, it is of doubtful validity and its supporters fade away.

[4] Some difficulties with a full and careful formulation will be discussed below.

[5] A minor exception to this is discussed in the next footnote.

occurs, then phenomenal quality terms could not in fact have any meanings for the epiphenomenalist. This follows because the impotence thesis requires that such terms refer to phenomenal qualities and denies that occurrences of the qualities are ever causes of anything.

This line of reasoning could perhaps be generalized to include all tokening behaviors that involve terms purporting to refer to mental states or events. On such generalization, the truth of epiphenomenalism entails that no mental term can stand in the appropriate semantic relations. In order for any mental event term to have meaning, STP requires that its referent be part of the causal history of the tokening behavior in which that term functions. But the very heart of epiphenomenalism is the denial of causal efficacy to mental events. Therefore, if epiphenomenalism is true, no mental event can figure as a cause in the history of any tokening behavior. From the conjunction of epiphenomenalism and STP, it then follows that no mentalistic term can have meaning. Of course, this conclusion is disastrous for epiphenomenalism, for even the meaningfulness of the statement of the theory presupposes that at least some mentalistic terms refer to inefficacious mental events. Thus, in the end, if STP is true, epiphenomenalism is an incoherent position whose truth preempts the possibility of its meaningfulness.

This important objection deserves careful consideration for at least three reasons. First, if the objection is sound, it is completely devastating for this major mind-body theory. It cannot be tolerated by the impotence theorist in the way in which, for example, charges of counterintuitiveness can. Any serious advocate of epiphenomenalism must meet this objection head-on. Second, the argument deserves attention precisely because it has *not* been carefully formulated and defended. An argument hiding from full view but thought conclusive by major thinkers in the field is likely to have an unwarranted impact on discussions. The interests of philosophical development are not served by the dismissal of important alternatives for reasons never carefully formulated or defended. If epiphenomenalism—or any view for that matter—is to be refuted, it should be refuted by a good argument, not by a hint, a whisper, or a mere suggestion. Finally, there is a third reason for examining this argument in detail. By showing how the epiphenomenalist might deal with such an objection, we can gain a better appreciation of the mature and full philosophical power of the position. Given the minimal serious attention the impotence view has received, this by itself is an important enough reason for our study.

Obviously, the focus of the argument is what we have called the "semantic tie principle" (STP). As we have already pointed out, this principle has not received a systematic formulation, much less a full defense, nor is it our purpose in this paper to provide that. Nevertheless, it is important to become somewhat clearer about what this principle is and what commitments are associated with it. It is unclear whether it is meant to be a general semantic principle or whether it applies only to raw feels, as Meehl's formulation suggests. As a working proposal, we can formulate STP with regard to raw feel terms as follows:

> A raw feel term is meaningful only if, if T is a tokening in which the term occurs, then T has the occurrence of the appropriate phenomenal quality as a part of its cause.[6]

Let us proceed at once to some preliminary comments. First of all, as will become clear later, a formulation of STP as a general semantic principle is not so simple a matter. But whether we take STP in its general or its restricted form, it is necessary to distinguish between tokening and nontokening uses of terms. As we understand Meehl's position, tokenings are only a subclass of all uses of a term. For him, they are the subclass of uses in which the specific semantic function of a term is to report the occurrence of some phenomenal quality.[7] If we generalize STP, then of course

[6] It should be noted that this does not require that the term actually occur in tokening behavior. We chose this formulation to leave room for cases in which such explicit synonyms as "red"-"rot" might be introduced, although "rot" has not occurred in a tokening behavior. Of course, the situation is much more complex if we try to construe STP as a general semantic principle.

[7] The same point can be made even if we allow all uses of a term to count as tokenings. We must then distinguish between those tokenings that have the appropriate phenomenal quality as a direct or immediate part of their causal

tokenings would not be restricted to reports of the occurrences of *phenomenal* qualities. It should be obvious at once, however, that many meaningful terms do not and cannot serve a tokening function. So-called syncategorematic terms, such as "the," "and," and "but," are meaningful but do not function in the reporting role for which STP is meant to lay down conditions.

Even if we restrict ourselves to terms like "red," we must distinguish between a statement like "I am now seeing red" and one like "I hope I will see red." The former is a tokening while the latter is not, at least as far as the phenomenal quality red is concerned. Obviously, the occurrence of the phenomenal quality red need not be part of the immediate causal history of the second sort of utterance. However, unlike the case of syncategorematic terms, STP can still apply indirectly to the second sort of case by maintaining that tokening uses of phenomenal quality terms are logically prior to nontokening uses. That is, it is only because we can or have used "red" meaningfully in the first sort of case that we can use it in the second.

If STP is to be offered as a general semantic principle, then some distinction between direct and indirect applications would be necessary to account for such terms as "unicorn."[8] Proponents of STP would have to maintain that insofar as such terms are meaningful, their meaning must ultimately be explicable by means of terms to which STP applies directly. If Meehl, Feigl, and the others were to accept this stance, they would be holding that tokening uses are logically prior to other, nonostensive uses of language. This would be true not only for the same terms occurring in tokening and in nontokening contexts (as with "red"

history and those that have it as an indirect and mediate element. See our discussion below.

[8] It is worth noting that any attempt to see STP as a general semantic principle would require a careful distinction between *learning* circumstances and *using* circumstances. Given such a distinction, it would be possible to contend that STP applies directly only to learning circumstances. We would thereby allow for uses of language in which no direct causal role is played by appropriate phenomenal qualities but which are nevertheless tied to actual occurrences of such qualities at some time in the causal history of the term's use. This way of developing STP leads in the direction of the concept empiricism discussed below.

above) but for all terms whether they occur in tokening contexts or not. This amounts to claiming that a meaningful language must contain at least some terms that can be and are used in tokening contexts and that are therefore governed by STP. Further, they would be claiming that the meaning of all other terms must be explicable in terms of these primitive or fundamental terms. Such a position is in effect a form of concept empiricism. In its expanded, general version then, STP amounts to asserting the primacy of ostensive definition for meaning and the grounding of all semantic relations in natural (causal) relations. Whether or not this is an acceptable cost for proponents of STP obviously depends on their assessment of concept empiricism.

Perhaps proponents of STP would like to avoid commitment to something like concept empiricism and thus would not want to expand it into a general semantic principle along the lines suggested in the previous discussion. There are in fact some reasons for believing that it is meant to apply to raw feels only. In the first place, the only explicit discussion of the principle, in the Meehl article, occurs in the context of raw feels alone. Second, it is advanced specifically in the context of the mind-body issue and by such philosophers as Feigl. For Feigl and other identity theorists, the crucial issues center on raw feels. Such thinkers typically do not propose a single treatment for all mental concepts. Some are taken to be topic neutral and are thus thought to present no problem for the identity theorist. Others are given some form of behaviorist analysis. The serious difficulties of the mind-body problem thus revolve around the residue of terms for which a behaviorist or other reductive analysis seems out of place. This residue usually includes sensation terms (or itches, pains, tickles) and terms for raw feels (or the occurrences of such phenomenal qualities as red).[9]

Now if the mind-body problem is to be stated in terms of the relation of sensations and raw feels to brain processes, STP need

---

[9] For this approach see J. J. C. Smart, "Sensations and Brain Processes," *Philosophical Review* 68 (1959): 141–56, and Herbert Feigl, "Mind-Body, *Not* a Pseudo Problem," in *Dimensions of Mind,* ed. Sidney Hook (New York: New York University Press, 1960), 24–36.

only apply to sensation and raw feel terms. However, even this restricted version of STP needs some qualification. We must at once ask the exact meaning of "tokening behavior." Are we to suppose that all tokenings are true? Suppose, for example, that the phenomenal quality blue occurs, but lying, I say "red." Is this a bit of tokening behavior? We can see no reason for saying that it is not. However, if it is, it constitutes a clear case in which a phenomenal quality is not a part cause of speech that betokens its presence. Proponents of STP will surely argue that I can lie by using "red" in this context only because "red" does in fact mean red and that can be true only if at least some tokenings in which "red" occurs have the phenomenal quality red as a part of their cause. Thus, my use of "red" on the occasion in question does have the occurrence of the phenomenal quality as part at least of its causal history, although admittedly not as part of its immediate cause.

The argument here is that cases of lying are parasitic on truthful uses of words. That is, I can use "red" to lie only because it does mean red; but for it to mean red, there must have been previous tokenings in which the term or a synonym was associated with the appropriate phenomenal quality in the way required by STP. Not only are such tokenings a condition of and thus logically prior to raw feel terms having meaning, but they are also causally and therefore temporally prior. That is, prior tokenings whose immediate causal history contained the appropriate phenomenal quality are themselves parts of the causal history of my present false tokening.

We can, of course, decide to use the term "tokening" so that only true uses count as tokenings. But this would yield nothing in philosophical clarity. We would then have to introduce some such term as "purported tokenings" and formulate STP in terms of that.

A revised and improved formulation of STP restricted to raw feels might run as follows:

> A raw feel term is meaningful only if, if T is a tokening in which the term occurs, then either T has the occurrence of the appropriate phenomenal quality as a part

of its cause or T has as a part of its causal history
tokenings that had the appropriate phenomenal quality as their part cause.[10]

More simply put, STP maintains that at least on some occasions,
my uttering "red" or a synonym is a direct consequence of the
occurrence of the phenomenal quality red. There may well be
further revisions necessary to polish STP into an adequate principle even in its restricted application. However, we have developed it sufficiently for our purposes. There can be no doubt
that in either its restricted or its general form STP seems incompatible with epiphenomenalism. If true, it is the foundation of a
compelling objection.

We want to be as generous to proponents of the objection as we
can possibly be. But it is worth noting at once that an argument is
only as strong as its premises or the reasons for it. As things stand
today, no reasons have been offered in support of STP. In fact, we
have already seen that development of it into a general semantic
principle entails commitment to views that are at least highly
questionable. The epiphenomenalist might well point out that
the burden of proof is on the proponents of STP to make it at least
plausible.

In the absence of formal defense by its proponents and in order
to get a clearer view of STP, it might be wise to ask about its
pedigree. What is its natural philosophical home? What intuitions
lie behind it? We do not have to look far for answers to these
questions. What lurks behind STP is the notion of the primacy of
natural relations to semantic or epistemic ones. The causal theory
of perception is perhaps the most familiar product of this line of
philosophical thought. How is it possible, proponents of the
causal theory of perception ask, for the data presented to consciousness to yield knowledge of the natural world unless they
stand in some nonepistemic, causal relation to the world? This is
precisely Meehl's "fascinating question," restated here to apply in

---

[10] By calling this "an improved formulation," we certainly do not mean to
suggest either that there are no other difficulties with it or that we find it acceptable
or true. Our concern here is not with STP per se but with its impact on epiphenomenalism.

the perceptual sphere. Once we have this in mind, it is not surprising to find STP proposed by the philosophers we have mentioned. Its natural home is a philosophical realism that gives primacy to the physical. Such a view frequently takes the form, on the contemporary scene, of a scientifically grounded philosophy of mind of the sort we normally associate with Feigl, Meehl, and Sellars.

By the same token, we should now have a good idea of where to look for those who deny STP. Bishop Berkeley was committed to denying it since he thought that no items in the physical world were causes, even though some of them were connected by meaning relations. Of course, Berkeley also rejected the causal theory of perception and with it the primacy of the physical. It may thus be supposed that his denial of the semantic tie principle can provide no solace for an epiphenomenalist since, after all, Berkeley's position is an idealism that seems at first blush to be at the opposite pole from the impotence hypothesis. But while it is clear that Berkeley's particular brand of idealism is incompatible with epiphenomenalism, it is not at all evident that every position that incorporates Berkeley's denial of STP would be. In particular, a thoroughgoing phenomenalism may well be compatible with epiphenomenalism. Our point in stressing this is twofold. First of all, the proponents of STP and of the attendant objection to epiphenomenalism have not offered positive reasons for adopting their principle. Second, as a result, we feel justified in thinking that there may well be nothing wrong with rejecting the principle outright. We have, in any case, not been shown what, if anything, is wrong with an epiphenomenalist simply doing without it, if he can. Until its proponents provide either reasons for STP in general or at least reasons why an epiphenomenalist must accept STP, the impotence theorist is free to ignore the argument.

But it may well be objected that although epiphenomenalism is not incompatible with phenomenalism and thus may not be incompatible with the denial of STP, the impotence hypothesis and the semantic tie principle are nonetheless natural bedfellows. As we indicated earlier, the natural home of STP is a philosophical realism that gives primacy to the physical. Exactly the same is true of epiphenomenalism, the thrust of which is to tie consciousness and mentality to the physical. As we have tried to show, that is also the thrust of STP. Yet we have seen that these two naturally allied views appear to be incompatible. At this point, a thoroughgoing materialist may suggest that the incompatibility is the result of the halfheartedness or ambivalence that is at the center of epiphenomenalism. He may point out that it is not enough to tie the ghost to the machine. The combination of an autonomous physical world with impotent minds naturally leads to inconsistencies. What must be done is to banish the ghost altogether. That is exactly what the materialist proposes to do. The incompatibility of epiphenomenalism with STP is the result, he is apt to charge, of the failure on the part of the impotence theory to carry to their conclusion the very principles that underlie it.

This line of argument requires the epiphenomenalist to make a more direct attack on STP or at least on its use in the argument against his view. To do this, we must look more closely at STP. Its essence is the claim that causal relations must undergird semantic relations. In order for there to be a semantic relation between the word "red" and a specific set of raw feels, there must be a causal relation between certain tokenings and raw feels of the appropriate sort. Since the semantic relation is direct, that is, there is nothing semantically intermediate between particular tokenings and the correlated raw feels, we may be led to suppose that the causal relation must also be direct. This, however, would make STP a much stronger and much less plausible claim than it needs to or ought to be. In fact, we have already seen that to make STP even minimally plausible, it is necessary to allow that the causal role played by phenomenal qualities can be quite indirect. In its weakest and probably most defensible form, the principle asserts only that each semantic tie presupposes some suitable causal connection. This does not specify the determinate character of the causal tie. Our strategy will be to argue that this weaker form of STP can be satisfied by epiphenomenalism, even if the stronger one cannot.

A full understanding of the situation requires that we develop the epiphenomenalist position in a little more detail. Consider a particular sort of brain event B. Such events will in many cases have, according to the epiphenomenalist, two distinct sorts of effects. In the first place, through a complex set of intermediate causes, *B*'s may generate some observable behavior. The behavior might well be the utterance of "red," i.e., tokening behavior. In the second place, *B*'s may give rise to mental events of the type Feigl and Meehl refer to as "raw feels." Of course, from the point of view of consciousness, only the raw feel and the experienced tokening are evident. The *B* involved is hidden from view in the recesses of the brain.

Now there are two things worth noting about this analysis. First, according to it, there is a causal tie that undergirds the semantic relation between experienced tokenings and raw feels, even though it is not the direct one we might originally have supposed. The causal connection does not run from raw feel to tokening; instead, both the raw feel and the tokening behavior are effects of a third, *B*-like event. This satisfies the condition set by the weak form of the semantic tie principle. Second, it is not surprising, at least from the point of view of consciousness, that we believe there is a direct causal relation between the raw feel and the tokening behavior. For in our experience, the raw feels and the tokenings occur constantly and intimately conjoined; by contrast, their intermediary, which is the real cause of both, is inaccessible in ordinary conscious life. *B*-like events do not appear in experience; their existence is discovered by scientific experimentation. It is, then, natural to suppose that the occurrence of the raw feel is the direct cause of the tokening and that the causal connection that grounds the semantic tie is this supposed direct one between raw feel and tokening. The epiphenomenalist would not want to deny that there is a causal connection, only that it is a direct one.

The current strategy is the same as that which allows the epiphenomenalist to fend off the charge of counterintuitiveness. There also, he does not deny that we believe in the direct causal efficacy of our conscious thoughts, feelings, hopes, and desires in generating subsequent behavior. He denies only that such opinions are true and then seeks to make his denial plausible by providing an account of how and why we come to possess such deeply entrenched beliefs.

It should now be clear that epiphenomenalism is not inconsistent with STP. The appearance of inconsistency is due simply to the mistake of supposing that every causal relation must be a direct one. Such a supposition is not generally warranted; in fact, once we have the principle clearly in view, we can find innumerable counterexamples to it. The correlation of *A* and *C* argues for some causal relation between them. But it takes a separate argument to establish that the connection is unilinear or direct.

So far we have made only negative or defensive points in response to the proponents of the semantic tie principle. However, the epiphenomenalist also has a more positive and more radical strategy open to him in answering these critics. The proponent of STP claims that there has to be a causal connection between our tokening behavior and sensory items to which our tokenings refer. The epiphenomenalist can respond by offering an analysis of the conditions under which the problem is supposed to arise for him. The analysis attempts to show that the very circumstances that are supposed to generate the problem for epiphenomenalism are misconceived. If they are reconceived in terms of a conceptual framework consistent with the impotence theory, the problem disappears without impairing the account we give of meaning and linguistic behavior.

The difficulty is generated by accepting the apparently simple dichotomy between tokening behaviors and raw feels. Tokening behaviors are physical while raw feels are supposedly mental. The argument proponents of STP advance rests on the claim that such behaviors cannot stand in a meaning-relation to raw feels unless the raw feels stand in a causal relation to the behaviors. But the epiphenomenalist rejects the very terms in which this problem is set. He begins by calling attention to the fundamental distinction between meaning and linguistic behavior. A central consequence of the impotence hypothesis is that linguistic behavior is explicable without any reference to nonphysical items. It consists in certain operations of highly complex physical organisms; as such, whatever laws prove adequate to explain the sequence of physical events are also adequate to explain the physical events that constitute speaking, writing, and other such behaviors.

By contrast, *language as experienced* is not a series of physical

acts. The palpable structure of meanings, the framework of connotations, the nuances of intended significance are all mental acts
or the objects of such acts. Counterintuitive as it might at first
appear, even perceived linguistic behavior is, by ontological status, mental. For the epiphenomenalist, it will not do to draw the
mental-physical line simply between linguistic behavior and raw
feels. Instead, we must begin by distinguishing between mere
linguistic behavior, which is a proper subject of scientific investigation, and linguistic behavior as perceived or experienced,
which is its mental counterpart.

This by itself may provide some insight into why the confusion
between the mental and the physical levels is so easy and persuasive. We are tempted to identify linguistic behavior with what
we perceive of it. Next, when we note that reports of red are
evidently correlated with perceptions or experiences of red objects, we naturally find ourselves impelled to ask how there could
be this report without that sensed quality. This question, however, is the result of inadequate analysis. In asking it, we telescope
a double inquiry into a single one. The result is a confusion that
creates the appearance of an insuperable difficulty for the epiphenomenalist.

The need for a double inquiry is the necessary consequence of
dealing with two disparate and ontologically irreducible levels.
On the physical level, we have the difficult task of explaining the
correlation of tokening behaviors with the physical counterparts
of sensed qualia. We know relatively little about how these hook-
ups occur, but the reason for our ignorance is not intrinsic un-
knowability. Brain physiology is still in its infancy. The important
consideration is that there is no reason why it has to remain there
indefinitely. Here we deal with the physical; our knowledge is
bounded by the time and effort we expend rather than by the
intrinsic limits of our faculties. There is no doubt some causal
connection between physical quality-counterpart and the behavior indicating its presence. But it is important to remember
that the quality-counterpart is not the sense quality and the
tokening behavior is not, intrinsically, its perceived counterpart.

On the second (mental) level, the inquiry has to focus on the
relationship that obtains between the spoken or written words *as*

experienced and the experienced quality to which they are supposed to refer. The words are experienced as having meaning, as
palpably referring to the quality sensed. It is a misconception to
suppose that the quality stands in a causal relation to the experienced words that refer to it. Since both the experienced tokening
and the sensed quality are mental, neither stands in a causal
relation to the other. Instead, both are the products of underlying
causal factors.

The relation between *experienced* tokening and raw feel is clearly
semantic. The words appear in consciousness as reporting or
referring to the quality. But it is important to keep in mind that no
causal tie is needed between the experienced quality and the
experienced tokening to undergird this semantic connection. The
total quality/experienced-tokening complex is what is produced,
for all of that exists at the level of consciousness. Of course, this
complex *is* undergirded by a causal relation, albeit not one that
obtains between the elements of the complex. The causal connection that makes this semantic tie possible is that between the
physiological counterpart of the sense quality and the tokening
as a purely physical act. When this latter connection obtains,
given an intact and normally functioning brain and nervous
system, it rises to consciousness in the form of the experienced
semantic tie between word and quality.

Perhaps it is wise now to summarize the central points of the
epiphenomenalist's main response. There are two negative
points and two positive points to note. (1) There is no semantic tie
between the purely physical tokening and the experienced quality. (2) There is no causal tie between the tokening behavior as
experienced and the experienced quality. (3) There is a semantic
tie between the tokening behavior as experienced and the experienced quality. (4) There is a causal tie between the purely physical
tokening and the physical counterpart of the experienced quality.
In short, the causal tie obtains between two physical items, and
the semantic tie obtains between two mental items. The real crux
of the epiphenomenalist's response is the claim that proponents
of STP do not take the mental-physical distinction seriously
enough and hence do not locate each relation on its proper ontological level.

The double inquiry to which we referred earlier requires that we explore both the physical tie and the experienced meaning relation. Each inquiry has its own point, its own method, and its own results. The first study is purely scientific in character, the second is descriptively phenomenological. Since our access to conscious relations, to structures that appear in consciousness is immediate, it is initially easier to focus on these and to deal with them. The temptation then presents itself to connect the structure of appearances too closely with the order of changes in the world. The natural assumption at this stage is to suppose that the causal relations that make for change obtain between the items that appear to us. It is only later sophistication, heavily reinforced by the success of manipulative science, that helps us understand that appearances themselves are only products of causal changes and never the efficacious factor in the change.

It might be supposed that the epiphenomenalist's analysis gives rise to a needless reduplication of entities. We end up not only with experienced tokenings and sensed qualities but also with physical tokenings and physiological quality-counterparts. It strikes us, of course, that there is nothing unnecessary about this duplication. But at any rate, to affirm that it *is* unnecessary is but another way of saying that epiphenomenalism is false. Whether it is or not may be difficult to decide. But it is well to remember that that is the question at issue; mere assertion of its falseness will not do.

Our point is that the epiphenomenalist can reasonably argue that the Feigl-Meehl-Sellars objection will not carry the day, simply because it is based on an inadequate grasp of the radical nature of the impotence hypothesis. The new analysis we have suggested enables the impotence theorist to account for the requisite causal tie connecting quality and tokening without introducing the need for causal efficacy on the level of mind. The radical nature of the impotence view is brought home once we gain an adequate understanding of the double-level view of language it requires. There may be arguments against the adequacy of this analysis of the components of language, just as there is considerable evidence in favor of it. But those arguments will have to be developed one at a time, and when they are developed in detail, we shall know whether or not the epiphenomenalist can answer them. Even if he cannot, however, his view will fail not on account of the Feigl-Meehl-Sellars objection, but on account of some new argument as yet unwritten or unthought.

CHAPTER 5

Two Concepts of God

PHILOSOPHERS have long debated the question of the existence of God. This is one of many philosophical issues in which the motivation for inquiry has come more perhaps from the side of human feeling than from disinterested scientific curiosity. Powerful emotions appear to prompt thinkers to devote effort to the attempt to prove or disprove the existence of God. The urgency of this task has made some of these philosophers pay less than adequate heed to the concepts they employ. It appears to have escaped the attention of many of them that the word "God" does not have a single meaning either in religious language generally or in philosophical theology. It is obvious that one of the important ways in which religious traditions differ is in their conceptions of the Deity. But a considerable number of different God-concepts may be distinguished in the Judeo-Christian religious tradition itself, and not even in Christian theology proper is the word "God" free of ambiguity.

On examination, it appears that "God" has stood for any one of a family of concepts. A brief comparison of St. Thomas Aquinas's concept of God with Tillich's, St. Peter Damian's notion of the Supreme Being with Bishop Berkeley's, and Hegel's idea of the Deity with Kierkegaard's should be sufficient to indicate the range of dissimilarity within this wide family. On the other hand, however, certain significant characteristics form a part of many, though by no means all, Christian God-concepts. The traits I have in mind are those of infinity, goodness, power, wisdom, and personality, among others. The skeletal God-concept that may be constructed out of these traits has, without doubt, been a central strand in the historical succession and superposition of conceptions of the Deity. It has been the dominant form of which perhaps the majority of the God-concepts of Christian philosophical orthodoxy were differently developed variants. According to this skeletal concept, God is an Infinite Being who is perfect and self-sufficient. He is a Person or a Trinity of Persons who showed infinite power and infinite goodness in creating the world, is infinitely well informed about the deeds of free agents in it, and will be infinitely merciful though immeasurably just in judging, rewarding, and punishing them.

I call this conception of God "skeletal" because of its generality; it is neutral with respect to the radically different views one may take of such central issues as the nature and extent of God's power, the relation of God's reason to His will, and the exact significance of characterizing the divine motivation as "good." Without answers to these and similar problems, it is impossible to have a fully developed view of the Divine Personality. I maintain that this skeletal concept of God has been of central significance in Western philosophical theology because of its ties with the general conceptual framework of Christian rational religion. My claim is that this central, skeletal concept of God is radically incoherent. My critical analysis of it may be looked upon as an attempted raid on natural religion in the tradition of Hume and Kant. But there are important differences between their enterprise and mine, not the least of which is that both Hume and Kant were primarily concerned with showing the inadequacy of the proofs for the existence of God. If my claim that the concept of God is logically incoherent can be substantiated, the question of the existence of God does not even arise. To ask it would be as senseless as to ask about the existence of square circles: the object of a self-contradictory concept necessarily does not exist.

There are at least two reasons why the traditional God-concept is logically incoherent. *The first reason* is that at least one of the essential attributes of God—omniscience—involves an internal inconsistency. Second, some of the attributes traditionally ascribed to God—the attributes of power and consciousness—are incompatible and cannot both characterize a single Being. It is worth remarking that if I succeed in establishing even one of these two contentions, the concept of God I am considering will have been shown to be of no theological value. That it is of dubious *religious* value is a point I hope to show a little later on.

It is virtually impossible to overestimate the significance of the notion of omniscience for theology. According to the traditional view, God's omniscience functions as an indispensable condition of His effective choice of the best. Without it, God's love would be half-blind: His power would verge on brute, undirected force. Divine Providence would be impossible without omniscience, and the Last Judgment would turn into an odious display of presumption and arrogance. The radical superiority of the Supreme Being resides in His precise knowledge of all there is to know. Only such intelligence can ensure full divine self-realization and serve as eternal guarantee that each one of God's acts is right.

Omniscience consists in knowledge of whatever is knowable. But knowable things are of many sorts, not all of which can be apprehended by the same sort of cognitive act. Knowledge by acquaintance of sense-qualities, emotions, and states of mind is different in kind from the propositional knowledge we may have of such objects as past events, scientific laws, and mathematical theorems. I do not wish to explore the relationship between knowledge by acquaintance and knowledge by description generally. I shall restrict myself to calling attention to the single fact that in certain cases, if not in all, presentational awareness is a necessary condition of propositional knowledge. I do not wish to rest my case on the general principle of empiricism according to which nothing can be in the intellect that was not first in the senses. The truth of my more limited claim is independent of the truth or falsity of this sweeping assertion. The relatively simple and clear-cut case of dependence I have in mind is the one in which we deal with the concept of some sense-quality or feeling. In such instances, it appears to me to be clear that prior cognitive acquaintance with the sense-quality or the feeling is an indispensable condition of forming a concept of it and, therefore, of understanding propositions that are about it. In plainer language, in the case at least of sense-qualities and feelings, experience is a condition of understanding. No one can have a concept of fear or love or the color red without the appropriate experiences, and no one can understand a proposition without grasping every one of its constituent concepts.

My objection to the attribute of omniscience, then, is this. On the hypothesis that a Being is omniscient, we can show that there are some things He cannot possibly know. The fact that He cannot know them is not the result of any inherent unintelligibility on their part. It is, rather, the outcome of God's postulated omniscience. Let us take doubt as an example. Evidential inadequacy is often the cause of doubt, but it is never identical with it. The consciousness that there is inadequate evidence for a proposition is also improperly called "doubt." I am conscious, for example, that there is inadequate evidence for the proposition that the last shot of the Second World War was fired in 2000 B.C. I cannot, however, be said to doubt its truth, for I know its falsity. Doubt is a psychological state of vacillation, a felt incertitude about what is true. God's omniscience precludes His having any such experiences. If He knows all truths, He cannot experience uncertainty about them. Since for any true proposition p He knows that p, it is impossible for Him to experience that felt inability to determine whether p or its contradictory is true, which is the essence of doubt. But if God cannot experience doubt, He cannot have a concept of it. And if He cannot have a concept of doubt, He cannot completely understand any propositions of which the concept of doubt is a constituent. And no person who fails to understand a proposition can be said to know it to be true.

What I hope to have shown so far is that omniscience makes impossible certain experiences without which omniscience itself is impossible. To put it another way, I contend that there are certain experiences, and therefore certain sorts of knowledge, that are the unique possession of finite, less-than-omniscient consciousness. The notion of an omniscient consciousness—one that is in actual possession of all possible sorts of knowledge—therefore lacks logical coherence.

There are three ways in which traditional theology might try to avoid this conclusion. First of all, it may be maintained that whatever is the exclusive property of the finite is destitute of value and reality. Since knowledge is of the real, to say that God knows whatever can be known is to assert that He knows everything that has reality. If doubt cannot be apprehended by the Perfect Being, the reason is that it is a privation. In His own way,

God knows whatever fragment of actuality there is in doubt; for the rest, doubt is not a proper object of cognition. And in order for God to know the kind of positive being there is in doubt, He certainly need not have been plagued with the experience. This escape route will not work. In taking it, the theologian commits himself to the totally unjustified dogma that there are degrees of reality. There is no earthly reason to suppose that, given their existence, doubt is any less real than certainty, the laws of gravity, or the Divinity. Being is not like excess body weight of which one can have more or less. Although existing objects may differ in kind and complexity, and different cognitive methods may be required to explore them, no one of them is any more real than the others, and they are all possible objects of cognition.

The second way in which the theologian might attempt to counter my attack is by the claim that God's ways of knowing are radically unlike ours. In God, there is no distinction between intuitive, presentational awareness and discursive, propositional knowledge. He has an "intuitive understanding": a faculty that combines in itself the universality of thought with the concrete immediacy of sensation. In God, therefore, concepts do not presuppose experience; the two are somehow united in a unique sort of cognitive act. But how is this synthesis of incompatibles possible? How can we understand this union of the abstract, discursive universality of judgment with the concrete, intuitive particularity of sensation? There is, it seems to me, only one possible answer to this question: we cannot understand it. God's ways are not our ways. He is beyond the limits of reason: in Him, contradictions are reconciled. If the theologian does not go this far, it is up to him to give a full account of the divine intuitive understanding. If, on the other hand, he does admit that God knows in ways unknowable to man, he has abandoned the enterprise of rational theology. Revealed religion is still open to him and so is silent worship, but he cannot claim to have an intelligible concept of his God.

The third and final attempt to escape the conclusion that God cannot be omniscient takes the form of the insistence that while God the Father knows whatever God can know, God the Son has access to whatever is uniquely finite. It is through the suffering of

Jesus Christ that God effected the reconciliation of finite and infinite. What, then, could prevent the theologian from claiming that it is the passion of Jesus Christ that provides God with the experiences requisite for His knowledge of human emotions, doubt, and suffering? In this argument, traditional theology begins by virtually conceding the point at issue. It is admitted that God as transcendent and eternal cannot know the suffering of man. In order to experience and thereby know human doubt and pain, He has to resign His infinity, His eternity, His omniscience. But now a serious problem presents itself. In order to make good his escape, our theologian has to present intelligible—and that means contradiction-free—accounts of the Incarnation and the Trinity. Without these, it could not be understood how the experiences of Jesus can contribute anything to the divine knowledge. And I cannot conceal my conviction that of the Incarnation and the Trinity no consistent theory will ever be advanced, for such paradoxes and such mysteries are essentially beyond the pale of rational explanation.

The second inconsistency of the traditional God-concept derives from the incompatibility of the attributes of power and knowledge. By the power of God, I presume that men of religion as well as theologians mean the ability of God to cause changes. The creation of the world itself (if any such event ever took place) may be considered a change, albeit a change of a very special sort, if we view it against the background of divine constancy. Change is most aptly characterized as the exchange of qualities or relations in an environment of relative permanence. We say that a change has occurred when some trait not previously present has taken the place of one that had been there before. To put this somewhat more precisely: we may properly say that a change has taken place if some object O is characterized by the quality Q_1 but not by the quality Q_2 at a time t_1, and if it is characterized by the quality Q_2 but not by the quality Q_1 at an immediately subsequent time t_2. Time, then, is unavoidably implicated in change. Not only is every change in time; there is also time in every change. For no single state of affairs is a change. Change must have terminal points, and it is essential that these termini inhabit different moments of time.

Time, therefore, is at least a necessary condition of change. If every change takes time and takes place in time, each cause of every change must share this property. In addition to whatever other connections there may be between them, the cause must stand in a temporal relation to its issue. Both cause and effect, both change and the being that is the source of it must have the property of temporality. God, if He has the power to cause changes, must be a Being who exists in time.

In addition to the ability to cause changes, the traditional view also attributes to God the ability to know what He has caused. How is knowledge of change possible? On one condition only: if there is a synthesis in thought of the termini of change. Cognition of an object O as characterized by the quality Q_1 but not by the quality Q_2 at time t_1 does not give one knowledge of change, nor does cognition of the object O as characterized by the quality Q_2 but not by the quality Q_1 at time t_2. In order for there to be consciousness of *change*, both of these states must be kept in mind. What is essential is that we think of the *terminus a quo* as prior to the *terminus ad quem* without thinking of it prior to thinking of the *terminus ad quem*. Knowledge of change demands that actual change be "arrested" in a vista: knowledge of temporal passage is possible only if the mind transcends the process and constructs an unmoving likeness of the moving flux.

An act that synthesizes time cannot exist in it; and time, whose essence is succession, cannot survive a synthesis. Knowledge of process is possible only through synthesis, but cognitive synthesis is not another process. It is not an event after the fashion of natural events. It has no temporal duration, no beginning, and no end; there is simply no time in it. It is only by the measure of external events that we can even say that it occurs at a certain time. No conscious act can be a part of the flux it surveys. If the act of knowledge must be free of time, the knower who consists of a series of such acts cannot have any temporal predicates. God, if His essential function is to know, is a Being who cannot exist in time.

The second inconsistency of the God-concept, then, is this. If God has power, He must live in time as an agent in the general flux. If God has knowledge, He must transcend time and cannot be a part of the flux He knows. Now it is clear that a single being cannot be characterized by two attributes, one of which requires and the other of which precludes the possession of a certain property. If we conceive God both as an effective agent and as a conscious mind, we endow Him with such attributes: the first demands His temporality, the second debars it. Knowledge and action cannot be combined: either God has power, or He is a mind. If He wields power, He is a being among beings in the natural world, a force unmindful of what it effects. If, on the other hand, He is a conscious God, He can be but a spectator of fate, an impotent witness of the cosmic dance.

The most obvious objection to this argument is that it is based on a misapprehension of the nature of divine agency. Only the philosophically primitive have meant by the power of God His ability to cause changes in the world. This popular interpretation can admittedly not stand serious scrutiny. Sophisticated theologians, however, have never thought of God's efficacy in quite this way. By divine power, many of them understood two closely related properties of God. The first was God's total independence of every other thing: His causeless self-existence. The second property, growing out of the first, was God's support of the world: His role as sustainer of a universe that could not exist on its own. The claim of these theologians was not that specific changes in the turning world should be credited to God's activity, but the far more radical one that the very being of contingent nature depends on God as its essential ground. The power of God, then, is His ability to sustain a changing cosmos by an act of will.

One of the clearest statements of this view of divine power is found in the work of René Descartes. The creation and the preservation of the world, Descartes explains, are the same activity. The world lapses from existence every moment: each time it takes a divine act of will to bring it back. From the standpoint of God, of course, there is no renewed volition at each moment: such multiplicity would make Him temporal. God, however, is not temporal; He is eternal. A single, eternal divine *act* of will, as distinct from temporal *action*, suffices to guarantee the continued existence of the world.

Whatever incidental value this objection might have in shoring up the cosmological argument for the existence of a Necessary Being, it does nothing to counter my contention. To demonstrate that my interpretation of divine power is wrong, it is necessary to show, first of all, that there is a cogent alternative. This the objection clearly fails to do. Power is the ability to act or do, and all deeds and all actions occur in time. The attempt, recurrent in the history of philosophy, to read dynamism into the eternal has been based on the almost perverse refusal to distinguish between doing and being. It is essential, however, that this distinction be drawn. Even if we were to admit that each temporal thing is a set of events or actions, it would not follow that eternal objects have to be active in order to be. The eternal can be said to *be* but not to *do*. This is clear from the nature of logical (as distinct from existential) dependence. If the fact that A logically depends on B means that B is in some sense active and has power, we would have to begin to talk absurdly of the activities of logical classes and the power structure within the syllogism. It is absurd to talk this way because it is not by virtue of anything the premises do that they imply the conclusion. Premises and conclusion are connected timelessly and changelessly by logical relations, but not even the fact that they are logically connected implies any activity of connec*ting*. There is no action until the implied conclusion is actually inferred, and such inference is a temporal act of man.

My contention is that the eternal cannot be a cause. It functions as a necessary condition of some actions, such as inference, not by virtue of what it does but on account of what it is. The notion of an eternal act is void of meaning. Inactive eternity, such as a system of pure geometry, is easy to conceive, and there is little trouble with the temporally dynamic. But nothing can act and remain changeless, or cause and not enter time. To speak of God's eternal act of will is to speak in terms that are self-contradictory. No consistent concept of divine power can be obtained here and, therefore, no intelligible alternative to mine.

A second possible objection to the argument that power and consciousness cannot characterize the same being is that it proves altogether too much. If agency and knowledge cannot be combined in God, is there any reason to suppose that they can in man? And if they cannot, what account can we give of the obvious fact that humans are both agents in the flux and conscious beings who know what they do? Clearly, if this argument is right, each man is a compound of two beings: his body lives and fights in space and time, while his mind is a spectator of existence. The ultimate result is an epiphenomenalism that holds that the physical organism is the source of all human achievement and that consciousness is a fertile body's impotent product.

I find the reasoning in this argument quite exemplary. It is entirely successful in drawing out some of the implications of what I said. But I fail to see why anyone should think that by themselves alone these consequences constitute a valid objection to my view. There is nothing inherently disreputable in dualistic theories of the nature of man. Their history has been a long and distinguished one in which some major chapters were penned by theologians. And as far as the theory of epiphenomenalism is concerned, many more thinkers say it is untenable than are prepared to back their claim with reasons. Let me make this point as forcefully as I can. I have never yet seen an argument that would be adequate to refute epiphenomenalism. The objections that have been urged against it do not even suffice to reduce its probability to a level below those of other mind-body theories.[1] Under these circumstances, I think it justified to disregard the current objection. It has not earned the right to be taken seriously since it merely shows that my analysis of consciousness and power implies a theory that may well be true.

The traditional core-concept of God that I have attacked is a patchwork of incompatible features. The patchwork character of the notion is clear not only from its logical inconsistency. Religiously, the concept is a monument to the futile attempt to combine the ideals of power and of love. The ambivalent character of God is reflected in the oscillating religious attitudes of the believer. The man who devotes his life to serving God can often

---

[1] There are intimate connections between epiphenomenalism and the entire argument of this essay, not the least of which is shown in the concept of God—modeled on epiphenomenal mind—presented in the following pages. Yet the theory of epiphenomenalism itself must remain unsupported here. The reader interested in seeing a defense of it may turn to "The Impotent Mind," pp. 16–28 above, and "Epiphenomenalism and the Notion of Cause," pp. 29–33 above.

not decide if he should fear the Lord's power or return His love. He cannot do both: it is impossible for him to fear the Person he loves or love the force he fears. God, conceived as such a hybrid of feeling and force, is an improper object of religious worship. The proper response to power is resistance, to irresistible power cession without complaint; the man who worships power is a knave. God's omnipotence does not make Him any more admirable than He would otherwise be: even when love controls the exercise of power, only love is of value, power is a means. This ultimate irrelevance of power is well expressed in the teachings of Jesus Christ and is symbolized in His passion, from which perhaps the ultimate and very important religious lesson to be derived is that only feeling and love, only what is of value, should be adored.

Many philosophers are of the opinion that there is no need for a concept of God today. To them, the attempt to understand, to criticize, and to revise the traditional notion may appear a waste of time and analytic skill. But needs vary with aims and purposes, and though the concept of osmosis is not needed to account for the motion of the earth, it is not for that reason useless. There are at least three different contexts in which an adequate concept of God may be of value. First of all, it may form part of a total conceptual structure or metaphysics. Second, it is important to provide for the religious man an object thoroughly worthy of his worship. Finally, it may serve as the public, unified expression of human ideals. The God-concept has traditionally been such an amalgam of accepted values; perhaps the time has come for us to sum up in the concept of a Superior Being some of the central ideals of the current age.

There are at least two requirements that any adequate God-concept must meet. The first is the logical requirement of consistency; the second, the religious criterion that the object of the concept should be unconditionally fit for worship. The notion of God I have attacked fails on both accounts. With certain changes, however, we could devise a concept that could readily meet both the logical and the religious tests. Whether we think of worship as admiration that breeds imitation or as devotion caused by deep respect, it is clear that its only ultimate object is a being of pure value. Only that which is of intrinsic worth may be a constituent of this Deity; power, therefore, is not His attribute. Everything that is of intrinsic worth must be a constituent of Him; only in this way can He be the Being than whom none greater, that is, none more valuable, exists. According to this conception, then, God is the totality of all achievements: the sum of all value attained in the present as well as in the past.

Since only experiences can have value, the ultimate constituents of God are conscious moments. He consists of all the feelings of joy and sympathy and ennobling sorrow that were ever enjoyed in the history of the world. God is the totality of which every member of the class of valuable experiences is a part. The parts do not stand in dynamic connection with each other or with the whole they compose. The constituents of the Supreme Being form only a logical unity: they are related to each other by resemblance and mutual class membership but not by direct generative bonds. If we take seriously the principle that what is perfect cannot be a means, we must think of God as the sum of created value and not as the Creator. If there is anything we should be content to leave causeless, it is the world: the God I speak of is brought into existence by complex portions of the flux of nature. He is the sum of the whitecaps on that restless sea.

Events assume the eternal status of truth after their occurrence. God's constituents are events thus detemporalized: He is the complete record of the world's achievement. Each part of Him is as unchangeable as the frozen past and no less time-independent than a syllogism. But the whole can "change" by accretion: each present adds new value to the Deity. God, then, is an ever-increasing whole to which each conscious being—human, animal, and whatever other kind exists—may make its contribution. Any experience that is of value permanently swells the aggregate.

The fact that it conceives God as constituted entirely of events under the form of eternity should suffice to distinguish this view from any other hitherto proposed.[2] On the one hand, it differs

---

[2] In what follows, I am concerned only with the comparison of views, not with their defense or refutation. I neither attempt to prove nor succeed in establishing that my idea of God is preferable to Feuerbach's or Hartshorne's. I concentrate on bringing out some of the ways in which these conceptions differ: assessment will have to wait for another occasion.

from such a conception as Feuerbach's in its insistence that God is not a figment of the human mind. He is conceived here as a real, though not spatiotemporally existing, Being: there is nothing subjective about the forms of events of which He consists. This conception differs, on the other hand, from such a view as Hartshorne's in its radical claim that in the last analysis the unity of God is but the unity of a logical class. Both Hartshorne's God and mine are cosmic repositories of value; but in his opinion, value can be preserved only in an active, unifying mind. The denial that there is any organic unity or inner dynamism in God is, however, a hallmark of the view I advocate.

If persons are organic unities that appropriate experiences into their living substance, the God I speak of is clearly not a person. On this theory of personality, however, human minds could not be persons either, for none is a self-organized, enduring unity. But it is misleading to suggest too close an analogy between human minds and the eternal consciousness of God. One significant difference between them is that the reason we have for calling humans "persons" is never present in the case of God. Both individual behavior and bodily structure form organic unities in man: such unities subtend each human mind. There is, however, no physical organism to serve as the single source of the Divine Mind. Speaking loosely, we might say that the world as a whole is the body of God, but there is little reason to think that nature in its totality is a single animal. If we are more precise, we must maintain that certain organisms within nature create the episodes that form God's life, but there is little reason to think that these individuals constitute a Superorganism that is God's body. Since no single organism supports God's consciousness, we cannot ascribe to it the simple economy of the animal mind. The staggering diversity of acts that constitute the Supreme Being is held together only by their shared quality of value—by the fact that each is a moment when through consciousness the flux touched the eternal.

Now is not the time to elaborate this new concept of God. I would have to eliminate difficulties, introduce qualifications, and answer some important objections before I could feel quite secure that the concept is of genuine value in metaphysics or theology. I feel a little more positive about two or three other questions. For one, I am satisfied that the God-concept I have presented is free of the logical inconsistencies of the traditional notion. I am also quite certain that a God of the sort I have described actually exists. For if there is a single experience that has intrinsic value, there is a sum or a totality of such experiences. Each feeling of happiness or joy, therefore, confirms the existence of the Deity. Finally, I am persuaded of the religious adequacy of this living God. Machines do not worship, but there are few men who do not find or look for a god to serve. The ideal of maximizing value that this concept of God expresses is thoroughly civilized and humane. If this notion of God took the place of the older ones in our great religions, the believer could adore a Being of pure value instead of a kindly tyrant. Then each time we achieved a suitable state of mind, we could rejoice in the certain knowledge that that small part of us will live forever as a part of God.

CHAPTER 6

Santayana's Philosophy of Mind

THE HISTORY of philosophy resembles a convention of deaf-mutes. Each participant attempts to communicate the secrets of his private imagination through a swirl of silent gestures. Intent on disclosing his own insight, each is confined in his own world: he has no ear for the language of others and often little knowledge of how to make them understand his. The carnival of controversy that ensues is grotesque in the eyes of the outsider but tragic for the thoughtful participant. For in the history of philosophy, many more messages are sent than are received, and the ones that are received come to us mutilated, infected by our own perspective and interests. In our own way, each of us distorts or discards the central judgments of almost everyone else. The dead sign language of the printed word is inadequate to span a century. Philosophers signal like wild semaphores that lost their common code.

If the philosopher who attempts precision and rigor is often misunderstood, the fate of the thinker who writes as though he were a poet is still worse. A picturesque style rich in metaphor invites misapprehension not only of its content and detail but also of the author's general intention. The result of such misunderstanding and of the frustration attendant upon the attempt to explicate poetry in prose is disdain and eventually the total neglect of the thinker's work. The supposition is soon advanced that the author did not mean to write serious, systematic philosophy or, at least, that his thought is not a significant aspect of his work. In precisely this fashion, George Santayana has long been celebrated as a consummate stylist, a poet, and a literary psychologist, while the view that his philosophy does not warrant serious study has been gaining ever-wider acceptance.

It has become fashionable to pay cursory homage to Santayana's "courageous naturalism" and, at most, to follow this by the expression of regret about the vague and almost mystical things he said about the realm of spirit. But, the official view runs, such mysticism, incoherence, and ambiguity should not surprise us, for Santayana was, after all, a poet, and it would be rash to look to him for philosophical enlightenment or to judge him by the rigorous standards of rationality. I contend that this "official" view of Santayana's philosophical achievement is radically mistaken. If my purpose were to present a general refutation of it, I would begin by arguing that style and content cannot be dissociated and that Santayana's picturesque mode of expression is not an accidental feature of his work. In his view, neither literary psychology nor philosophy is a source of clear and adequate knowledge, and it would be vain pedantry to affect precision of language where such is inappropriate. An imaginative style that evokes in us the intuition of particularly rich and comprehensive essences is singularly appropriate for Santayana, who believes that existence is ultimately unintelligible, knowledge is always symbolic, and one of the tasks of philosophy is to articulate "the large facts."

I will, however, not take this occasion to present a general rebuttal of this most influential of the current appraisals of Santayana. Instead, I hope that the destructive task of showing the inadequacy of this appraisal will be accomplished in the course of the constructive enterprise of developing a central segment of Santayana's philosophical thought. The segment of his system that I wish to explore is what may be called "the philosophy of mind," viz., his views on such subjects as the nature of mental acts, the nature of the immediate objects of consciousness and, in this paper especially, the relationship of mental acts to the animal organism. In essence, I propose to do three things. First of all, I intend to point out some of the fundamental concepts of Santayana's philosophy of mind, along with the technical terms that fix these concepts in the public language. Second, I shall exhibit the structure of Santayana's thought, the strong skeleton of a system that may be discerned once the bedizenments of style, all embellishment, and vagary are cut away. This will be the major task of my paper. In order to accomplish it, I shall attempt to clarify his language, systematize his statements, and throw some light on his scattered arguments. Whenever necessary, I shall introduce distinctions or make explicit the ones Santayana drew. In some discussions, I shall be reduced to conjecturing what he would or might say: in all such cases, I shall try to stay within the largely unstated intent of his thought. Finally, by a critical examination of some of its concepts and theories, I hope to demonstrate that Santayana's philosophy of mind has a unity of purpose and structure that is a considerable source of strength. Even though I shall not hesitate to level serious criticisms against it, I hope to show that the easy dismissal of this aspect of Santayana's mature thought is as unjustifiable as it may be injurious to future progress in the philosophy of mind.

By careful and elaborate ontological analysis, Santayana distinguishes four "realms" or irreducibly different kinds of being. First in order of being, there is an infinite number of essences; this infinity of the forms of definiteness Santayana calls "the realm of essence." Essences are universals, and as such, they do not exist. By existence, Santayana means location in a space-time network with the consequent possibility of causal action. Essences do not exist because neither spatial nor temporal properties may be predicated of them. They are timelessly and hence changelessly self-identical forms of every degree of determination. Such timeless, changeless universals, Santayana maintains, are necessary conditions of the possibility of time and change and action and, therefore, of the world as it exists.

In the order of generation, matter has primacy, even though its operation presupposes the availability of a plenum of essences. Matter is the principle by virtue of which essences are instantiated: it is the incalculable force that confers existence on the forms. In a fundamental sense, matter has no characteristics or nature. As the principle of selective instantiation, it is merely the undifferentiated and inarticulate other of essence. No essence can yield an adequate description of its inner dynamism, and it does not derive its inexhaustible creative power from participation in some form. Matter is a primordial existential flux; it is an indescribable and unintelligible surd.

The world of substance, of physical objects acting and reacting in space, can be analyzed into the two components of matter and essence. The blind thrust of matter embodies, "existentializes," set after set of essences. And we must be careful not to put narrow limits on the conception of essence: Santayana claims that even events have essences. The essence or form of an event as distinct from its occurrence he calls a "trope." Substance may, then, be described as a set of instantiated tropes or, in plainer language, a large number of physical events. The realm of truth is the total inventory of essences instantiated by matter. It consists of the possibly infinite set of universals that have been, are being, and will be exemplified in the history of the world. In Santayana's view, then, truth is fully objective: it does not presuppose the existence of a knowing subject or mind. On the contrary, truth as an objective standard is a necessary condition of the possibility of true opinions. Judgments are true if and only if they faithfully reproduce a portion of the descriptive properties of the world process.

The fourth irreducibly different realm of being Santayana distinguishes is that of spirit. By "spirit," he means nothing more mysterious than consciousness. However, the notion of consciousness, I am afraid, is mysterious enough for some philosophers. For this reason, I shall presuppose in my discussion as little as I can, perhaps no more than their and my human experience. Human experience consists of a series of conscious acts, and consciousness is the total inner difference between being asleep and awake.[1] This difference itself is never the sole object of consciousness, but in retrospect it can be discerned with sufficient clarity. In conscious events, we must draw a distinction between the objects of consciousness and our consciousness of these objects. The consciousness or conscious*ing* of the object is a pure act of apprehension. As such, it exists only in being enacted and can never be its own object or the object of another conscious act. It is because the act of consciousness is never, and can never be, among the objects of our experience that so many phi-

[1] George Santayana, *The Realm of Spirit* (New York: Charles Scribner's Sons, 1940), 18. Hereafter referred to as *RS*.

losophers tend to deny its existence. But its presence, though not all its properties, is undeniable even on a Humean theory of mind: it is a necessary condition of experience and the correlate of every object of awareness.

Spirit in a man, then, consists of a series of conscious acts, each with its own manifold of objects. Santayana calls these conscious acts "intuitions." The objects of consciousness are always changeless and impotent essences. Since no conscious act can exist without some objects, and since any essence implicates through the internal relation of difference an infinity of other essences, the entire realm of essence is a necessary condition of the possibility of intuition and hence of spirit. In another and even more fundamental way, intuitions presuppose the existence of both matter and essence. Although consciousness is first in the order of knowledge, it is a late arrival in the causal order of nature. Its emergence presupposes the instantiation by matter of a set of enormously complex essences. This system of tropes, the hereditary movements and physical organization of an animal, Santayana calls "the psyche." The psyche is the mythological unity of the sum total of significant tropes embodied in the life history of an animal. Since it is wound up to aim at self-development and self-maintenance, the psyche has diverse groups of functions that conjointly define its nature. Since it is present in the seed, the psyche's first function is embryological and vegetative. Biologically, it is a self-regulating and self-repairing mechanism. In the search for food and shelter, it is the source of locomotion. It surrounds itself with a web of organs and acquires the psychological function of being perceptive and intelligent in its responses. Socially, it is the agent in all interaction and the cause of all behavior. Morally, it underlies all choice, impulse, and interest and is the natural ground of the distinction between good and evil. Its physiological and endocrinological function is to maintain the internal health and equilibrium of the organism. Finally, one of its neurological functions is to give rise to consciousness.

Spirit is thus totally dependent for its existence on the system of embodied tropes that constitutes the psyche. "Spirit, or the intuitions in which it is realized . . . [requires] the existence of nature to create it,"[2] Santayana says. And again, "The life of the psyche, which rises to . . . intuition, determines all the characters of the essence evoked."[3] In the light of this generatively second-ary or derived character of intuitions, it is important to remark that even though spirit is causally reducible to the psyche and exerts no causal influence over anything, it nonetheless con-stitutes an ontologically irreducible and ultimate mode of being. At a later stage, I shall discuss Santayana's reasons for maintain-ing the irreducibility of consciousness to neurological process, of spirit to psyche. At this point, however, I must content myself with an unembellished statement of what Santayana holds.

The significance of Santayana's distinction between psyche and spirit is best brought out by directing attention to the properties and functions of each. The psyche as a set of embodied tropes is a relatively stable vortex in the universal flux. Each psyche is a system of vital events: each system of this sort is a material organism. To say that something is material is to assert at least that it is publicly observable, that it is in a field of action continuous with the human body, and that under favorable conditions its behavior may be predicted and even controlled. To say that some-thing is in a field of action is to say at least that it has a specific locus in physical space and a specific locus in physical time, that the behavior of its spatiotemporal neighbors may bring about ·changes in it, and that its changes may modify the behavior of its neighbors. A psyche, then, is an observable, spatiotemporally located system of operations that stands in close and constant interaction with its environment. No psyche is a substance. Only the physical universe as a whole is a substance in the sense of being an enduring and independent existent. Psyches are modes of substance, limited centers of dynamic equilibrium that the flux of existence temporarily sustains.[4]

By contrast with its material organ, spirit is immaterial and

---

[2] George Santayana, *Scepticism and Animal Faith* (New York: Charles Scribner's Sons, 1923, reprinted 1955), 274. Hereafter referred to as *SAF*.

[3] *SAF*, 130.

[4] George Santayana, *The Realm of Matter* (New York: Charles Scribner's Sons, 1930), 140. Hereafter referred to as *RM*.

imperceptible. It is "the actual light of consciousness,"[5] "the light of discrimination,"[6] or "intelligence in act."[7] The essence of spirit or mind is cognitive awareness. Let me warn at once against two possible misunderstandings. First of all, by "spirit" Santayana does not mean a single individual being or some cosmic Consciousness. Instead, he uses the word to refer to a category or type of being, the class of occurrences of which every particular thought, feeling, and sensation is a member. Second, the fact that he speaks of "minds" should not mislead us into supposing that he thinks of minds as substantial, independently existing things. Nothing could be farther from Santayana's intention than to admit the existence of enduring mind-substances or mental continuants. Consciousness exists only in the individual acts Santayana calls "intuitions." A mind, therefore, is simply a set of intimately connected intuitions. The intimate connection between the intuitions that constitute a single mind is at least of two sorts. First, all of them share the same psyche as their source of origin. Second, the essence disclosed in any intuition of the set is qualitatively similar to, or in some sense continuous with, the objects of intuitions that precede and succeed it. Since the occurrence of intuitions and their specific objects depend on the psyche, it is clear that the continuity of our experience is due to the continuity through change of the animal organism, and the unity and identity of the mind are but reflections of the unity and identity of the psyche.

Intuitions are intentional acts directed upon objects. The objects of intuitions are nonexistent essences of varying complexity. At this point, a problem arises. If all intuition is of essence but knowledge is always of some state or process of substance, how is knowledge possible? If nothing that is presented to the mind exists, how can we discern the phases of existence? If the immediate is, without exception, a changeless and eternally self-identical universal, how can we perceive the growth and the corruption that gnaw at the heart of each particular? Let me begin an answer

[5] *RM*, 139.
[6] *SAF*, 273.
[7] *Ibid.*, 274.

to this problem by expanding the act-object terminology that has been adequate for our purposes until now.

Santayana needs a threefold distinction here. He cannot be satisfied with distinguishing the act of consciousness from its immediate object. He must also draw a sharp line of separation between this immediate or "immanent" object of consciousness and its transcendent object in the knowledge-situation. The framework of distinctions Santayana has in mind parallels rather closely Meinong's act-content-object scheme. Intuition is the act of consciousing, changeless essences constitute its content or immanent object, and the enduring substance of the physical universe functions as its most frequent, though by no means only, transcendent object. It is important to insist that by speaking of intuited essences as the "content" of experience, I do not mean to imply that for Santayana experiences form total and inseparable wholes of which such essences are parts or in which they are in some way contained. On the contrary, Santayana is a realist in the extreme sense of maintaining that both the immediate and the mediate objects of consciousness, both essence and substance, are logically as well as causally independent of mental acts.

Under what conditions will an intuited essence constitute knowledge of material substance? Intensely aware of the overwhelming difficulties of any copy-dualism, Santayana claims that knowledge presupposes neither the qualitative identity nor even the resemblance of what is "in the mind" and what physically exists. There are no reasons to suppose and there are excellent reasons to doubt that the simple, dramatic pictures of the eye trace faithfully the movements of the flux. If the animal organs and occasions of knowledge are taken into account, the probability of such a reproduction of the world in sense is at once seen to be infinitesimal. Literal possession of the object or of a replica of the object, however, is not a necessary condition of knowledge. The relation between the immanent and the transcendent object of consciousness is symbolic: the data of sense function as symbols of the presence and processes of physical objects. Santayana has never made a sustained attempt to explain the nature of symbols or to formulate the rules of symbolism. I suspect that in the claim that essences appearing in intuition are symbols of the modifications of matter, the word "symbol" is used in a quite nontechnical sense. It is used primarily to call attention to (1) the fact that the intuited essence and the properties of the encountered physical object are not numerically identical and (2) the fact that the animal whose psyche gives rise to a series of conscious acts does not accept the essences intuited at face value but habitually deputizes them to stand for and report the movement of ambient forces. As a test of the adequacy of such symbolism, we do not need to compare the given with what is physically real and hence irrevocably beyond the reach of mind. The ultimate criterion of successful symbolization is appropriate action.

Knowledge, then, is always symbolic in character. Intuited essences serve as the vehicles of symbolism: the movements of substance, the phases of the world process, are symbolized. I will not concern myself with special problems that arise in this connection, but I cannot avoid dealing with at least one issue of general significance. Intuition in its pure form is enjoyment of self-identical essence. How is it possible for an essence, intuited in its meaningless aesthetic immediacy, to acquire meaning and become a symbol of something other than itself? What is the factor or force that transforms the contemplation of essence into knowledge of substance?

In its current form, the question is misleading. It can readily be interpreted as implying that there is some mysterious psychic force that harnesses, at a certain point in our development, innocent intuition to the practical life. This interpretation of Santayana's point is incorrect for two reasons. First of all, common human experience does not consist of a string of pure intuitions. Probably even the earliest conscious experiences of the child are symbol-cognitive; for the adult, at any rate, the uncommitted contemplation of essence is an infrequent and difficult achievement. Second, since most of our experiences are substance-directed and hence involve symbolic cognition of facts or things beyond the experience, it would be clearly inappropriate to speak of the intuition of essences and of the factor that makes it possible for the essences to function as symbols as if they were in some sense separable. The factor present in all experiences that are symbol-cognitive and in no experiences that are not, Santayana calls "intent." Now even though intuition can exist independently of intent, as it does in moments of aesthetic enjoyment, on occasions of symbolic cognition the two exist inextricably interwoven. When our consciousness is symbolic, intent and intuition are at best distinguishable elements in the experience; it would, however, be a mistake to speculate about the way in which intent transforms essences into symbols. Strictly speaking, such a transformation does not occur. A pure intuition exists while it lasts; it can never be transformed into an act of knowledge. Similarly, moments of symbolic cognition cannot be stripped of their referential element and transformed into pure essence-directed acts. Like Athena out of Zeus's head, each moment of consciousness springs into existence full-grown out of the psyche's substance.

What then, it might be asked, is the nature of intent? It is the expression on a mental plane of the outdirected concerns of the psyche. Intent is the counterpart in consciousness of animal fear and the psyche's natural urge to live. The hidden agencies of the environment must be feared and fought: animal life is eternal preparation for the impending blow. This preoccupation of the psyche with the distant, the absent, and the latent is reflected in the mind in our tendency to take the qualities of the given as revelatory of what is not presented. Intent thus is an agent of animal faith; it is external reference, unthinking belief in the not-given. Such tacit reference to what is not presented or what is yet to come is an essential condition of all perception, memory, and science. In the case of perception, intent takes the form, first of all, of the supposition that the essence presented stands for a physical object and, second, of the belief that this object far outstrips in complexity the essence that is its symbol. In the former instance, intent deputizes an essence to stand for an existent; in the latter case, one or a small group of properties is taken as the symbol of a larger set. In general, intent is the animal urge to use what is present and presented for the representation of the absent; by its means, essence may become the symbol of existence, and the changeless may be made to yield knowledge of change.

In view of the central significance of the concept of intent in his account of the conscious life, one could reasonably expect Santayana to be detailed and specific in his explication of it. Unfortunately, however, such expectations are disappointed. Santayana leaves the matter on a level of high generality with almost all the technical details missing. Here Santayana might argue that since the major task of philosophy is the evocation of particularly comprehensive essences, once such an essence has been elicited little more can or should be done. This argument sounds hollow, and I suspect it had little to do with Santayana's scanty attention to the theory of intent and symbolism. A far more obvious explanation is at hand. Santayana was simply not interested in issues relating to the nature of intent. Even though he showed intense interest in certain special fields of symbolic activity such as religion and art, he had never managed to develop any great concern with the general problem of how symbolic cognition is possible.

The reason why Santayana has so little to say about intent is that its study does not further his central interests in the nature of spirit and of the spiritual life. The study of intent gives practically no direct insight into the nature of spirit. Even though intent can exist only in conscious experiences, it is not for that reason indigenous to consciousness. Spirit in its purest form is pure intuition. Pure intuition is free of all symbolic reference and all belief in the absent. Intuition with intent is a form of spirit, but it is not spiritual. Intent strips intuition of its spirituality by subjecting it to the principle of practical interest, the prejudices of its psyche, the grotesque limitations of a single perspective. If a mind could ever be fully spiritual, it would have no special interests, no predilections, and no preferences. If a life of detached contemplation could ever be sustained, it would consist of the impartial readiness to conceive without the urge to posit or possess. "All essences are grist for the mill of intuition"; spirit, as the principle of universal sympathy, would never be motivated on its own account to go beyond what is immediately presented.

As spirit is purified, it approaches the ideal of what it would be if it were left alone: pure contemplation of essence or *Wesenschau*. In a strict sense, of course, if spirit were left alone, it would not even exist. The psyche, after all, is the sole and adequate source of consciousness, and it is this humble origin of spirit in the heat of organic adjustments that makes prolonged spiritual living an unattainable ideal. If it were free of external influence, intuition would be fully and solely essence-directed. Intent represents alien interests, the interests of the struggling body, in the realm of mind. It diverts the attention of spirit from essence to substance and impels it to follow the fortunes of its organ. Santayana's interest in intent is slight because it is only the study of intent-free intuition that yields an insight into the nature of spirit. Once the nature of spirit is clearly conceived, the ideal of the spiritual life becomes inescapable. The central concern of Santayana's philosophy is with life, not theory, and specifically with the uniquely human, or divine, life of disinterested aesthetic enjoyment. In this subordination of theory to practice, Santayana is in the best tradition of the Ancients. As a consequence, the standard by which his work is to be judged cannot be the single one of theoretical adequacy. Like any philosophy that has at its heart a conception of the good life, it has to be judged at least partly by the satisfactoriness of the life it advocates.

Santayana uses a general argument to show that mind and matter, knowledge and object known cannot be identical. The physical world is a spatiotemporal process. Change, coming into being and passing away, pervades the innermost recesses of every material thing. Change is substitution of event for event and quality for quality in relatively permanent surroundings. In the material world, this substitution is total in the sense that the termini of change cannot coexist: whenever there is a change from any state S_1 to another state S_2, there is a time at which S_1 is actual and S_2 is not yet, and a later time at which S_2 is actual but S_1 exists no longer.

If the mind mirrored this total physical substitution of state for state, knowledge of change would not be possible. Change can be known only by "arresting" its temporal passage. Since it is a relation, it cannot be conceived unless its terms, separate and successive in physical time, can coexist in the conscious mind. The state that is no longer must be remembered, and the state that is not yet must be anticipated; only by such time-spanning, synthetizing actions of the mind is knowledge of temporal process made possible. Change and knowledge of change differ, then, in a fundamental way. Apprehension of the changing is synthetic and hence exempt from alteration and passage; change, on the other hand, involves successive substitution that is possible only in physical time. But the temporal and the nontemporal cannot belong to the same ontological realm, Santayana maintains. The act of intuition is not an event located in physical time, nor do the essences intuited in any way undergo substitutive passage. Each act of consciousness occupies what Santayana calls "the transcendental position appropriate to viewing";[8] each is "withdrawn from the sphere of the categories which it employs."[9]

This argument appears to me to be an exceptionally strong one. It is a reason sufficient by itself to justify the initial distinction between mental act and physical event, quite irrespective of what our ultimate theory of the mind-body relation will be. Santayana contends that no theory of the relation of consciousness to the physical world can disregard the difference between the temporality of change and the time-spanning vision or time-independence of the cognitive act. The pair of concepts that seems most succinctly to express Santayana's view of the contrasting nature of physical existence and mind is that of agent and spectator. Agency in a space-time field is the very essence of substance, and spirit consists of nothing but cognitive acts. Since all causation and generation belong in the sphere of action, it is here that we must look for the origin of consciousness. Since all cognition belongs in the realm of spirit, it is to spirit that we must look to discover the organ of consciousness and the laws or circumstances of its emergence.

No reasonable philosophy can ignore the fact that cognitive awareness arises on the occasions of physical existence. Santayana contends that consciousness emerges as a by-product of the activities of the psyche. This appears to be a difficult view to uphold. What specific sense can be attached to the claim that the spirit depends for its existence on the psyche? Since all generation

---

[8] George Santayana, *The Realm of Essence* (New York: Charles Scribner's Sons, 1927), 128.
[9] *RS*, 46.

is material, the psyche-dependence of spirit must be total: each moment of consciousness must be produced individually by some process in the physical organism, and no cognitive act can sustain itself in existence, change anything, or beget its own successor. The correlation of neural events with conscious acts, no matter how complete, would never suffice to establish such generative dependence. By the claim that *a* generates *b*, we mean more than that *a*'s and *b*'s are highly correlated, although it is by no means clear what more. In any case, it is evident that if by causation Santayana meant nothing more than constant conjunction or regular sequence, he could not consistently maintain that all generation is physical. Consciousness precedes physical changes no less regularly than psychic process ushers in mental acts.

It is clear, then, that no science, not even the ideally complete unified science of physical nature whose possibility Santayana foresaw, can adequately support a theory of the unilateral generative dependence of consciousness on the material organism. There appear to be at least two reasons why Santayana's epiphenomenalism is not a scientific hypothesis. The first is that in speaking of the generation of spirit by psyche, Santayana means to convey more than that there is a functional relation between the two: he wishes to maintain that in addition to the discoverable correlation between mental acts and physical events, there is also an imperceptible though real derivation of the former from the latter. All such generation occurs "in the dark" of the realm of matter. As such, generative process is, in principle, unthinkable. Since only forms or essences may be intuited and they are the termini of change, the actual process of alteration, the process that renders essences existent, the process of the embodiment of forms is closed to inspection by the mind. Such generative process permeates the psyche and surrounds it. The body encounters it at every turn, even though the mind finds its existence conjectural and can at best adumbrate it by the use of symbols. Generation is matter itself, and matter is the unintelligible other of essence. The unintelligible cannot be an object of scientific inquiry.

The second reason why epiphenomenalism is not a scientific

hypothesis is that it is a theory about the relationship of two types of occurrences, only one of which falls properly within the field of scientific investigation. Conscious acts are private in a way no physical object or particle is: their imperceptibility is not on a logical par with the imperceptibility of electrons. There is something logically odd even about the correlations between physical events and mental acts, for a direct correlation can be established only in the single case of the investigator's own experiences. For the rest, we must be satisfied with the indirect and tenuous method of attempting to correlate physical events with experiences through the verbal, introspective reports of others. Santayana's theory of the mind-body relation, then, cannot look to science for confirmation because one of the terms of the relation cannot be investigated by the scientific method, while the relation itself cannot be understood by the mind.

I will not hold it against Santayana's mind-body theory that it is not a scientific hypothesis; no mind-body theory is. However, I do wish to call attention to the difficulty Santayana has to face in his attempt to give an account of the relationship of consciousness to the physical organism. What appears to be needed first and foremost is a theory of causation. Santayana rejects the entailment view,[10] and his epiphenomenalism makes it impossible for him to hold either the activity theory or the regular sequence view.[11] He is left with the conviction that constant conjunctions are signs of causal connections, but that the generative act itself is beyond the pale of mind. When late in life he noted the fact that on the issue of the emergence of consciousness he has "not seen much new light,"[12] he should have felt no surprise or regret. There is nothing new to be discovered here for the simple reason that there is nothing to be known about the causal process that gives rise to intuitions. The most we can hope for is a more adequate knowledge of the physical occasions and the phys-

[10] *RM*, 111.

[11] On this issue see "Epiphenomenalism and the Notion of Cause," pp. 29–34 above.

[12] George Santayana, "A General Confession," in *The Philosophy of George Santayana*, "The Library of Living Philosophers" (La Salle, Ill.: Open Court Publishing Co., 1940), 17.

iological antecedents of the emergence of consciousness. But no matter how much we may eventually learn about the psychic tropes that are the necessary and sufficient conditions of consciousness, we will never be able to understand the dark process by which something new, a mental act, is brought into the world.

It is tempting to terminate Santayana's credit at this point and file for theoretical bankruptcy. There is good reason to be dissatisfied with Santayana if this is all he has to offer. I tend to think he is quite correct in his contention that reality outstrips the human mind or that existence is a surd. But this single contention does not constitute a philosophy. In fact, if it is not to be construed as an outright denial of the possibility of philosophy, all avenues of rational inquiry must be explored until exhausted. If the principle of the ultimate unintelligibility of existence is not to beget wild mockery of reason, we must avoid seeking its protection at every turn.

I now wish to argue that Santayana in fact does not have direct and immediate resort to the unintelligibility of generation in his attempt to explain the relation of spirit to psyche. He conceives the mind-body relation in terms of concepts that, while they are inadequate to render a complete account of the generation of consciousness, at least confer upon it a degree of intelligibility by connecting it to the coherent system of concepts and theories that constitutes his ontology. The key to my argument is Santayana's distinction between what belongs in the realm of spirit and what is properly spiritual. Every type of consciousness belongs in the realm of spirit, but only intuition free of intent or animal faith is truly spiritual. Feeling, belief, and memory are forms of consciousness, but they do not possess the spirituality of pure intuition. Unbiased and uncommitted contemplation, aesthetic enjoyment of the immediate reveals most clearly the inner, spiritual nature of spirit. Spirituality is freedom from the concerns of animal life, release from the anxious selectivity of the psyche, liberation from the practical intelligence that is incessantly at work adapting means to ends. It is precisely this temporal separation of means and ends that is the most pervasive feature of the physical world. By contrast, for spirit in its purity each mental act is its own end: each is whole and complete in itself and a means to nothing beyond itself.

The difference between the physical and the mental is best expressed in terms of the contrast between the Aristotelian concepts of process and activity. A process (*kinesis*) is an event or series of events with internal reference to time. By this I mean that each process is temporally diversified: each consists of heterogeneous segments or parts and cannot be considered complete until its last part has occurred or its end product has been brought into existence. No part of a process can meaningfully stand alone, for a process is complete only when completed. It is "whole" only in the whole time required for its occurrence. But since processes are changes or motions, there is an important sense in which they are never whole at all. For although they are "whole" in the whole stretch of time necessary for their existence, that stretch of time never exists as a whole. Being temporally variegated, processes are condemned to move from birth to death, from beginning to end, essentially incomplete.

An activity (*energeia*), by contrast, is a being or an occurrence with no essential or internal temporal reference. Activities contain no heterogeneous or separable parts. They are complete and self-contained at each moment of their occurrence: their actualization is not accomplished piecemeal and by parts. Although an activity may be said to last a shorter or longer period of time, such time is not an intrinsic measure of it; the profound irrelevance of time to act is clear if we recall that activity is whole not only in the whole stretch of duration through which it exists but also in every measurable part of that duration. Activity, in brief, is act without motion (*energeia akinesias*) or an occurrence that is not a change.

The relation of spirit to the world of nature generally is that of activity to process. Borrowing further from Aristotle, Santayana describes the system of operations that is the psyche as the first actuality of a natural body possessing the power to live.[13] Consciousness, accordingly, is the second entelechy of the living body, or the psyche in act.[14] The relation of a particular spirit to its organ, then, is that of the second entelechy to the first or, in what is perhaps a less precise but more direct way of putting the matter, that of the actual to the potential. The ideal of spirit is pure

[13] *SAF*, 217.
[14] *RS*, 94.

actuality; Santayana models the spiritual life on the divinely active but unproductive existence of Aristotle's Prime Mover. Such divine perfection will, of course, be powerless in the sense of being unable to create change. Impotence is the price of perfection. For if existence is the movement from potentiality to act,[15] pure actuality once reached cannot give rise to any more existence. When the laborious process of physical life is transmuted into synthetic vision, existence achieves its aim and apex in actuality. In actuality, motion ceases and existence comes to rest. The actual light of consciousness is a terminus of life; beyond this act of final consummation, existence has nowhere to go.

In the last few pages, I have presented what I take to be Santayana's constructive account of the mind-body relation. On the whole, I have refrained from raising objections; I have reserved until now the task of critical assessment. The first difficulty that appears to be involved in Santayana's view is that the Aristotelian concepts he adopts have acquired their distinctive significance in a framework of teleological explanation. Concepts cannot readily be torn from the context that is their natural habitat. Aristotle is very plain in stating that potentiality exists for the sake of the actual and that the soul is the formal and final cause of the body. But Santayana, as an epiphenomenalist, cannot and does not leave room for formal or final causes, even though he wishes to retain the notion of the mind as the form or actuality of the body. Now what explanatory force do the concepts of potentiality and actuality possess if they are divested of all connotations of purposiveness and hence of value? Is purposiveness not tacitly assumed even in Santayana's own attempt to account for the impotence of mind by the claim that once existence achieves the actuality that is consciousness, it has nowhere to go, or that the end of a causal chain can only be something that is an end-in-itself (note the ambiguity of "end")?

This objection is readily answered by recalling Santayana's distinction between scientific and literary psychology. The science of the psyche consists of the description and explanation of the behavior of animals. Psychology can be scientific only if it

---

[15] *RM*, 93.

aspires to be a part of biology: its aim is a system of theories that would be ideally adequate to explain the vital operations of animals in space. Since consciousness does not consist of publicly observable events in space and time, it cannot be an object of scientific inquiry. In clear contrast, then, to the behavioristic or physiological science of the psyche, the art of literary psychology is the imaginative exploration of the feelings and intentions of other minds. The literary psychologist divines the existence of thoughts and purposes in nature; the hallmark of his art is that it yields a reading of the flux of nature in terms appropriate only to spirit. The result of literary psychology is myth.

Now myth, properly understood, is adequate to convey a moral about regions of fact that are opaque to the intellect. It is, in reality, the only means at the disposal of the mind for gaining knowledge of what is recondite. If it is taken literally, however, it presents a grotesque and untenable view of the world. Teleology is a myth of the literary psychologist; it is the interpretation of nature in spiritual terms, the projection of desires and aspirations into the flux. Reading the fortuitous concourse of events from its own perspective, spirit might easily see a moral direction to history and believe that its own existence has from the first been the goal of evolutionary change. Such myths should be taken seriously but not literally. They should be made to yield whatever insight they can, but we ought to be wary of accepting them as accurate descriptions of reality.

Santayana's defense on this point consists, then, of the claim that the relation of consciousness to the body belongs in the sphere of literary psychology. Here the mystery of the generation of spirit by matter is transformed into the myth of the attraction of matter for the ideal and its potentiality to make it actual. It must be remembered that this is no more than a myth and, therefore, less than knowledge, and even this myth has to be discounted and stripped of its teleology to bring it to fighting weight. But, it may now be objected, does the claim that psyche and spirit are related as first and second entelechy, or as the potential is related to the actual, in any way help us attach clear meaning to the "generation" of intuitions or specificity to the psyche-dependence of spirit? Is the concept of potentiality of any theoretical significance, or is it merely the ponderous expression of our conviction that things manage to bring into existence what we think they do?

This objection is well founded. A statement *ex post facto* that X had in itself the power to generate Y is not an explanation of the occurrence of Y. The claim that consciousness is the operation of a psychic power conveys no information about methods of action or modes of generation. But what kind of information are we looking for? What sort of "explanation" of the generative process would satisfy us? Santayana urges, rightly I think, that there are no ultimate explanations[16] and that sooner or later we must face the facts and make our peace with the insane and inexplicable emphasis that arbitrarily raises some possible state of affairs to the status of existence. It is certainly true that we can think of generation only as "a transformation of one thing into another, involving two natural moments, and leaving the bond between them obscure."[17] If this is the best the human mind can do, it would be thoroughly unreasonable to ask for more. I, for one, do not find it difficult to conceive that the human mind may identify the unintelligible without understanding it, and that it lives by framing spontaneous myths to assimilate each recalcitrant fact into its structure.

Santayana's positive contribution to a better understanding of the mind-body problem was his recognition that epiphenomenalism is incompatible with any of the significant views of causation. While he was by no means the first philosopher to abandon the category of causation in the attempt to explicate the precise connection between consciousness and the animal organism, his introduction of the potentiality-actuality framework in its place was both adroit and auspicious. Not only was his epiphenomenalism made self-consistent in this way; the concepts of process and activity made it possible for his view of the mindbody relation to be incorporated in a coherent and comprehensive system of theories that derives its strength from, among

[16] *SAF*, 208.
[17] *RM*, 90.

others, a cogent ontology and a persuasive view of the nature of the good life.

The strength of epiphenomenalism is that it preserves the experienced duality of consciousness and physical fact, while it leaves the material world exempt from interference by non-physical agencies and therefore open to total scientific scrutiny. The epiphenomenalist takes full account of the obvious facts of the physical dependence of consciousness, as well as the no less obvious fact that consciousness as we know it is a product of evolutionary, biological advance. There is no theoretical reason why any physical action or change could not be explained in terms of previous physical actions and changes, or why science could not develop a system of concepts and theories ideally adequate to account for the behavior and distribution of all physical things. Santayana's philosophy of mind has the advantage of allowing for this autonomy of science in the physical realm while it retains as categoreally different the private and intentional mind. I also consider it a strength of Santayana's position that it avoids the pitfalls of the view, now in vogue, that phenomenalistic language and physicalistic language differ only in connotation but agree in referent, and that introspection and the observation of brains are but two ways of examining the same thing. Epiphenomenalism has its difficulties, and it will certainly not appear plausible to the man who has not seen himself forced out of other, initially more promising positions by overpowering objections, but these difficulties are relatively slight when compared with the problems of the monistic identity view.

The weakness of Santayana's philosophy of mind is the weakness of any system. No system is an open-ended set of theories that leaves room for investigation or research. There is nothing tentative about a system; it is not a dynamic tool or a stimulus to inquiry, for it is nothing if it does not claim to give a full and authoritative account of all the facts. A system is a clear and total crystal; it may be beautiful, but it is dead. Since it has to account for everything, it tends to establish an orthodoxy or a status quo and become a harassment to much-needed research. To cite only one example, Santayana's concept of intuition cuts across the distinction between thought and sensation. The system tends to sanctify the concept, and the significant differences between sensing and thinking are suppressed. The result is that the little known and rather complex similarities and divergences of sense and thought are no longer deemed worthy of serious investigation. The issue is considered resolved once and for all. The instances could be multiplied, even though in such systematic dogmatism Santayana is by no means the worst offender.

I shall not use his dogmatism, clearly an unavoidable attendant of every philosophical system, as a general argument against Santayana's philosophy of mind. For the weakness of systems is at once also their strength: like castles and manor houses, they are recognizable landmarks for the mind. A hundred or five hundred years after the architect has died, we may still study the structure of the walls and spend an evening in his living castle. What is of import is not that we divine with accuracy the builder's every thought. His work belongs to the public treasury of mankind, to be used by each as his wits will allow. In this way, history sometimes converts the voiceless monuments into starting points for another age. New thinkers will begin where Santayana left off. They will transcend or reject him; they may distort his thought or not even know that they are in his debt. All of this, I am certain, matters not the least; all of them will have profited from Santayana's work, and it is such facts that justify the man, not our eulogies.

Philosophy, like the human mind itself, lives only in being continually refashioned and recreated. The question of ultimate historical accuracy is irrelevant to the progress of philosophical thought. What matters is the continued integrity of the inquiring mind. What matters is that we should use the past the way we use food, for the sustenance of life. If in the last analysis our intuition discloses essences different from those that constitute his philosophy, Santayana would have no regret. Man is not a disembodied searcher after truth: each must mirror the world in his own way. Every man must seek to make his thought the adequate expression of his personality; this is the sum and substance of philosophy. In this enterprise of self-fulfillment, Santayana would be the first to wish us luck.

CHAPTER 7

The Proofs of Realism

I T MIGHT SEEM difficult to imagine a more disappointing essay than Santayana's contribution to the well-known manifesto of critical realists.[1] The cursory reader is encouraged by the title to expect rigorous proofs of realism. Yet the essay contains neither compelling logical arguments nor overwhelming empirical evidence in favor of the realist hypothesis. Much of what Santayana says is interesting, and some of it is important, but one has the feeling throughout that none of it has the least tendency to demonstrate the truth of realism. One's worst suspicions seem to be confirmed at the end of the article, where the author appears to make a mockery of his own exertions by the disarming confession that his position cannot at all be proved to sceptics or idealists. If only he had thought of this at the beginning, we may feel, he could have saved himself the effort of writing such a thin, confused essay. Incidentally, he could also have spared us the embarrassment of seeing through the threadbare thought of an allegedly great philosopher.

We may be inclined to file away some mental notes on Santayana and perhaps on critical realism, and then let the matter drop. Yet this would be a mistake. The hypothesis that Santayana set out to prove realism but later recognized the impossibility of the task is too easy to be credible. And the view that he would allow the damning record of such a change of mind to be published is so improbable as to deserve no serious attention. The reason why the essay might seem baffling at first is simply that it presupposes too much. Because he is a systematic philosopher, each element of Santayana's thought is organically connected

---

[1] George Santayana, "Three Proofs of Realism," in *Essays in Critical Realism* (London: Macmillan, 1920), 163–84. Hereafter referred to as "Three Proofs."

with every other. It should come as no surprise, therefore, that his theory of perception is largely unintelligible in abstraction from the system as a whole. Because he is exceptionally single-minded, almost every one of Santayana's essays is a portrait in cameo of his system. Since the depiction is unannounced and in miniature, it should come as no surprise that much of what he says seems at first incoherent and becomes clear only when the general context is supplied and the fine lines have been sketched in.

The function of this essay is to provide the context and the refinements necessary to see Santayana's critical realism as a consistent, though not fully defensible, whole. Since the appearance of Marten ten Hoor's study over half a century ago,[2] there have been only scattered and minor attempts to present a critical assessment of Santayana's theory of knowledge. Even those who paid particular attention to his epistemology showed only passing interest in his theory of perception. He has received not so much as the uncertain compliment of attempted refutation; Lovejoy and Drake have long been singled out as prime targets for raids on critical realism. I hope to convince the reader that Santayana's version of the theory is well worth serious study by showing that it is a sophisticated, and in some respects persuasive, attempt to give an account of the facts of perception. I shall try to do this without concealing the difficulties of the view; only in that way will it be possible for us to understand the sort of proof Santayana proposes to give of realism, and to assess the force and adequacy of his arguments.

If realism, in the widest sense of the term, is the view that there is nothing whose *esse* is *percipi*, Santayana must be counted among its most determined and single-minded advocates. His realism has its historical roots in Plato and, to a lesser extent, in Aristotle; its closest contemporary analogue is the G. E. Moore of "The Refutation of Idealism," with whose analysis of consciousness into diaphanous act and nonmental object Santayana fully concurs.[3] But there are two forms of realism we must distin-

---

[2] Marten ten Hoor, "George Santayana's Theory of Knowledge," *The Journal of Philosophy* 20 (1923): 197–211.

[3] G. E. Moore, "The Refutation of Idealism," in *Philosophical Studies* (London: Harcourt, Brace, 1922), 1–30.

guish. One is a theory about universals and their relation to thought; the other is a theory about particulars and their relation to sense. The first maintains that universals are neither mental in nature nor dependent on thought for their being or existence. The second contends that spatiotemporal particulars are nonmental and exist independently of our perception of them. The theories are similar in making the essential realist claim that consciousness does not create its objects. They differ only in the type of consciousness, and hence the type of object, concerning which their claims are made.

It is worth remarking that the two types of realism are logically independent of each other. Either one could be maintained while the other was denied, without involving us in self-contradiction. Descartes, for example, was a realist in his view of perceptual knowledge, but he maintained that universals were dependent on the mind. At least one reading of Spinoza, on the other hand, would have us see him as a realist about the universals that were the objects of his second and third kinds of knowledge, while he held that the time-bound objects of perceptual cognition were creatures of the human imagination. Santayana is explicit in subscribing to both theories of realism. One the one hand, he insists that essences or universals are independent in their logical being of the intuition that summons them to mind. He spends long chapters, on the other hand, in the attempt to show that there are enduring, substantial things whose existence is independent of, and unaffected by, our knowledge of them.[4] In this paper, I shall not spend time on Santayana's Platonic realism about essences. I shall concentrate on his realistic view of sense perception. To focus our inquiry, let me begin by discussing his two central, and apparently contradictory, methodological commitments.

The two methods to which I refer structure and dominate the first and the second parts of *Scepticism and Animal Faith*, respectively. The first is the sceptical method of refusing to assent to any proposition whose certainty has not been demonstrated. The

---

[4] See, especially, George Santayana, *Scepticism and Animal Faith* (New York: Dover, 1955), chaps. 18, 19, and 20. Hereafter referred to as *SAF*.

second is the method of accepting, after some rational reconstruction, the beliefs of sound common sense.

Sceptical doubt leads Santayana to solipsism of the present moment, in which nothing beyond the immediately given is admitted. Since the existence of a past, of a future, and of outlying contemporary events is always subject to doubt, we are left with the changeless qualities and relations we intuit. They justify no inference to anything beyond themselves. If to exist is to stand in changeable, external relations,[5] the features (essences) that constitute the only possible objects of consciousness themselves turn out not to exist. This does not mean, of course, that what is given in the specious present is *nothing*, but only that any such complex essence is simply what it is and stands, as essence or group of qualities, in no temporal or dynamic relation to anything. Essences, not being enduring objects, cannot be changed: a "changed" essence in the field of attention is one that has been exchanged, viz., one whose place has been taken by quite another.

Consciousness of the immediate objective manifold, then, yields only acquaintance with essence, not knowledge of existence. Intuition that is free of the transitive force of intent is, indeed, incorrigible; but this certainty is bought at the price of significance. In pure intuition, nothing is meant and nothing is asserted: since no judgments are made, no mistakes can be committed, and all is open-eyed trance and docile enjoyment. Santayana's sceptical method thus leaves him stripped of the knowledge of change, existence, mind, and God. Even the possibility of knowledge evaporates as the world contracts to the moment's changeless essence and the silent self is swallowed in the object. Ultimate solipsism ends without an *ipse*; although as a theory scepticism ends with the singular conclusion that all theories are unjustified, as a method it is successful in reducing us to ignorant and ignominious silence.

Now the point that may be the source of great puzzlement in the reader is Santayana's repeated claim that scepticism is both irrefutable and untenable. On the face of it, this involves an

[5] *SAF,* 42.

outright contradiction. To say that a theory is untenable is to contend that someone is in a position to refute it or has already done so: to say, on the other hand, that a thorough investigation has failed to reveal any compelling argument or evidence against a view is to commit ourselves to considering it eminently tenable. If Santayana is in fact guilty of such a contradiction, we have good reason to maintain that his concessions to the subjectivistic, sceptical tradition of modern philosophy are incompatible with the positive tenets of his ontology. And if this incompatibility can be substantiated, it is evident that the most distinctive element of his philosophy, the attempt to implant the private life of spirit in the rich soil of the natural world, must inevitably end on the rocks.

A close reading of Santayana should make it clear that he is careful to avoid the imputed contradiction. He holds that from the standpoint of rational argument scepticism is irrefutable. From this point of view, it is not only a tenable, but the only tenable, position.[6] When he says, by contrast, that the sceptical stance is insupportable, he speaks from an entirely different frame of reference. Just as the reflective man cannot escape scepticism, the active man cannot escape belief. Suspension of belief is an impossibility for the animal engaged in action: his impending actions, his expectations, the rhythmic patterns of his life impose beliefs on him or express his tacit commitments.

The sceptical method hinges on the rationalistic criteria of knowledge. If only what is self-evidently true or demonstrably certain may be known, we shall end by knowing nothing. Although this is the note on which the first part of *Scepticism and Animal Faith* closes, it would be a mistake to construe it as a conclusion of Santayana's philosophy. It is, instead, to be read as a *reductio ad absurdum* of scepticism, and hence of the rationalistic criteria of knowledge. The fact that these criteria leave us with no knowledge and no justified belief[7] is enough to show their absurdity; it is clear that in beginning with them we have made a false start. Doubt, as the voluntary withholding of assent in the ab-

---

6 *Ibid.*, 101.

7 *Ibid.*, 110–11; George Santayana, "Literal and Symbolic Knowledge," in *Obiter Scripta* (New York: Scribner's, 1936), 129. Hereafter referred to as "Literal."

sence of ideal evidence, is an intellectual exercise which can show only that our ideal of evidence has been set too high, viz., that natural knowledge of the natural world cannot meet the demands of unbridled reason. But scepticism does not suspend life; doubt is not disbelief. Belief is the involuntary active attitude of an animal engaged in the business of life, as well as the expression of that attitude in consciousness. On its physical side, it is the psyche's attitude of expectation and her readiness to react. Mentally, it is neither a quality of ideas nor the vivacity of our conception of them,[8] but the felt presence of intent or transcendent reference, which is the counterpart in consciousness of the vectorial energies of the psyche.

In sum, then, scepticism is irrefutable so long as we move in the realm of reason or discourse, but untenable if we take three-dimensional man and ubiquitous action as the starting points of our philosophy. Though reason finds all doubts legitimate, good sense and candor pronounce the sceptic dishonest. The dishonesty comes of an essential conflict in the sceptic's life: in his theory he suspends his commitments, while in practice he happily acts them out. A philosophy that will not abandon us the moment we take it out of the study must be based on the "large facts" of temporal existence, it must be free of crippling discrepancy between theory and practice, and it must include a criterion of rational belief that allows for legitimate (though not indubitable) natural knowledge.

"Animal faith" is the phrase Santayana uses to denote the commitment, the confidence in the constancy and plasticity of the environment, which is tacit in spatiotemporal action. When we act, we silently assume the truth of such principles as (1) there is a world that consists of enduring things, (2) there is a future that will resemble the past, (3) the things we seek can be found, and (4) the things we see can be eaten.[9] These and other principles implicit in action are the tenets of animal faith. Their progressive unraveling, careful formulation, and organized presentation are the tasks of the second method to which I have alluded. This

8 *SAF*, 16.
9 *Ibid.*, 180.

constructive enterprise undertakes the restoration of the views of common sense, using as its criteria the beliefs tacit in animal action. Everything Santayana says about the general features of the natural world is meant to have its justification, directly or indirectly, in the natural beliefs unavoidably implicated in action. These beliefs, in their turn, cannot be justified by evidence or argument: their validity is assumed in the acts of collecting evidence as well as in the processes of reasoning. Although practical success often bears them out, they have the status of ultimate, inescapable commitments. They are the natural beliefs of the active man; if they are false, human action and the world of flux are radical deceptions, and we are back at a feigned scepticism.

That the two methods Santayana uses are not incompatible or contradictory should now be obvious. They are not coordinate and rival methods at all: Santayana's positive conclusions are all reached by the method that may be described alternately as the critical reconstruction of common sense or as the eduction of the principles of animal faith. Scepticism is used exclusively with destructive intent: it clears the field of dogmas, establishes the impossibility of rationalism, exposes its own criteria of knowledge as irrelevant to life, and ends in a self-stultifying silence that invites neglect. Once the sceptical phase of his investigation is completed, Santayana can begin the positive enterprise of framing a natural philosophy. Scepticism has served to eliminate blind alleys, to set limits to his inquiry, and to focus his task.

The sceptical phase of Santayana's analysis leaves him with essence only. Since essences, the immediate objects of consciousness, are logically prior to the cognitive acts that apprehend them, Santayana is led naturally to hold the realistic position that universals are neither mental nor dependent on intuition. But essences are changeless qualities and relations, not existing material things: they cannot be the objects of natural knowledge. The existence of a world of substantial and enduring things is, accordingly, the primary assumption implicated in action. In affirming the existence and detailing the properties of such a world, Santayana pays special heed to the realistic assumptions of common sense and animal action. When the notion of substance is first introduced, it is simply that of whatever exists independently of thought but is open to cognition.[10] It is only later that this realistic skeleton of the concept of substance is fleshed out to become that of being with "a place, movement, origin, and destiny of its own,"[11] namely, that is, at least potentially, both agent and patient in a field of action.[12]

We thus find ourselves with the classic trichotomy of dualistic realism in the theory of perception. There is a mental act (intuition) directed upon nonmental immediate objects (essences). The immediate objects serve in some way as the vehicles of perception: the ultimate object of knowledge is the independently existing physical world (substance). It is at this point that the critical realist must face his two most fundamental problems. The first is the provision of a general account of the nature of knowledge and a formulation of its criteria. The second is the explication of the relations that obtain between intuited essence and perceived substance in veridical as well as in erroneous perception. Although the two problems are intimately connected, I shall consider Santayana's answers to them singly and in succession.

Let me begin with the problem of the nature of knowledge. In light of his view of the realm of truth, it might seem rather simple to provide a Santayanan account of knowledge. Facts are existing things or events we run into:[13] as such, they are objects not of intuition, but of belief. Such belief must be the outcome or expression of living in the flux. Now a proposition p that serves as the vehicle of belief about some fact a is true if and only if it consists of essences that also occur in the standard comprehensive description of a. The standard comprehensive description of a fact is the truth about it: it is a part of this truth that is or can be brought to a person's mind when he is said to know that fact. It may appear, therefore, that knowledge, for Santayana, is simply true belief founded on experience.[14]

10 *Ibid.,* 182.

11 *Ibid.,* 203.

12 For a more complete treatment of the notions of substance, see my "Matter and Substance in the Philosophy of Santayana," *The Modern Schoolman* 44 (1966): 1–12.

13 *SAF,* 229.

14 *Ibid.,* 180.

Unfortunately, this view will not do as it stands. Knowledge, Santayana assures us, is symbolic in character. The relation of the essence intuited to the essence embodied, therefore, need not be that of identity, as the strict form of the correspondence theory of truth would demand. The two essences need have no intrinsic connection for the one to constitute knowledge of the other, and in fact they rarely do; the only thing important is for the one intuited to be taken as the symbol of the one actually instanced. If this view is taken as seriously as Santayana's repeated insistence on it demands,[15] the nature and limits of knowledge must be sought in the rules of symbolism. But we search in vain for a clear and complete theory of symbolism in the works of Santayana. He places no limits on appropriate symbolization and presents no criteria by which the adequacy of a symbol may be determined. Instead, he shows the greatest permissiveness about what may with legitimacy be considered symbolic knowledge. Any essence intuited in the presence of an object upon which we react is an acceptable sign for it, he informs us.[16] And since any object has, "at least partially and relatively,"[17] the characters we assign to it, we are apparently free to assign any feature to anything without running the risk of being found in error.

This view raises serious problems, to which I shall come presently. For now, however, we may welcome it, for it eliminates the apparent contradiction between the symbolic nature of knowledge and the criterion that demands that knowledge, as true belief, repeat a part of the truth about some fact. The truth about a fact *a* is *a*'s standard *comprehensive* description. As such, it is infinitely extended and includes all *a*'s relations to everything existent and eternal.[18] The essences, therefore, that constitute the perspectives of any and every being on *a* are all parts of the truth about it. Now whenever some being takes a view of *a*, it intuits exactly those essences that are enshrined in the realm of

[15] *Ibid.*, 176–78; "Literal," 141–46.
[16] George Santayana, "The Unknowable," in *Obiter Scripta, loc. cit.*, 181. Hereafter referred to as "Unknowable."
[17] "Literal," 131.
[18] *SAF*, 267.

truth as constituting its view of *a*, and those essences are a part of the truth about *a*. The obvious but disquieting conclusion is that in spite of all the ignorance and stupidity in the world, no one can be in error in any judgment he makes about anything.

The most remarkable feature of this view is its tendency to move away from judging the adequacy of knowledge by an ideal standard. The truth as the ideally accurate description of facts seemed, at first, to be such a standard. But the comprehensiveness of the description strips it of its value as a norm, and the condition and circumstances of the knower appear to assume supreme importance in determining the adequacy of knowledge. The excellence of a representation is thus a function of the situation that gave rise to it: to judge it good or bad apart from that context is simply meaningless. It is, accordingly, not as a matter of irony that Santayana calls a blatantly inaccurate assessment of his opinions fair and good, in view of the fact that it is a photograph "taken of my system in a bad light at a great distance."[19]

This view, held without a corrective, ends in irremediable relativism. If the circumstances and limitations of the knower are allowed to enter into our assessment of the adequacy of a piece of knowledge, cognitive achievements become incommensurable, understanding cannot be enhanced, and the collective enterprise of science is ruled impossible. To avoid such a vicious relativism, Santayana introduces two criteria in terms of which we may establish the comparative excellence of cognitions. The first is the test of action. Given two beliefs about the same configuration of circumstances, one is more adequate than the other if it traces the generative relations of the substances involved more accurately than that other. The measure of accuracy is the degree of success that may be achieved by acting upon the belief, since such success is thought to depend upon the correct estimate of the balance of ambient forces. It is this compelling structure of power that constitutes the "control by outer facts" Santayana considers essential for knowledge.[20] Since prosperous animal operation is the only

[19] George Santayana, *The Realm of Spirit* (New York: Charles Scribner's Sons, 1940), 273.
[20] *SAF,* 180.

possible touchstone of the relevance and appropriateness of the symbolic cognition of the dynamic, Santayana's claim that "knowledge of nature is a great allegory, of which action is the interpreter"[21] may readily be seen as a perfect *précis* of his position.

The second criterion should be prefaced by the comment that even though he sometimes speaks of their "ultimate elements," Santayana does not distinguish between the essential and the accidental properties of existing objects. Any and every property that characterizes an existent is enshrined in the realm of truth as pertaining to it: none is more relevant to it than any of the others, save in the eyes of an observer with special interests. Every part of its standard comprehensive description is equally and irrevocably a truth about it. For this reason, it is impossible to characterize advance in knowledge as movement from the apprehension of peripheral properties to cognition of the object's central features. Santayana's second criterion for judging the adequacy of knowledge is designed, therefore, as an alternative to this characterization. It is simply the claim that, without there being degrees of truth, there are degrees of knowledge.[22] On this view, the adequacy of knowledge must be judged by its completeness. The completeness of a piece of knowledge, in turn, is a matter of how much of the truth about a fact it manages to include. Since the truth about any fact is infinite in extent,[23] complete knowledge must always remain an ideal limit for mortal man.[24] But the finite segments of truth we rehearse are susceptible of comparison on the simple quantitative scale of greater or lesser inclusiveness, viz., they are essences of greater or lesser complexity.

It should now be possible to formulate a relatively precise description of the nature and criterion of knowledge, as Santayana conceives them. As we have seen, we can accept the view that knowledge, for him, is true belief aout facts, if we introduce the necessary qualifications and place the right interpretation on this

21 "Literal," 140.
22 "Literal," 132.
23 *Ibid.*
24 George Santayana, *The Realm of Truth* (New York: Scribner's, 1938), 79. Hereafter referred to as *RT*.

general formula. Thus, the detailed description might run as follows. A belief may be said to constitute knowledge if and only if (1) it is the projection by intent into a bounded region of existence of more or less complex intuited essences, (2) the essences thus projected are parts of the standard comprehensive description of the given region, and (3) the belief, if it were translated into behavior, would make it possible for the animal to engage in action that is both successful and relevant to the region. It is important to note that knowledge is always of some past, present, or future segment of existence, that it is always mediated by projected essences, and that the segment of existence or fact that is its object is always logically prior and dynamically independent of it. Both the intuition and the projection of essences are mental acts, and the mental realm is that of free construction and discourse, for Santayana. It is for this reason that (3) is of central importance in his account of knowledge: only through the medium of action can a conscious belief make contact with the hard facts that constitute its only check and control.

Knowledge, then, is a cooperative enterprise of body and mind—the "intellectual transcript" of the reaction of an organism to its environment.[25] The concept of belief itself is amphibious in the work of Santayana. Sometimes it stands for a mental act; on other occasions it designates a behavioral disposition or bodily attitude. Since beliefs in the first sense are units in discourse, consistency—a requirement of organized thought—is a necessary condition of knowledge. The ultimate test of the truth of a belief in the first sense (as act of mind), however, is the successful discharge in action of the corresponding belief in the second sense (as latent tendency). The unfailing correspondence of beliefs as occurrent acts of mind and as behavioral dispositions, which is necessary to maintain this view, is a postulate of Santayana's philosophy of mind; its defense properly belongs under that head. Finally, the ideal of knowledge, as imposed by the prolixity of the realm of truth, is unattainable omniscience. But as much knowledge as is requisite for us not to be entirely in the

[25] "Literal," 115.

dark about nature[26] or to enlighten us about our natural good[27] or to develop a useful but tenuous natural science[28] should suffice for human beings whose bodies were forged for action and whose minds have been framed for contemplation and not for belief.

The most remarkable omission in Santayana's account of knowledge is the lack of reference to evidence or reasons. We would not normally be said to know *p*, unless we were able to offer some evidence for it or some good reasons for thinking it true. Now Santayana is, I am quite certain, in full agreement with this view. He fails to make much of it, however, for a simple and perfectly good reason. His view is that perceptions and beliefs, with the exception of totally deceptive ones, are the causal consequents of their intended objects. For this reason, the very occurrence of a perception or belief must be taken as prima facie evidence of the existence of its objects, and hence of its own truth.[29] Given this view, it is not surprising that Santayana does not think it important to stress the evidential element in knowledge. The tenability of this view, however, turns on the fate of Santayana's beliefs about the connection of mental acts to antecedent physical processes in general, and on the case for his causal theory of perception in particular. Since I have already considered the former issue elsewhere,[30] I now turn to the theory of perception proper.

At first sight, Santayana appears to be of two minds about the relation of intuited and embodied essences in perception. Since essences are repeatable universals, the way is open for the identity of the perceived features of the epistemological object with the characteristics of the surface of the independent substance. And indeed, Santayana often writes as if veridical perception consisted in just such a reduplication of essence in two distinct realms of being. At one point, he identifies the ideal of realism as the view that appearance and substance are distinct in existence but identi-

---

26 *Ibid.*, 134.
27 *SAF,* 102.
28 *Ibid.*, 178–79.
29 "Literal," 131.
30 See my "Santayana's Philosophy of Mind," pp. 67–88 above.

cal in essence.[31] In another place, he firmly maintains that perception, if adequate, describes the whole essence of its object: the diversity between perception and natural substance then amounts to no more than "the separable existence of each."[32]

In direct opposition to the above view, we have the Santayana who spoke of the "fantastic inadequacy of our perceptions,"[33] who wrote an entire chapter to show that nothing given exists, and who boldly affirmed that "no quality in the object is like any datum of sense."[34] For this Santayana, all knowledge is symbolic, and the most we can achieve is "appropriate description," which is "no incorporation or reproduction of the object in the mind."[35]

I attribute this apparent contradiction to Santayana's free and evocative use of language, which verges, on occasion, on the philosophically irresponsible. I call the contradiction "apparent" because a study of our author's general intent makes it relatively easy to detect his deliberate position. If it conceived veridical perception as consisting of the reduplication of the world in sense, Santayana's theory would be subject to all the obvious and fatal objections to copy-dualism. Santayana knew the force of these objections too well not to have taken them into account: his repeated insistence on the symbolic nature of cognition was in fact prompted, at least partly, by the desire to sidestep such difficulties. The claim that knowledge is symbolic,[36] the reminders that there is a great disparity between human ideas and natural things,[37] and the reason he gives for the fact that intuited essences are seldom, if ever, identical with the essences embodied in substance[38] are the best indications of Santayana's actual belief. If we add to this his claim that sensation works "in a conventional medium, as do literature and music," and is pre-

---

[31] "Three Proofs," 165.
[32] "Literal," 114.
[33] *SAF*, 6.
[34] *Ibid.*, 84.
[35] *Ibid.*, 178.
[36] *Ibid.*, 103.
[37] "Literal," 133–34.
[38] *Ibid.*, 133.

sided over by the Muses,[39] no reasonable doubt can remain that he repudiates the view that in veridical perception envisaged and embodied essence are identical.

Santayana's reason for thinking the qualitative identity of the data of sense with the properties of substance vastly improbable is not only the negative one of avoiding the difficulties of a Lockean view. He hints at his positive reason in several places where he speaks of the discrepancy between the scale of nature and the scale of our senses. Since he nowhere discusses the topic in detail, I am forced to fill in the missing steps in his argument. The scale of our senses is established, he maintains, by "the interaction of gross living bodies."[40] Nature, by contrast, is minute in the scale and texture of her ultimate processes. Now it is highly probable that processes whose scales differ do not embody or give rise to intuitions of the same essence. For this reason, Santayana appears to conclude, it is highly probable that human perceptions cannot capture the essences embodied in the ultimate natural units of substance.

This argument involves too many unsupported assumptions to be convincing. First of all, that the scale of the senses is established by the interaction of macrobodies is both a vast and a dubious simplification. It is, of course, true that to the best of our knowledge there are always some medium-sized bodies involved in perception. But it is rather probable that the ultimate causes or immediate conditions of intuition are not gross objects but submicroscopic processes, whose scale may be not very different from that of the ultimate units of substance. And, further, even if the difference in scale were granted, it remains dubious that processes of different magnitude cannot embody at least some of the same essences. Mathematical and geometrical properties are examples of essences that may be embodied on various scales, and there are many more among those most familiar in our experience.

The weakness of Santayana's argument on this point convinces me that we should leave open the possibility of the identity of

39 *SAF,* 102.
40 "Literal," 133.

intuited and embodied essence in veridical perception. However, I feel inclined to agree with Santayana that even if the identity ever obtained, it would be impossible to verify it. At any rate, he assures us, qualitative identity is not the usual relation between intuited appearance and substantial reality when perception is said to be correct in its deliverance. Their relation is that of a symbol to what it symbolizes. To say this, however, and no more, is singularly uninformative. What we need is a theory of symbolism, and although Santayana claims to have made use of Peirce's work in this field,[41] his scattered statements are not easily collated into an adequate, consistent, and defensible view.

The two greatest hindrances to understanding Santayana's theory of symbolism are its incompleteness and its verbal boggles. It is best perhaps to begin with the remark that Santayana considers the data of sense to be symptoms of changes and adjustments in the psyche.[42] In another place, he calls such intuited essences "signals to the animal of his dangers or chances,"[43] an unhappy locution since the "signals" are sent by the psyche to the spirit that, consisting of intuitions only, has no Ego to receive, interpret, or act on them. Then, again, essences are "messengers" or "signs" for existences of which they provide descriptions.[44] But messengers presuppose an audience and signs some interpreter; consciousness can provide neither, since it consists only of momentary acts. Once more, sense qualities, like exclamatory words, are elicited from the psyche by the pressure of external events; by another unhappy turn of phrase, Santayana calls such qualities "spontaneous symbols."[45]

Verbal and conceptual confusion seem to rise to a crescendo when Santayana introduces the notion of an index without the least explanation and quickly proceeds to tell us that an index, when used, becomes a symbol.[46] If we take this in conjunction

[41] In a letter quoted in Justus Buchler, "One Santayana or Two?" *The Journal of Philosophy* 51 (1954): 52–57.
[42] *SAF*, 64.
[43] *Ibid.*, 102.
[44] *Ibid.*, 155.
[45] *Ibid.*, 56.
[46] "Literal," 141.

with his claim, made elsewhere, that an index used becomes a sign,[47] we must inevitably conclude that Santayana makes no distinction between symbols and signs. This conclusion is borne out by his constant and easy shift from "symbol" to "sign" throughout his "Literal and Symbolic Knowledge" and else-where, as well as by the frequency in his work of such phrases as "sign or symbol."

Can we disentangle any positive account of what it means for an essence to be a sign or symbol of existence from Santayana's cryptic and perplexing suggestions? The bare outlines of such an account may be detected in his hints, I believe. His use of map reading as the model for symbolic cognition suggests that he conceives of symbolization as a four-term relation.[48] In the case of the map, the terms are obviously the chart itself, the countryside, an interpreter, and the interpreter's conception of the relevance of the chart to the countryside. In the more general case, the essence as symbol and some substance as thing symbolized are clearly two of the terms. The other two terms, however, are not as easy to identify. The key is in Santayana's insistence that in symbolic cognition there is always some "material instrument of information."[49] The remaining terms, therefore, must be the "momentary map" drawn somewhere in the nervous system of the organism and the active psyche that fills the role of inter-preter.

Now in reading a chart we do not assign its properties to the geographical region it represents: the features we project are ones correlated with the properties of the map and suggested by them. Similarly, the essences we read into nature in symbolic perception are not those embodied in the brain-region that probably serves as the material instrument of information, but those whose intui-tion that activated brain-region creates. There need be no pictorial or qualitative similarity between symbolized substance, brain-region, and intuited essence. The connection between a sub-stance and our brain-"map" of it and a brain-"map" and its

[47] SAF, 87.
[48] "Literal," 141.
[49] Ibid., 142.

associated intuition is a dynamic or generative one. The foundation of symbolism is thus the natural or dynamic correspondence
of certain material objects with certain intuitions. Any essence
may become the sign of any substance, therefore, so long as
(1) the presence and activity of the substance regularly evokes
(through intermediary brain-"maps") intuitions of that essence,
(2) the absence or inactivity of the substance is regularly accompanied by the absence of intuitions of that essence, and (3) relevant changes in the substance regularly evoke changes in the
intuition of that essence. The central role of the dynamic tie
between the significate and the sign of its presence it creates, and
the lack of resemblance between them, exhibit this concept of
symbolism as closely similar to Peirce's notion of an index.[50]

The relationship I have so far described suffices for a perception
to be minimally symbolic of its object. Since it was caused by its
object, the perception may be called a "symptom," "signal," or
"index" of what it cognizes. However, in favorable circumstances
we claim to know more than the mere presence or absence of
substances. Such knowledge is based not on any simple pictorial
or qualitative similarity, but on some "methodical correspondence" between the sign and its significate.[51] What Santayana
seems to have in mind is a structural correspondence: certain
systems of relations that obtain between symbols in perception
are supposed to match, point for point, systems of relations in
existing objects.[52] Such one-to-one correspondence of selected
groups of relations is the basis of our closer knowledge of nature,
and particularly of the dynamic interactions of substances. The
fact that appearance is the child of reality guarantees the frequency of their, at least partial, correspondence; when such analogies
are exploited, appearance yields representative knowledge of
reality.[53]

My first objection to this theory derives from the peculiarity of

---

[50] Charles Hartshorne and Paul Weiss, eds., *Collected Papers of Charles Sanders
Peirce* (Cambridge: Harvard University Press, 1932), 2: 160–65, 170–72.
[51] "Unknowable," 172.
[52] "Literal," 139–40.
[53] *Ibid.*, 141.

introducing the material psyche as the symbol interpreter in cognition. Since the psyche is not conscious and consciousness is not a material thing, the view makes it impossible for the symbol interpreter to be in any way cognizant of the symbols it is supposed to interpret. The symbols are intuited essences; since the psyche's organic intelligence cannot detect their tenuous presence, it cannot interpret their message or use them to light up the darkness of nature.

The difficulty is clearly a result of Santayana's epiphenomenalism, but he never attempted to deal with it explicitly. A possible answer to it may run as follows. When an animal encounters another natural thing, a "map" corresponding to that thing is established in the creature's brain. But the reaction of the animal to such an external influence goes far beyond the creation of a transient brain-"map": the entire organism is vibrant with nerve and muscle movements, chemical changes, and rapid bodily adjustments. Physiological processes decode the brain-"map" and compute the location and potentials of its external cause; others use the brain's memory-stores to calculate the form and magnitude of the appropriate response. This or something like this may be a fair general description of what, on the basis of its "innate instinct" and "training and experience,"[54] the psyche does to the material instrument of information in the symbol relation. All the intelligent "symbol-interpreting" occurs at this point and on the physical level: the actual symbol and its felt projection on the environment are but mental "transcripts" of the psyche's activity. The intuited essence is the counterpart or reflection in consciousness of the brain-"map"; the intent or belief that seems to project the essence unto a region of existence is the mental, and hence only apparently active, counterpart of the psyche's attempts to decode and respond to the information carried by the brain-"map." Since consciousness reflects the activities of the psyche without reenacting them, the symbol, as it appears to us projected unto the world, must be but an image in a pellucid medium of action in the dark: its ground is the reaction of the psyche to the outside world.

[54] *Ibid.*, 115.

This defense of Santayana's position suffers from the vagueness of the notion that consciousness is a "reflection" or "transcript" of the psyche's movements, as well as from a surfeit of speculative physiology. Instead of pressing these points, however, I shall move on to my next objection, which raises even more serious difficulties. All the immediate objects of our experience are nonexistent essences. These essences, Santayana tells us, serve as symbols of ambient substances. Yet, symbolization presupposes some form of contact between symbol and thing symbolized. The simplest form of contact is the sort of juxtaposition of thing and symbol that we establish when we teach the meaning of words by ostensive definition. The contact between the two elements may, of course, be much more tenuous, but everything symbolized must be tied, directly or indirectly, to something that appears in our experience. Without some such point of contact, we end with a free-floating system of symbols, which have neither relevance nor application to existence. Now since on Santayana's view nothing given exists, there seems to be no possibility for an existing substance to enter the sphere of consciousness or of experience. The system of our perceptions forms a charmed circle: no symbol can break out of it to touch the ebbing flux, and no substance can break in without being turned, as if by magic, into the bloodless essence of itself. Even if we were inclined, therefore, to accept the testimony of animal faith and to construe the existence of an independent world as unavoidably implicated in action, we could not claim to have the least knowledge of that world. Ideas can have no relevance to substances that always elude them, and symbols have no application to what cannot be tied to some object of consciousness. If nothing given exists and if cognition is symbolic, knowledge of nature is impossible.

This objection, if it remains unanswered, is devastating for Santayana's realism. A first attempt to give an account of the way symbols link up with the reality they depict may be built on the distinction Santayana draws between intuition and intent. Intuition is passive consciousness: it is the contemplation or enjoyment of essences without commitment and belief. In perception, by contrast, we find that presented essences are taken as indicative of absent existing things. There the immediate objects of our consciousness are not enjoyed for their intrinsic nature: they are used in the attempt to characterize some segment of a complex and changing world. The belief element present in such perceptual (and other) judgments is what Santayana designates by the word "intent." This belief element is the detectable difference between the receptivity of intuition and the active symbolic cognition that occurs in perception. Intent seeks out and fixes in attention the region of existence we are moved to explore; by projecting intuited essences unto a dynamic field, it establishes the indispensable contact between substantial thing and its finespun symbol.

The analysis of judging into the element of intuition and the element of intent bears close resemblance to Descartes's view.[55] Tacit in it is a theory about the constituents of judgments. Although he never explicitly defended this theory, it seems that, for Santayana, intent identifies the subject of the judgment (some existing thing or event), and intuition provides the predicates assigned to it (intuited essences). This view is borne out by such claims as that we posit existence first and then color it with whatever essences the mind can provide.[56] However this may be, it is clear that intent alone cannot tie symbol to substance. In focusing on an object, intent can no more escape the charmed circle of experience than can direct intuition. Its sensible endeavor does not carry it beyond the object of experience: it falls far short of reaching independent substance. The essences it seems to project on nature are projected only on a specious backdrop of pictorial space and sentimental time: intent is impotent to further the cause of correlating sensed time and space with the space and time that characterize substance.

Santayana's main attempt to link symbols to their existing objects takes the form of a theory about the role in perception of bodily attitudes.[57] He appears to realize that nothing purely

---

[55] Compare with Descartes's account of judgment in his *Meditations on First Philosophy*. René Descartes, *Philosophical Works* (New York: Dover, 1955), 1: 171–79.

[56] *RT*, 51.

[57] "Three Proofs," 169–73; *SAF*, 172–79.

mental, such as intent, can bridge the gap between intuited symbol and independent substance. It takes an amphibious being, part mental and part material, to connect a system of symbols with a system of things or events. Santayana believes that, luckily, man is just such an amphibious creature. The human mind provides the symbols of perception, the human body identifies the substance that is the cause of that perception and of which those symbols may form relevant knowledge. The object of perception lives and moves on the same plane as the body; its influence on our organs is what makes us respond by pointing at it or assuming some posture of pursuit or avoidance. This discoverable direction and attitude of the human body picks out and fixes the object of the mind's concern. Once the body's endeavor and heed are riveted on the foreign substance, intent projects alternative or complementary essences on the region of the field of action that existent occupies. In this way, the relevance of knowledge is assured, and we can safely proceed with the task of choosing the most adequate among alternative descriptions.

I am afraid this solution simply will not do. If no existent ever enters the sphere of our consciousness, the human body cannot play the role Santayana ascribes to it. In order to play this role, the body would have to fulfill two requirements: (1) it would have to exist in a field of action continuous with external substances, and (2) it would have to be presented or presentable to the mind. But according to Santayana himself, the two requirements are incompatible. If nothing given exists, the body presented to consciousness is but a complex essence within our perceptual field. As such, it cannot be the body that is an existing substance in its own right within the field of action. The body whose "discoverable attitude" identifies the object of intent is, therefore, the phenomenal body: it is a unit in discourse that occupies a position in pictorial space and is devoid of dynamic properties. This body is the only one we can observe, and it is altogether unable to escape the charmed circle of our thoughts. The attitudes of this perceptual object can be directed only upon other objects in perceptual space; its motions, changes, or developments all take place in sentimental time. It could be used to identify the existing substances that surround the *material* body only if we could show, on independent grounds, that there is an exact correspondence between the elements and the relations of pictorial and physical space, sentimental and physical time, and the phenomenal and the physical body. Yet, since only one of each of these three pairs of terms is a possible object of consciousness, there is no way such a correspondence could be established.

Santayana's attempt to tie the symbolic terms of perception to their putative objects thus fails on account of the impossibility of using the specious endeavor of a phenomenal body to fix in mind the movements of a substance. But in addition to this difficulty, Santayana's theory of perception suffers from another serious weakness. The complication to which I refer springs from his claim that any sensuous image that fills the mind when the body reacts to a substance is adequate to express that reaction and to signal the presence of an alien force.[58] But any sensation that expresses some actual relation in which an object stands to the self is said to be true of that object.[59] An immediate consequence of this view is that perceptual error is limited to total delusion. "An animal vision of the universe is . . . never false":[60] so long as there is some object that confronts the self on the plane of action, it is impossible to attach an essence to it that will not yield a true description. A perceptual judgment can be false only if its constituent essences have been bred spontaneously in the psyche, viz., if their presence in intuition is not causally tied to immediately preceding motions in external substance.

Now it may well be true that the presence of material things is open to the test of action: what we can or cannot do is often adequate indication of the existence of substances in our environment. The way to find out about what appears to be water in the desert is to try to drink it, and it is reasonable to be sceptical about the existence of pink rats that cannot be touched or caught or caged till a sober morning. But this by itself is not enough to establish Santayana's position, which remains open to two serious objections. First of all, it seems wrong to insist that no

[58] "Unknowable," 181.
[59] *SAF,* 180.
[60] *RT,* 50.

perception that has an object may be in error. The truth, borne out by the common and correct distinction between error and delusion, appears to be the very opposite. Since error is failure in rendering the nature or properties of some existing thing, only perceptions that have such objects may be liable to it. Second, it is unfortunate to suppose that, given an external object, any essence is as good as any other to characterize it. In addition to being counterintuitive and abolishing the well-established difference between the more and the less accurate in the realm of sense-experience, the view that all the perceptions of an object are equally veridical leads to one or another of two conclusions. The first is that physical objects possess no properties other than those attributed to them by the senses: perceptions are true of objects because they or their components constitute them. The second is that each perception is relative to the position and predicament of a percipient animal; as such, it yields knowledge only of some of the relational properties, but none of the hidden core characteristics, of its substantial object. The first conclusion tends to undercut Santayana's realism; the second moves from total perceptual relativism to scepticism about the power of the senses to give knowledge of reality. Both, therefore, are evidently incompatible with Santayana's views; they are also objectionable on independent grounds.

Santayana may try to avoid the first objection by claiming that action is a test not only of the presence but also of the dynamic properties of perceived objects. This, however, will not work. The dynamic properties of substance are potentialities or dispositions that, in the nature of the case, cannot be perceived. A disposition is not the sort of thing that is sensed or experienced or encountered; it is, rather, suspected or posited or inferred. We usually take the presence of a certain group of sensible qualities as evidence of the existence of a certain disposition in an object. When the evidence is adequate and the object actually has such a disposition, our inference is warranted and our belief is true. But this conviction, although based on perceptions, is not itself a perceptual belief. An invalid inference from sensible qualities to disposition does not turn the consciousness of those sensible qualities into an erroneous perception of the disposition for the simple reason that they were not a perception of it in the first place. To perceive the dynamic properties of substance is impossible in the same way and for the same general sort of reasons as it is impossible to walk or sneeze or store a jump. Since no such perceptions can exist, it is absurd to invoke them in the attempt to expand the class of perceptions that may be erroneous.

In answer to the second objection, Santayana introduces his theory of the degrees of knowledge.[61] He appears to be of the opinion that we can avoid the view that all the perceptions evoked in the presence of a substance are equally veridical by arranging our perceptual experiences in a hierarchy of greater and lesser adequacy. There seem to be two independent measures of the adequacy of perceptions. Both of them measure the magnitude of the segment of the realm of truth reproduced in a given experience. The first concentrates on the range of truth encompassed: the wider the context of "substantive being" in which the perception places its material object, the truer the perception will be. The second gauges the articulateness of the essences intuited: the more richly developed and minutely specific the essences, the truer the perception will be. A view of Monticello from a high-flying airplane may give us range without much articulateness: the house is seen in its relation to a large number of other physical objects, but most of the details of all of them are missing. A close-up picture of my right thumb, by contrast, may yield minute articulateness with not a great deal of range: the pattern of lines detected is richly elaborate, but the breadth of "substantive being" encompassed is negligible. Most of what I have said so far is a development of mere hints in Santayana; how he would rate the relative weights of the two criteria, however, is an issue about which I cannot even hazard a guess. All one can say is that the measures are additive: any perception that has both range and articulateness is more adequate than a perception that has one of them only, and any perception that has one of them is more adequate than a perception that has neither.

I am afraid these criteria, no matter how far or how well they may be developed, cannot remove the grounds for my second

---

[61] "Unknowable," 181.

objection. It is only by a subtle, and perhaps unintentional, slip that Santayana may speak of perceptions as being more or less true.[62] In his own view, truth is not a matter of degree: any judgment that repeats a part, no matter how small or large, of the standard comprehensive description of a fact is true, and any judgment that contradicts a part is false.[63] For this reason, range and articulateness cannot measure how true our perceptions are, but at best how much of the truth (standard comprehensive description) about a fact they reproduce. They are thus gauges of the information content of our perceptions. But it is evident that truth and information content vary independently: the richest perceptions and the most articulate judgments may be false, while many true perceptions remain stark and unadorned. It is not open to Santayana, therefore, to argue that his two suggested criteria suffice to avoid the unwelcome consequences of the view that all perceptions that have objects are equally veridical. The criteria do not measure the accuracy of perceptions; the adequacy they do measure is not that of the perception to its object, but of the intuition to the total truth about the fact upon which intent directs it. And that the accuracy of a perception has no significant correlation with the amount of information it conveys should be evident to anyone who wishes to invest a few minutes of his time in reflection on this topic.

Two additional points need to be made here. The first is that there seems to be an element of absurdity in the attempt to hinge the accuracy of sense-experience on the complexity of the essences that appear in consciousness. I am reasonably certain that whatever absurdity there may be here was unintended, and remained undetected, by Santayana. The reason for this is that his mind, moving in a characteristically intuitive and verbal medium, has probably never worked out the discursive details of his position. The combination of imaginative sweep and relative carelessness about detail is frequent, and perhaps unavoidable, in synthetic thinkers whose first goal is a vision of the world.

The second point is that as far as internal elaboration is con-

[62] *Ibid.*, 181–82.
[63] *SAF,* 267.

cerned, I can see little difference between such perceptions as that of Monticello from an airplane and that of my right thumb from a distance of two inches. The essences intuited appear in both cases to be vastly complex; there seems, in fact, to be no ready way of determining which of the two has more components or is more articulate. Nor is it possible to decide, on the basis of the perceptions alone, which of the two encompasses a greater range of "substantive being." The difficulty that arises from this is the following. The criteria of range and articulateness are meant to be ways in which the adequacy of a perception may be measured by reference to the essences present in sense-awareness alone. However, the articulateness of the essences frequently does not reflect the complexity of the physical objects they report, and the range of substantive being encompassed cannot be known by a study of essences only. For this reason, range and articulation cannot function as epistemic measures of the adequacy of perceptions. We can use them to gauge the adequacy of a perception only if we have more information than that perception, or any group of perceptions, can provide. To know if the articulateness of our essences is relevant to judging the adequacy of sense-experience, we must know the articulations of substance. And to know the range of substantive being our essences depict, we must have independent information about the landscape of ambient substance. I need hardly remind the reader that Santayana himself maintains that neither one of these requirements can in fact be met.

This last point leads me to what I think is Santayana's only possible defense against the sort of difficulty I have been urging. Most or all of my objections, he might argue, are subjectivist in nature: they are based on the anomalies of the private knowledge-situation. But he condemned and abandoned the attempt to do epistemology by beginning with the knower and his ideas when he condemned and abandoned systematic scepticism. His interest, Santayana might continue, was in founding his epistemology on ontology, and not vice versa: he wished to begin with a world populated by animals engaged in dodging, fighting, and eating one another. He framed all his theories, and hence also his theory of knowledge, by viewing active beings in a moving flux from the standpoint of an objective observer. How they perceive and know was sketched as if it were a story told by an omniscient third person or a report of his findings by a biologist. Objections, Santayana might conclude, that are based on the peculiarities of the epistemic situation or on the difficulties of the egocentric predicament are, therefore, irrelevant to his account of knowledge and perception.

The final judgment of the adequacy of this defense must rest with the reader. If the reader agrees that my objections are based on peculiarities of the egocentric predicament, he must decide whether or not he thinks it possible and legitimate to found epistemology on ontology, and to treat the subject matter of the theory of knowledge with the same objectivity with which we can treat the objects and processes of biology. Whatever the reader's convictions on this account, I cannot forego the remark that Santayana himself appears more deeply committed to a subjectivist (or at least a "privatist") emphasis than he would, at times, like to admit. He holds, after all, that intuitions, the ultimate units of cognition, are the invisible fruition of life. They cannot be observed as essences are observed, and they cannot be encountered as natural objects are encountered;[64] they are not even events after the fashion of natural events.[65] These undetectable, evanescent moments of consciousness constitute our being as minds. Privacy and total isolation are thus the burden not only of each mind but of each separate intuition; and it is with these intuitions and the panorama of essences open to them that our account of knowledge must begin. It seems, therefore, that Santayana is no less pledged to the "modern" subjectivism, which takes as the ultimate data for its theories whatever private consciousness reveals, than he is dedicated to the task of resuscitating the sound naturalism of the Ancients. If his philosophy fails at this point, its ill success is due to precisely this attempt, arduous but perhaps unavoidable, to marry Cartesian commitment to the inner life to Aristotelian insistence on the primacy of nature, and

[64] *Ibid.*, 274.
[65] George Santayana, "Some Meanings of the Word 'Is'," in *Obiter Scripta, loc. cit.*, 208.

to see the world as an amalgam of public substances and unapproachable mind.

Our discussion has now come full circle, and we are in a position to answer the question with which we began. What sort of proof does Santayana propose to give of realism? It is evident that by "proof" he means the provision neither of compelling arguments nor of overwhelming empirical evidence. His view is that no arguments are so compelling as to withstand the onslaught of scepticism and that philosophical theses cannot be confirmed by observation. What Santayana wishes to show is not that realism is absolutely or demonstrably right, but that it is among the theories animal faith reinstates after sceptical doubt has been abandoned as self-stultifying. The object, thus, is to exhibit that realism is a tenet of animal faith. The method of proof must, therefore, take the form of showing that realistic knowledge is implicated in action. And this in fact is what Santayana attempts to do in the first and most important of his three proofs of realism. This "biological" proof consists in showing that pursuit and flight, animal desire, and intelligent action all involve realistic, viz., transitive and relevant, knowledge of a moving environment.[66] The knowledge is transitive, because its objects exist independently of it in the physical flux; otherwise action on them would be impossible. The knowledge is relevant, because appearance cannot leave us entirely without a clue as to the nature of surrounding substance; otherwise successful action would be impossible. The animal engaged in the business of life naturally believes, or acts as if he believed, in the existence of a knowable external world. To show that realism is such a "natural opinion" implicated in action is all the proof an honest philosophy can or need give of it.

The second proof is a characteristically Santayanan attempt to show that critics have succeeded in the verbal denial of realism only: realistic commitments and distinctions inevitably reappear in their rival theories. The modern denial of realistic knowledge in the physical sphere, Santayana argues, was possible only on the assumption of it in the psychological realm of minds and their

[66] "Three Proofs," 172.

ideas. Even those who wish to maintain that a changeless Absolute Spirit is the only reality must make room for a world in which
action and transitive knowledge are possible.[67] This proof is
clearly ancillary to the first one: its function is not to show that
realism is a tenet of animal faith, but to buttress the biological
proof, and perhaps to secure its flanks, by the capsule demonstration that the facts of practical life and the tenets of animal faith
permeate even the theories specifically designed to prove them
illusory. To prove a proposition p in this context, then, is not to
exhibit that the truth of p is implicated in action, but to display that
if p is a corollary of action, it will be inevitably present in any
theory that can lay the least claim to plausibility or adequacy. The
proposition may appear in many guises. It may be denied in its
usual formulations while it is affirmed in uncommon language,
or it may be overtly rejected while it is covertly unwittingly embraced. But, Santayana believes, in one way or another the proposition must be present in or implied by every theory: that
knowledge is transitive, for example, is a view to which each
philosopher is unavoidably committed by the claim that his theories are true of a world they did not create. The latent materialism
of idealists may thus be supplemented by their latent realism, and
we see at once that, for Santayana, every philosophy, with the
exception of total scepticism, consists of the same hard core of
honest beliefs, along with varying amounts of verbiage and
dross.

Santayana's third proof is an attempt to show, by a method not
unlike phenomenological reduction, that the immediate objects
of thought are universals of mind-independent status. Since the
realism he wishes to prove there differs from the one that has
been my topic, I shall not spend time on it now. Instead, I shall
sum up by remarking that it should now be clear why Santayana
ends his essay with the admission that his proofs are not compelling to sceptics or idealists.[68] Scepticism is an irrefutable position,
and it is always open to the idealist to suspend the hard facts of
practical life in a solvent of what Santayana preferred to call

[67] *Ibid.*, 176.
[68] *Ibid.*, 184.

"egotistical" theories. To the "honest" man, who wishes his philosophy to accord with his daily practice, scepticism has always been a forced pose, and idealism will always remain an implausible construction. His "natural opinions" that, though logically indefensible, are "honestly expressive of action"[69] make him a realist in epistemology, as they make him a materialist in metaphysics. His "belief in nature, with a little experience and good sense to fill in the picture, is almost enough by way of belief. Nor can a man honestly believe less."[70]

It is very difficult to disagree with Santayana on this last point. To see the spectacle of nature as a play of which spirit is the gay or bemused spectator[71] is not without its attractiveness and satisfactions. To see ourselves as parts of a great flux whose ways we vaguely trace in our terms is a condition of due measure and fit modesty in human beings. To admit that the mind is a weak, fitful beam in the encircling dark is sanity itself. In its inspiration and in its outlines, Santayana's view is indubitably right; it is only when we begin to work out the details of his critical realism that severe problems arise. But here Santayana may at once reply that in philosophy no less than elsewhere, we may have to be satisfied with a general picture that furthers scope in contemplation and harmony in life. And in this contention he may well be right.

[69] *SAF,* 308.
[70] *Ibid.*
[71] *Ibid.,* 274.

CHAPTER 8

Santayana's Moral Philosophy

W
HAT G. E. MOORE called the "naturalistic fallacy" consists in a confusion of the "is" of predication with the "is" of identity. The statement "pleasure is good," for example, should be taken as asserting not that pleasure = good or that "good" means "pleasant," but that pleasure is a member of the class of good things or that whatever is pleasant is also good. Good is an indefinable and unanalyzable quality, attaching to things, events, and courses of action independently of our cognition or volition. If two men disagree about the goodness or badness of things, events, courses of action, or persons, at most one of them can be right; if they contradict each other, one of them must be right—though it is difficult to know which one.

Santayana wrote an article entitled "Hypostatic Ethics"[1] in which he criticized this view severely. It is indeed true that good is good and not another thing, just as yellow is yellow and as such indefinable. But from the fact that a thing is indefinable we cannot conclude that it is unconditioned. The quality good attaches to things not arbitrarily and for no reason, but only under certain specifiable conditions. The prime condition is that someone take a positive interest in or a pro-attitude toward the object. Thus, things we consider good are good not absolutely and in themselves, but only relative to us. Value in all cases presupposes an act of valuing: an evaluator subject as well as a treasured object. This point seems to be valid, and it is a little surprising that it has not gained universal acceptance among moral philosophers. "One man's food is another's poison" the proverb has it; what is

---

[1] Section IV of George Santayana, "The Philosophy of Mr. Bertrand Russell," in *Winds of Doctrine* (New York: Harper Torchbooks, 1957), 138–54. Hereafter referred to as *Winds*.

good for one man may conceivably be, and often is, bad for another. Shall we then conclude that one of them must be wrong: that an object that is bad for a man is not *really* bad for him? Shall we say that the object *in itself* is good, and it is only perversion of nature or error in cognition on his part if he fails to see its goodness?

The case is analogous to that of sense perception. To say that objects are good or bad independent of our cognition of them is the equivalent, in morals, of naive realism. If we decree that some object is green regardless of circumstances, we are faced with the prospect of having to call the color-blind "depraved," the physicist "mistaken," and types of lighting other than the customary "unnatural." It is evident that we are setting up a norm: we shall call "green" that which, to the majority of human beings with sound vision, under standard conditions, looks green. Similarly, we can decide to call only that "good" which normal human beings under ordinary circumstances value. This standard is fairly compelling so long as the belief in a single, fixed human nature is retained. It may be held that the normal man under ordinary circumstances—the "man of practical wisdom" or "the good man"—knows the value of the object truly. Moreover, it may be considered obligatory to become as much like this standard of what a man should be as one's nature will permit. But as soon as we recognize that there is no such constant and universal human nature, it becomes evident that the ideal of one man or of one age can have no authority over another man or another age. Different natures make for different ideals; it would be just as ridiculous to expect an oyster to obey the fifth commandment as it would be impertinent for me to demand of shoemakers that they become heroes, saints, or composers of inspirational music. There is no reason to believe that the normal man's color judgment or his value judgment is more apt to be true to the object than anyone else's. The statements "object S under circumstances T looks green to a" and "action X under circumstances Y seems good to b" say nothing whatever about the object or the action as it is in itself. Value, like color, is a relational predicate: to say that X is good is an elliptical way of saying that X is good for somebody b.

Santayana distinguishes four realms or kinds of being: essence, matter, spirit, and truth. An ontological "realm" should not be confused with a cosmological region: the latter is a part of the natural world, as the heaven and hell of Catholic mythology would be if there actually were such places; the former is the result of a reflective analysis of experience. A cosmological region is one that may someday appear in our telescopes or in our microscopes, or one that astounded travelers to other worlds may find.

The four realms of being must evidently be present in every facet of our experience, and I shall now go on to elucidate how. In doing this, I wish to remark that Santayana has never developed a systematic and comprehensive view of ethics, nor has he made the attempt to relate his scattered statements about the nature of morality to his ontology as a whole. For this reason, a good deal of what I shall say cannot be supported by reference to explicit passages in Santayana's works. The aim of this paper is not to present a summary of Santayana's views on ethics but to develop and enlarge upon the ethical position that is the natural complement of his ontology.

We have already noted that Santayana agrees with Moore that good is a non-natural quality that is both indefinable and unanalyzable. As such, good is an essence. The realm of essence is the ultimate answer to reductionism of any type; to say that a thing is not what it is, that it is "nothing but" something else, is manifestly absurd. Good is good, and this is all there is to be said about *what* good is. It is a different question to determine under what conditions anything will be, or will be judged to be, good.

"By [morality] I mean the principle of all choices in taste, faith and allegiance," Santayana says,[2] and the principle of choice has its basis in matter. The animal organism with needs and drives of its own and a nature that is not infinitely plastic does not welcome all things, all events, all states of affairs equally. Selectivity is of the very essence of the animal: the psyche, which is a mythological entity invented to symbolize the subtle material organization of the body, endeavors to secure and maintain optimum conditions for expressing and discharging all that is latent in it.

---

[2] George Santayana, *The Genteel Tradition at Bay* (New York: Scribner's, 1931), 54.

The fact that certain things are preferable relative to the nature of the individual psyche is the basis of morality. If all things were equally valuable for me, nothing would be valuable—desire, will, and aspiration would pass out with a cozy sigh; life would cease. This is indeed, as we shall see, virtually the case in the spiritual life; but the spiritual life, Santayana believes, is supramoral. In general terms, the non-natural quality good will attach to an object if a psyche takes a positive interest in that object.

I should immediately warn against two possible misunderstandings of this view. First of all, the interest taken in the object does not have to be occurrent; it may be dispositional. This means that the object does not cease to be good for the subject as soon as it is not directly attended to. The value relation is based on a disposition of the psyche to aim at the object in question and a disposition of the object to satisfy the psyche's impulse directed toward it. Second, the interest does not have to be conscious. I may or may not realize that an object is good for me: the object may be good (in the sense of being impulse appeasing) without my realizing it, or alternatively it may be bad or indifferent despite the fact that I believe it is good. In general, interest is organic in nature and, as such, subconscious, preconscious, or unconscious. Morality originates in and is primarily relevant to the field of action; the fact that interest, the organic equivalent of value, is conferred on the object unconsciously in the darkness of the realm of matter explains why we naturally think that goodness and badness inhere in things objectively and that we *discover* them in the object instead of projecting them there. This view is indeed correct so far as it goes, but it does not go far enough. It stops on the level of consciousness without venturing below, to consider the conditions of consciousness that, Santayana maintains, are material.

One important upshot of the above discussion is that good and bad are not subjective in the obvious sense of being relative to knowledge or opinion. The realm of truth is the indelible witness that an object with some nature X will not satisfy a psyche with the incompatible nature Y, no matter how much that psyche desires or how hard it pursues the object. Although by virtue of the interest a high value will accrue to the object, the fact that the psyche's true good lies elsewhere will not be changed. The adoption of the view that possible perfection is determined by nature, well known from Aristotle, thus enables Santayana to distinguish between "apparent" and "real" goods. Of course, no good is good merely "apparently"—what is good is good. Santayana realizes this, which makes the issue more complicated but its resolution more satisfactory. I shall discuss that matter under the heading of the role of the realm of truth in moral experience.

Sketching the function of the psyche in moral life and thus staying within the realm of matter, I have occasionally been forced to use moral terms such as "good," "bad," "value," "perfection," "satisfaction." Strictly speaking, this is unjustified and should now be corrected. Moral terms do not apply to matter in motion as considered apart from a conscious*ing* mind. The river does not denounce the dam blocking its course as inherently evil. Stones fall, walls shatter without complaint; for nature, flowering gardens are no better than a scorched siliceous desert. If the psyche did not give rise to the spirit, moral feelings and a language of morals would be impossible. Only "moral action" would persist, but it would not be considered moral—it would be blind behavior. "Good" and "evil," "right" and "wrong" are spiritual terms: they are essences that the conscious mind apprehends but matter cannot embody. To prefer X to Y, to select, pursue, and possibly attain an object is a matter of the interplay of substances describable in purely behavioral terms. To think of X as *better* than Y, in addition to having selected it in preference to Y, brings into play a radically new and irreducibly different mode of being. Conscious acts and their contents are transcripts of physical changes, Santayana maintains[3] in accordance with his epiphenomenalistic theory of mind. This raises a question that is perhaps the outstanding difficulty of his ethics. If moral terms, i.e., certain types of essences, are expressive of the state of the psyche, there should be some discoverable transformation law governing the change of specific kinds of physical state into corresponding kinds of conscious state. However, such a mentalizing transformation rule or

[3] George Santayana, *Realms of Being* (New York: Scribner's, 1942), x; *Scepticism and Animal Faith* (New York: Dover, 1955), 277, hereafter referred to as *SAF*.

set of rules is nowhere provided by Santayana, nor is it at all easy to see how it could be provided.

In metaphysics, the problem is that of how a brain event or a brain process can give rise to a mental act. In ethics, the issue is that of how *ought* can be derived from *is*. "The life of the psyche, which rises to . . . intuition, determines all the characters of the essence evoked, and among them its moral quality," Santayana states,[4] but fails to expatiate on the nature of this determination. Why should a budding material tendency in its organ appear to the mind as an obligation or an imperative instead of as a rival inclination? More generally, how can the natural give rise to the ideal? The problem is a standard difficulty of naturalism, and Santayana has but one answer to it: "Ab esse ad posse valet illatio."[5] If we make existence the test of possibility, the generation of the ideal from the natural will seem no great mystery. Now I readily grant that actuality is a reasonable test of potentiality, but this to my mind does not in the least facilitate the elimination of the mystery. The question we are asking is not whether that which *is* the case may not after all be impossible, for that is a silly question; we are, rather, inquiring as to what is the case. No matter how convinced we are that the ideal has a natural ground, if a plausible account of the interrelation of the two cannot be produced, the position will have to be abandoned. Thus, Santayana's answer is not an argument: it is a statement of his conviction that the ideal must have a natural ground. This conclusion is in harmony with his general position: he never claims more than that he is a *dogmatic* naturalist.[6] However, when we are confronted with the task of pulling an *ought* out of a hatful of *is*'s, there is some doubt about the inherent preferability of dogmatic naturalism to some equally dogmatic version of psychologism.

I shall not press the point, although it is an important and interesting one. We cannot turn to science for an answer to the

[4] *SAF,* 130.

[5] George Santayana, *Reason in Common Sense,* vol. 1 of *The Life of Reason* (New York: Scribner's, 1905), 282.

[6] George Santayana, "Dewey's Naturalistic Metaphysics," in *The Philosophy of John Dewey,* ed. P. A. Schilpp (Evanston and Chicago: Northwestern University Press, 1951), 260.

question of the transformation laws that connect the physical with the psychical and the natural with the ideal, for science is concerned only with one term of the relation, viz., the regularities of the physical world. One would suspect that the answer, if there is one, would have to come from the side of philosophy. It is unfortunate that Santayana neither provided an answer nor acknowledged the insolubility of the problem.

Santayana agrees with the emotivists that moral terms have no descriptive significance.[7] Moral "judgments" are hybrids containing truths about matters of fact, together with the expression of a preferential attitude. The clue to the distinction between expressive and descriptive statements in Santayana is, I think, to be found in his "causal" theory of perception. Santayana is a critical realist. The sense datum (immanent object) and the surface of what C. D. Broad calls the "ontological object" are not for him numerically identical. The content of a perceptual act is one essence or a set of essences; the objects of perception are material substances. All knowing is in terms of the symbolic language of fancy, of essences appearing in intuition. The symbols have no intrinsic reference to what they are made to stand for; it is only intent, the compelling force of animal faith and urgency, that converts an essence into description of a substance. In themselves, all essences intuited are equally expressions of states of the psyche. Those that can be legitimately used as descriptive differ from all others in this crucial respect: they stand in causal connection with substantial objects external to the psyche and repeat some part of the standard comprehensive description of some fact about that object. But moral essences repeat no part of the standard comprehensive description of any fact; they cannot be instantiated by matter. Moral qualities or their equivalents in the psyche are not members of any direct causal chain linking the animal with its environment. They are spontaneous (though not uncaused) attitudes or the results of such attitudes on the part of the psyche. Whereas intuition of essences correctly used as descriptive of the ambient world is the last event in a series beginning with certain material changes in some external object, the

[7] George Santayana, *Dialogues in Limbo* (New York: Scribner's, 1925), 39.

intuition of moral essences is the last event in a series beginning with certain self-originated changes in the psyche, and is thus expressive of states of the psyche due (at least in part) to ingrained dispositions of the animal. There are difficulties here that a detailed discussion could eliminate. For our present purpose, however, it is sufficient if we have a general understanding of what I take to be Santayana's point. Santayana himself is not at all explicit on the issue; so most of what I have said regarding the nature of the distinction between "descriptive" and "expressive" essences is conjectural and tentative.

If moral essences are thus expressive, it would seem that they can be neither true nor false of the world and that the realm of truth has no function in moral experience. "An ultimate good is chosen, found, or aimed at; it is not opined."[8] Opinions we hazard may be true or false; preferences we feel can be neither. However, there are various ways in which moral "judgments" may, nevertheless, be true or false, and it will be of importance to list them in order to clarify the difference between Santayana's position and that of the emotivists.[9]

1. "Moral" judgments that concern means and not ends may certainly be true or false. Such judgments are not moral in the strict sense of the word at all; the proposition "X is good as a means" tells us nothing about the more properly ethical question, What is good in itself? or What ought to exist? If I say that something X will bring about a desired result Y, I may certainly be mistaken. The mistake, however, will not be a moral one; it will be a mistake about matters of fact.

2. We may say that a moral judgment is "true," meaning that it is true that it was made. "Jim a contemptible liar?" we may ask with incredulity. "That's right. That's what he said." Here "that's right" simply means "correct" or "true," but true once again not morally but factually.

3. A moral judgment may be said to be "true" if it is made *bona*

[8] *Winds*, 144.

[9] See chapter entitled "Moral Truth" in George Santayana, *The Realm of Truth*, vol. 3 of *Realms of Being* (New York: Scribner's, 1942), 473–84.

fide and "false" if it is uttered with intent to deceive. I may, for instance, claim that the ultimate good of man is forgetfulness and the only acceptable means to this end is the liberal consumption of opium. Now if I only *say* this without meaning it, the moral judgment will be "false," for then no interest exists on my part by virtue of which value would accrue either to forgetfulness as an end or to opium as a means. Similarly, the judgment will be "true" if I am honest and mean what I say.

4. The moral judgment "X is good" may be true in the sense that for the person the non-natural, relational quality good really attaches to the object X. But on reflection this is seen to be a not very significant form of moral truth, for unless a judgment is "false" in the previous sense of being willfully deceptive, it cannot fail to be true in the current sense. If you honestly say that X is good (for you), you cannot possibly be wrong, just as if you honestly say you see red, you cannot fail to be right. This does not, of course, mean that X is good in itself or at all times or for everyone or even for you in the long run; it just means that X now seems good to you, which is a fact no later experience can annul, nor the shrillest chorus of dissenters affect. Thus if you say "X is good," the correct answer is "If you say so. . . ."

5. Finally, a moral judgment may be "true" in the sense that it expresses the central and long-range interests of a man. This raises the issue of the distinction between real and apparent goods, which I shall now proceed to discuss. As I have previously remarked, on a primary level every good is a good. If to love my neighbor is a good, and so is, by hypothesis, to tell an occasional lie, the question of which, if any, of these is a "real" good and which, if any, is an "apparent" good cannot even arise. A good can be an "apparent" good only relative to other, more pervasive, or more compelling goods. Thus, to tell a lie is an apparent or short-range or lesser good, because it interferes with the acquisition or achievement of other goods more comprehensive or more satisfying. Generally, it may be laid down that the "true" value of an object for a subject is a function of the comprehensiveness,[10]

----

[10] *Winds*, 146.

permanence, and biological utility[11] of the interest of the subject in the object.

If the most general question of ethics is, What ought to exist for its own sake? Santayana's answer is simply "Nothing." In themselves, or ontologically, essences have neither right nor claim to existence, and there is no *reason* (though there is a *cause*) why certain selected sets of essences are actualized instead of other sets or all sets or no sets at all. From the human point of view, however, groups of essences acquire selective emphasis, and it may legitimately be said that for human beings or human beings of a certain type, these essences ought to exist. Whatever would satisfy the animating or overriding impulses of a psyche ought to exist for that psyche. The standard of what would truly satisfy a given impulse is, since it is based on definite potentialities in matter, enshrined in the realm of truth. Thus the good of a man, viz., that which would satisfy his impulses, though relative to his nature, is nevertheless absolute and objective in at least three senses.[12] It is absolute in the sense that it is not relative to opinion but is predetermined by the fatal material constitution of the animal. Second, it is absolute in the sense that it is fixed and varies only concomitantly with changes in the nature of the organism or the structure of the environment. Finally, it is absolute in the sense that it is all-sufficient and total; it encompasses everything that is of the least value to that man.

The good in this sense is evidently a standard, an ideal that can never be fully realized. What can be realized is a harmony of our most persistent interests. Of course, such harmony itself is of value only if it is the object of an interest. The interest in harmony is what Santayana calls "reason."[13] Thus, reason is not a slave of the passions; it is one of the passions. Being an impulse for order, it works to harmonize, to rationalize, and to humanize all other

---

[11] George Santayana, *Platonism and the Spiritual Life* (New York: Harper Torchbooks, 1957), 248.

[12] *Ibid.*, 232.

[13] *Common Sense*, 267.

impulses. A conflict of interests is made possible in men with a
passion for harmony by the fact that fancy often suggests momentary and incompatible goods. In general, a "moral" judgment will be false if it places the satisfaction of an impulse that is
less comprehensive, permanent, or advantageous before that of
an impulse that is more comprehensive, more permanent, or
more advantageous. Thus, the problem of "real" and "apparent"
good is solved by being reduced to a question of better and worse,
of comparative value. The standard objection against interest
theories of value is also answered in this way. The interest theory
maintains that an object *o* is good (bad) if and only if a subject *s*
stands in a relation *R* to *o* so that *sRo* is the unit of value. Now it is
generally supposed that by pointing to the fact that the relation of
interest connecting the subject with the object may itself be good
or bad, the position has been refuted. To be able to say that the
positive interest taken in an object is itself good, we would have
to posit a second interest having that first interest as its object. It
appears that in this way we could be forced into the situation of
having either to deny the commonly accepted view that desires,
too, can be good or bad, or to admit that an infinite regress of
interests is necessary in order to avoid the awkward situation in
which desire for a good object will be neither good nor bad.

The difficulty falls into two parts. First, we must consider how
an interest by virtue of which the non-natural quality good attaches to an object may itself be good. Next, we must consider
how an interest underlying the inherence of the non-natural
quality good in an object may itself be bad. The former difficulty
is eliminated by looking upon the long-range, comprehensive
interests of a man as systematically ordered and harmonized by
reason. Impulses that promote or at least fit in with this harmony
of goals are welcomed, and positive value is conferred on them;
others are rejected as undesirable. The general impulse for harmony is, thus, an impulse for everything that serves to further
that harmony. But it may now be asked whether this impulse *itself*
is good or bad. Santayana's answer is, as I have already noted
above, that it is good only if desired. The admission seems to give
the case away, but in fact does not. It points to two essential

features of Santayana's theory of morals. The first is that the good ultimately rests on arbitrary preference, ethics on animal nature. The distinction between a humanistic ethics and the ontological consideration of morals is one of point of view adopted. What from the perspective of the former is both valuable and necessary appears from the latter's perspective arbitrary and dispensable. More specifically, when the desirability of the ultimate principle of a rational human ethics is brought into question, we have left the sphere of ethics altogether and adopted the point of view of the universe. Unless the preexistence of at least one contingent preference is allowed, human morality will be altogether impossible.

This leads to a second important feature of Santayana's view. If ethical principles, though necessary in order that there be a moral life, are only contingent from the point of view of the universe, they will have no authority over anyone not professing them. If I do not desire the oyster's life of safe, private pleasure or the ant's life of service to the community, their goods will have no compulsion over me. If I do not desire to live the life of a martyr, it is in vain to insist that I *ought to* live that life. Obligation, Santayana insists, must be internal and vital. It is based on self-knowledge, on the recognition of one's good as distinct from, and equally legitimate with, the goods of others. Santayana's imperative is identical with that of the Stoics. It is: "Act in accordance with nature," where by "nature" is meant the nature of the agent. Hence, the first and ultimate commandment of morality becomes the Socratic dictum: "Know thyself."

This view with a single stroke eliminates moral fanaticism. Recognition that the different goods of others have as much—or as little—right to existence as our own is the first step in the direction of tolerance based on understanding, and of moral sanity. But it may be objected that such an ethics, being both relativistic and naturalistic, leads on the one hand to moral anarchy and on the other to an acknowledgment of the incommensurability of values.

The first objection can at once be seen to be unfounded. Santayana does not believe in a single fixed and immutable human

nature.[14] In spite of all individual variety, however, he thinks that
human beings have enough interests in common, a sufficient
constitutional similarity, to avoid the danger of moral anarchy.
Though human nature varies indefinitely, human morality is the
inevitable hygienic bias of a race of animals.[15] As a contingent
matter of natural history and a necessary condition of classifica-
tion, there is a measure of overlap of the significant characteristics
of various individuals of a species; this is indeed why we classify
them as members of the same species. But as nature determines
perfection and the psyche selects her individual good, the core of
these various goods will coincide sufficiently to make social organization possible and to provide the basis for a workaday
morality.

It still remains to deal with the second objection, namely, that
on this view values are incommensurable. Santayana here adopts
the only position open to him—which seems also a sensible
one—maintaining that different types of good are indeed *essentially* incommensurable.[16] How are we to judge whether it is
better to be Socrates than a village idiot? To say that it would be
better for an oyster to be a philosopher than a mere dull mollusk
is not only silly; it is probably incoherent as well. Uniform standards of excellence for species of animals are unlikely though not
impossible, but it is totally implausible to claim a universal standard of excellence for all things. Nonetheless, this brave stand on
the incommensurability of values will not go all the way. We find
that comparisons of value are made every day; no honest philosophy can ignore this. Santayana tackles the problem in two
places[17] and suggests the following solution. Values can be compared only in the private imagination. The good of another is
apprehended by imitative sympathy, or "empathy," as it is sometimes called. It is brought before the mind in the form of an ideal
representation: a representation that may or may not be accurate
but is essentially imaginative. Comparison is then effected, and

14 *Ibid.*, 289.
15 *Platonism*, 274.
16 *Winds*, 148, 150.
17 *Winds*, 149; *Common Sense*, 240–43.

in people who are receptive, whose imagination is vivid, and whose sympathies are generous, the represented alien good may be deemed superior.

The question of appreciating the incompatible good of another raises the problem of egoism. "Egoism is not [a] thin and refutable thing," he claims.[18] Self-centeredness, uncompromising pursuit of a selected set of private objectives, is of the very essence of the psyche. The egoist holds that he himself—and, in general, any man like himself—is qualitatively superior to any other. Thus, all intolerant men are egoists, as are moralists subscribing to absolute codes of value. Santayana himself is, in this sense, certainly not an egoist. The question, however, is not a simple one and involves an explanation of how the psyche, automatic self-seeking machine that it is, can act disinterestedly. To be disinterested means to be interested in the goods of others, and eventually in all possible goods. Generosity is one of our primitive passions;[19] genuine altruism and a sense of justice are impulses as real, though sometimes perhaps not so powerful, as any others.[20] The growth of sympathy is parallel to the development of spirit and reaches cosmic proportions as spirit is gradually emancipated and approaches the ideal of a spiritual life. Though spirit is substance-directed, its ultimate good is sympathy; through tears and the intensity of feeling, it is champion of every cause. Sympathy, purged of its element of feeling and become tolerance and quiet understanding, is retained even in the mind's essence-directed stage, which is the spiritual life. Thus, the development from egoism to a partial altruism coincides to an extent with the progression from the moral to the spiritual life. I shall not now discuss the distinction between the two types of life and the problem of the *summum bonum* attendant upon it. This will be my last topic in this paper. Suffice it to say that the problem of how the psyche can act in a disinterested way is in the closest

---

[18] *Winds*, 150.

[19] George Santayana, *Some Turns of Thought in Modern Philosophy* (New York: Scribner's, 1933), 96.

[20] *Reason in Science*, vol. 5 of *The Life of Reason*, 246.

possible connection with the problem of how it can give rise to spirit.

Santayana's treatment of this problem is brief.[21] It is by exploring the possibilities of organization, by the spontaneous involution of matter that the psyche acquires a capacity for sympathy. The material sensitivity to events far off leads to an eventual sensitivity to possibilities that are not possibilities *for me here*, but represent the autonomous though genuinely different goods of others. Sympathy is, of course, limited by the fact that we can represent *sub specie boni* and assimilate only what we find intelligible and congruous with our mind. Nevertheless, even after this reservation has been made, sympathy still remains either a wholehearted sharing of the interests of others, as is the case in some communities and, I venture to hope, in most families, or at least an appreciation of the legitimacy and inward right of the objectives of other men, even of our enemies, as occasionally manifested in chivalry in war. Such an enterprise, on the part of the psyche, of increasing the appreciation of alien harmonies, this "interest in things not edible," may well prove fatal. There is nothing strange or surprising about this; no experiment of matter is everlasting, and the experiment of the psyche—making, among other things, a high degree of social organization possible—is not lacking in momentary successes. It was neither a mistake nor a good for the psyche to have generated the spirit and acquired a capacity for sympathy. Moral terms do not apply in the realm of matter, where, in the flux, what comes to be will soon pass away and where things in their inevitable movement have not the mind to call each other vile.

It will be in order here to remark briefly on Santayana's relation to hedonism. First of all, being an epiphenomenalist, he cannot be a psychological hedonist. Psychological hedonism is the doctrine that pleasure alone can be the final and the efficient cause of action. Now final-cause terminology in the sphere of matter, which is coextensive with the field of action, is purely mythological. Once again, I must refrain from a discussion of Santayana's views on the problem of mechanism versus teleology. It

---

[21] *The Realm of Spirit*, vol. 4 of *Realms of Being*, 614.

will be sufficient to note that he is essentially a mechanist. To postulate purposes and intentions guiding nature is the spirit's way of rendering intelligible the spectacle of the blind motion of matter. Thus the final cause of action is always whatever we happen to conceive the objective of the action to be. On this basis, it is simply not the case that the final cause of actions is without exception pleasure; we often think we do things to gain ends other than mere agreeable feeling. The hedonist's counterargument that such ends are the final causes of actions "only apparently" is without avail.

The case is even clearer with the claim that only pleasure can be the efficient cause of action. The epiphenomenalist is committed to the proposition that no conscious event is causally efficacious. Pleasure thus becomes a concomitant of action, but under no circumstances a cause of it. It is, of course, true that the physiological counterpart of pleasure may well be a cause of action; but the state of the psyche that *corresponds to* the consciousness of pleasure and that is probably a material equilibrium and harmony is not *identical with* that consciousness. The denial of causal efficacy and thus of biological utility to pain, however, yields an argument against epiphenomenalism, the psychological hedonist will here protest. This is certainly correct, but the argument from pain is easily met. I can see no way in which it could be proved or even made probable that the biological utility of pain— its functioning as a deterrent to actions of certain types, for example—is due to the conscious state of *feeling* pain rather than the corresponding physiological state.

Not only is Santayana no psychological hedonist; he is not an ethical hedonist either. By subscribing to the view that good is an indefinable essence, he avoids ethical hedonism with a single stroke. Generally speaking, his position with regard to pleasure[22] is Aristotelian. Pleasure is certainly a good, but it is not the highest good. Agreeable feeling is a concomitant, at best a component, of the good life, never the whole of it. Nothing is good unless it involves, directly or indirectly, the life of the feelings— thus, in the long run, the morally good life is also a pleasant life.

---

[22] See *Reason in Science,* 269, and elsewhere.

Moreover, although happiness is pleasant, it is not for that reason identical with pleasure, nor is it valued only for the pleasure it yields. Goods are numerous, individual, and irreducible.

It is unfortunate that Santayana says almost nothing about the rightness and wrongness of actions or about the relation of the right to the good. From his general approach, it seems evident that he has very little in common with the deontologists. A discussion of their work, however, would have been very helpful, both from the point of view of making explicit his objections to their view and as throwing additional light on some difficulties of his own position. Without trying to arrive at a complete and precise formulation, we could say that a right action is, for Santayana, without exception one that is in accordance with nature. In a sense, of course, we cannot fail to act in accordance with our nature, and thus, the formulation should be modified to read as follows. From a set of alternatives, the right action will be the one that under the circumstances best accords with the most pervasive and permanent interests of the self. As we have seen before, this does not entail egoism. It is unfortunate that altruistic action is sometimes said to be disinterested. The interest in another's good is no less an interest of the self than is the interest in one's own good. Santayana would, of course, have to acknowledge a distinction between the objectively and the subjectively right action. One of the aims of the morally good man is to make the latter approximate as closely as possible the former. The two crucial conditions for success in this are the knowledge of Nature and the knowledge of human nature.

This concludes my discussion of points connected with the first part of the problem raised above, namely, with the question of how interest in a good can itself be good. With this general background, I am now in a position to present a brief solution to the second part of the problem, which is: How can desire for a good itself be bad? The first point to note is that no desire can of itself be either good or bad. It is only with reference to other desires that a desire can be pronounced bad or, sometimes misleadingly, a desire for what is bad. No impulse has an object that is bad *from the point of view of that impulse*, though it may well be denounced as morally despicable from the point of view of another, rival interest. Thus, any object of any striving will have an inalienable interest attached to it; though the comparative value of one may be less than that of another, both will, nevertheless, be genuinely valuable.

Once again we see that the question of how desire for a good can itself be a bad desire reduces to the problem of how we can make judgments of comparative value. Comparative value judgments are based on conflicts of interests and presuppose ultimate adherence to one group of interests in preference to all others. From the perspective of any one impulse, all conflicting impulses are categorically pronounced evil. But in the nature of the case, one of the strongest impulses of a well-knit, healthy man is the impulse for a rational harmony of impulses. Long-range interests, desires that are life-enhancing and comprehensive, compatible and biologically sane, are combined in a system with the formal impulse for harmony supervening. It is by reference to this humanized and harmonized mass of interests that we judge of the goodness or badness of individual desires. A desire will be good if it is compatible with, or conducive to, the enhancement of this core of dispositional interests, and evil if it conflicts with it. Santayana's distinction between happiness and pleasure will serve to illustrate the point.[23] Pleasure is the result of satisfied instinct, happiness of satisfied reason. The satisfaction of any stray impulse is accompanied by pleasure. To a bored, lonely sailor, the consumption of methyl alcohol may be an immediate good and decidedly pleasurable. This fact is in no way changed by the additional fact that the sailor will go blind in two weeks. But because methyl alcohol causes blindness, the value of satisfying the impulse to drink it is small when set side by side with the disvalue it creates by impeding the satisfaction of more permanent and more comprehensive impulses. In contrast with pleasure, which attaches to the satisfaction of desires generally, happiness is the fruit of a sane, rational life. It is essentially a satisfaction of long-range impulses; it is serene rather than ecstatic; disciplined, not unrestrained; lasting, not momentary. Happiness involves pleasure, but not a surrender to pleasures.

[23] *Ibid.*, 251f.

The happy man has achieved a rational integration of objectives, an ideal harmonious with his nature.

There is, of course, nothing compulsory in reason. Moral objectives are optional and acquire value only when preferred. We cannot forbid anyone to be mindless. Some people do not wish to be rational, and so long as we do not get in each other's way, it would be silly to insist that they ought to adopt our good. The situation is more difficult when physical contact sharpens the conflict of interests into a clash in the sphere of action. The question then arises whether we have to be fatalists and accept whatever happens with resignation, as absolutely inevitable. Can we not iron out our differences by rational means, and is there no hope for reforming the unprincipled? Santayana's answer would seem to be that the only way of doing this is not by absolute moral legislation but by setting a good example. The first imperative of morality is to know oneself. Not even this is an unconditional rule, however, and thus it is not prescriptive for anyone who does not wish to acknowledge its authority. To the renegade we can only point out that, insofar as our natures and our needs as human beings are similar, he is not choosing the better part. If an Aristippus still persists in his preference for the immediate pleasure, or some more steadfast Raskolnikov contemplates decades of exquisite crime, profitable argument will have come to an end.

The question, What ought I do? is thus answered "Thou shalt know thyself and act accordingly." Self-knowledge is only partially a matter of physical (or social) science. It also includes an introspective self- examination that, for Santayana, is a part of the *art* of literary psychology and not of the *science* of nature. Socratic and Freudian[24] types of soul searching are further ways in which self-knowledge may be increased. The *summum bonum*, the highest good, is "to have expressed and discharged all that was latent in us."[25] The task is always definite, and it is imposed on us by nature. What Santayana conceives this definite task, the nature of the good life, to be is of the greatest interest. The characteristic perfection of human life is not moral. It is spiritual. This con-

24 *Genteel Tradition*, 57.
25 *Some Turns*, 100.

clusion has its logical basis partly in Santayana's conception of human nature as dual, as involving both psyche and spirit, and partly in his epiphenomenalism. Its closest affinity is with Aristotle's distinction between moral and intellectual virtue and his emphasis on the contemplative life as the good of man.

The moral life is concerned with action, and the sphere of action is the uneven flux of the realm of matter. No enduring satisfaction is possible here. Nor is the spirit satisfied with the pathetic partiality of the psyche, with its savage loyalty to a few selected objectives. The spirit sympathizes with all goods everywhere, repudiates the violent perspective forced upon it by the natural necessity of having to view all things from a particular, limited standpoint. If preference is a necessary and indispensable condition of value, universal sympathy eradicates the distinction between good and evil, altogether removing the ground of value judgments. It consists in the intuition of essences for their own sake; it is what may be called "the essence-directed stage" of spirit. This intuition, free of distraction and of the compulsive animal faith that hypostatizes its object, is somewhat like Spinoza's third kind of knowledge, cleared of its mystical and intellectualistic overtones. It is immediate possession of the ultimate, but this ultimate is a self-identical essence or set of essences, without meaning, efficacy, or contagious emotive significance. Though a form of contemplation, it is very like aesthetic enjoyment. To live the spiritual life is to lose all fear, haste, insecurity, but also all compulsive and demanding love. It is to lose oneself in the object and to gain not Pure Being in its infinity, but at least finite being in its purity. To live a spiritual life is to live in the eternal and to see all things under the form of eternity.

The fact that for Santayana consciousness has no place in the direction of action, viz., his epiphenomenalism, is the logical groundwork of his theory of the spiritual life. Since the mind fails to find its satisfaction in the world of nature—in experience, moral action, social living, or even natural knowledge—it must look beyond, or rather in front of (essence is the luminous foreground, the immediate object of consciousness), matter and attain its perfection in the uncommitted contemplation of the play of essences. Perhaps if Santayana had had a different view of mind, if consciousness had been given a role to play in nature instead of being relegated to the position of an impotent by-stander, his doctrine of the *summum bonum* would also have been different. As it is, the spiritual life is essentially one of resignation. To the spirit, no essence is preferable to any other, and ultimately the intuition of essences is not preferable to the dumb oblivion of death. "We talk of 'life' as if it were unquestionably something precious," Santayana says, and continues, "perhaps a part of the vocation of the spirit may be to overcome this prejudice."[26] The end of life is death, and to live spiritually is to have no painful and no binding attachments, to be always ready to die.

It is not clear whether Santayana considered the spiritual life *livable*. It must be livable, to some extent at any rate, if it is not to be a wholly delusive ideal. But it seems paradoxical in the extreme that the good *life* should be that in which one feels that one might as well be dead. And even if this uncanny indifference to death be acceptable, the spiritual life, desiccated angelic existence that it is, seems utterly remote from and unattractive to human nature as we generally know it. The pose of the sage reflecting on the tribulations of life from a distance is not without its seductive charm, but somehow I cannot help suspecting that it is never more than a pose. No one would care to, and for that matter no one could, live spiritually for forty or fifty years of one's adult life. Thus, Santayana's point may be that perfection, like husbandry, is seasonal: spring is spent in sowing, the summer in cultivating the fields, and moral action brings spiritual fruit only in the fall when the harvest is gathered and the soul prepares for the long winter journey. The spiritual life may be the perfection of old age, and old age may well be the consummation of a full life. But it is never the whole of it.

[26] *Realms of Being*, 615.

CHAPTER 9

Belief, Confidence, and Faith

SCEPTICISM AND ANIMAL FAITH is Santayana's most complex and most ambitious philosophical book. In execution no less than in its scope and conception, the work invites comparison with the philosophical classics. Unfortunately, like many of the classics, it is compressed, difficult and, in some fundamental ways, unclear. *Scepticism and Animal Faith* has an additional problem: its structure, though neat and natural, is seriously misleading. The evidently logical sequence of its chapters hinders the reader from seeing that the structure hides Santayana's method and obscures his most characteristic claims. This is the reason why in a book devoted to its introduction and elaboration, the concept of animal faith remains unclear.

Santayana's initial aim in the book is to determine if we can know anything. An adequate answer, any answer in fact, presupposes an idea of what it would be to know. Fully conscious of what he is doing, Santayana considers the problem on the basis of what may, not inappropriately, be called *the* classical standard of knowledge. According to this view, widely accepted since Plato's day or before, the scope of knowledge is restricted to those items concerning which certainty is possible. Certainty here has nothing to do with feelings or the manner in which we entertain propositions; instead, it is the impossibility of being in error. To know, therefore, is to grasp a fact beyond the shadow of a doubt.

This rationalistic criterion of incorrigibility is hard to satisfy. Santayana's point, in fact, is that it can be satisfied only at intolerable cost. The price of certainty, he argues, is significance; only by relinquishing all claims to knowing anything *about* anything can we achieve freedom from possible error. What we can have is indubitable nonjudgmental grasp of momentary, self-identical objects. In solipsism of the present moment the possibility of error is eliminated, but only the blank stare of consciousness takes its place. A hardy sceptic may think this acceptable or even fine; for Santayana, however, it betokens the bankruptcy of the rationalistic standard.

"Solipsism of the present moment is a violent pose," he says, "permitted only to the young philosopher, in his first intellectual despair."[1] A violent pose is not one that cannot be assumed: Santayana does not provide a logical *reductio* of the rationalist criterion. His claim is simply that using such a standard is pointless. It cannot be part of an *honest* philosophy, viz., one that speaks to the conditions and concerns of humankind. Santayana repeatedly uses the word "honest" and as early as the Preface announces his intention to develop a philosophy that will follow and articulate the common sense we all share. With the exposure of the rationalist criterion of knowledge as unsuited for a relevant and humane philosophy, Santayana concludes discussion of it. He feels he has shown the need for a radical departure from this part of Western philosophical tradition.

His next task is to introduce and elaborate an alternative criterion. Instead of proceeding to do this immediately and in a straightforward fashion, however, he takes another route and gets to a discussion of his own standard only seven chapters later.[2] His actual strategy is to start from the pure and unmeaning intuition of essence, expanding the scope of belief little by little. This procedure of gradually reconstructing the edifice of our knowledge has all the advantages control and due measure confer. By adding beliefs one at a time, Santayana can make sure of the nature and pedigree of each and arrange them in a pleasing logical sequence. But there is a grave disadvantage. This manner of proceeding creates the false impression of continuity between the destructive and the constructive sides of Santayana's project. One comes away with the feeling that having demonstrated the strength of the sceptic's position, Santayana is now somehow

---

[1] George Santayana, *Scepticism and Animal Faith* (New York: Scribner's, 1923; reprinted New York: Dover, 1955), 17. Hereafter cited as *SAF*.

[2] Chapter 18, "Knowledge is Faith Mediated by Symbols." But even here his discussion is far from complete.

beating him at his own game. What typically remains absent is recognition of the magnitude of the break between scepticism and animal faith. The reader is not likely to note that the former is the end of one philosophy, the latter the beginning of quite another.

As a result, at least partially, of this strategy in *Scepticism and Animal Faith*, not a single published commentator has managed to develop an adequate account of the notion of animal faith. This represents a lamentable record for philosophical scholarship. It is not that only the scholars are to blame. Santayana shares the responsibility for confusion by providing, as I have suggested, the wrong initial clue and then reinforcing it with a variety of misleading, if not actually mistaken, comments.

Another fact contributes to the misleading impression of continuity. Since Descartes's time or before, the search for certainty has focused on the inner life. Philosophers have typically agreed that nothing in the external world can answer the strict demand of indubitability. For this reason, they have usually started with consciousness, the self, or the facts of experience, working their way from the center to reach the periphery of an independently existing physical world. Santayana himself pays particular attention to the inner landscape in his treatment of the rationalist criterion. What strikes one as remarkable on reflection is that when he abandons the rationalist criterion and embarks on the development of his own philosophy, he does not concurrently jettison the subjectivist starting point. This is all the more surprising since it is simply not possible to make any sense of the idea of animal faith without thinking that it involves a radical shift away from all philosophy that views consciousness as either causally or evidentially central.

The reason for starting his reconstruction of belief at the dead center of pure intuition must surely be literary. If it were philosophical, it would put him in league with Descartes, attempting to roll back the tide of scepticism standing on the sure ground of some inner truth. This is not what he wants to do, although there is a sentence that appears to lend credence to the view. I quote it in full largely to show that Santayana's work deserves and re-

wards a careful reading no less than the work of those who affect
greater precision.

> Starting, as I here should, from absolute certitude—
> that is, from the obvious character of some essence—
> the first object of belief suggested by that assurance is
> the *identity* of this essence in various instances and in
> various contexts.[3]

The superficial impression is that Santayana attempts to derive
beliefs from or to justify them by the certainty we get in isolated
moments of consciousness. In fact, however, he says nothing of
the sort. His verb is "suggested," not "proved" or "implied,"
revealing that the principle of his reconstruction is literary or
psychological instead of philosophical or epistemic.

This last conclusion, one might argue, however, is in direct
contradiction with Santayana's reflections on his enterprise. In
Chapter 12, he distinguishes between the orders of the genesis,
discovery, and evidence of human beliefs. His own project, he
indicates, is to arrange our ideas in the last of these. It would
seem, then, that he intends to order them in the way in which
they support one another and justify the movement of our
thought. This initial impression is borne out by the studied and
gradual manner in which he constructs the edifice of human
knowledge.

But is the movement from the mindless certainty of intuition to
belief in nature and beyond that to the discernment of spirit really
evidential? In fact, the indubitable character of essence does not
justify any beliefs. On the basis of pure intuition, each subsequent belief is a new and unwarranted dogma. Could Santayana
have supposed that starting with changeless objects of consciousness, of which not even their being such objects can rightly
be affirmed, one could somehow justify belief in a changing
physical world? Could he have overlooked the fact that solipsism
of the present moment entails none of those later beliefs?

These questions are evidently rhetorical. Santayana himself
emphasizes that certainty about essence yields no conclusion

3 *SAF*, 111.

about existence. And a closer look at his words quickly convinces us that in talking of the order of evidence, he had in mind something a little less ambitious than a full deductive scheme. "I have absolute assurance of nothing save the character of some given essence; the rest is arbitrary belief or interpretation added by my animal impulse,"[4] he says. There is no indication here of a gradual evidential chain stretching from essence to embodiment. The distinction is simply between two sorts of evidential status: "absolute assurance" and "arbitrary belief." Absolute assurance (about essence) is achieved by meeting the requirement of the rationalist standard of knowledge. Belief is called arbitrary only from that perspective. The beliefs Santayana later develops have their own justification, but that justification is not in accordance with the rationalist criterion and is not to be derived from "the bed-rock of perfect certitude." It is justification by the standard of "animal impulse" or, as Santayana elsewhere christens it, "cognitive instinct" and "practical reason."[5]

If we read Santayana's claim that he is arranging human beliefs in the order of evidence as a commitment to producing an evidential chain from essence to existence, and the constructive part of *Scepticism and Animal Faith* as the execution of this plan, we are bound to be misled. The order in which beliefs are introduced in that book is convenient for Santayana to give the appearance of literary continuity in working his way out of solipsism. This obscures the fact that he has shifted to a new method for justifying beliefs. The arrangement of our beliefs in the order in which they are justified by the new standard of animal faith would, in fact, look very different from what we find in *Scepticism and Animal Faith*. Santayana never fully worked out that arrangement, although he came close to it in the early chapters of *The Realm of Matter* in discussing the indispensable and presumable properties of substance.

Let me now put my point more positively, which might then serve as an introduction to my account of animal faith. *Scepticism*

---

[4] *Ibid.*, 110.
[5] Paul A. Schilpp, ed., *The Philosophy of George Santayana* (Evanston: Northwestern University Press, 1940), 586. Hereafter referred to as *Philosophy.*

and Animal Faith consists of two unequal and discontinuous parts. The shorter, destructive part is designed to show that commitment to the rationalist criterion of knowledge inevitably leads to scepticism and that scepticism is a philosophical blind alley. Extricating himself from where this false start has taken him, along with much of the rest of modern thought, Santayana launches in the second part on an exploration of the philosophy of animal faith. He means this philosophy as an alternative to the subjectivistic systems that have dominated modern thought since Descartes. The foundation of the difference, and the key to Santayana's mature thought, is the new method of justification he proposes for our most general, one might want to say "philosophical" beliefs. The new method of justification consists in relating, in the appropriate fashion, each proposed general belief to the tacit commitments of the animal in us.

Why the animal? Knowledge, especially knowledge of general propositions, is after all a function of intellect, a capacity not typically associated with animals. The answer to this must be framed in terms of Santayana's belief that modern philosophy has put undue stress on intellect at the expense of intelligence, on mind to the detriment of the whole man. If life does not begin in ideation, neither should philosophy. Intelligence shows itself in action, and action subtends the world of representation. We must revert, Santayana maintains, to pre-Cartesian modes of thought and enter upon our philosophical reflections from the accepted fact of the reality of action. And by "action," Santayana does not mean activity as it has entered and is represented in a mind, nor act (as in Fichte) in which mentality has entered to capture the citadel. The insistence on *animal* life, then, is designed to stress the importance of starting from what Santayana was fond of calling a "natural" ground, viz., a mind-independent world surrounding us in space and surviving us in time that is the field, source, and butt of our actions.

If the initial focus is on the animal struggle to cope with an indifferent world, one may well ask why Santayana speaks of faith. "Faith" has overtones of greater sublimity than we deem appropriate for simple beasts. Yet the word is particularly apt for what Santayana has in view, especially if we keep the rationalist criterion of knowledge uppermost in our minds. For from that perspective, the animal's confident action presupposes unwarranted and unwarrantable dogmas; it is a matter of final and unjustifiable trust. As Santayana himself points out, once we accept the fact of animal confidence and countenance his method, we can find excellent reasons for many of our beliefs. But how can we justify the confidence and vindicate the method? From the standpoint of hard rationalist standards, we simply cannot. The confidence is based on faith, which is another way of saying that it has no foundation.

What, then, is the nature of animal faith? On the objective side, it is the unthinking boldness with which the animal, chased or chasing, takes its next step. Santayana tends to make statements of this sort and leave the matter, assuming that everyone will understand his meaning. For our purposes, this assumption is not reasonable. One gets an intuitive sense this way, but no precise account of the nature of animal faith. One cannot, for instance, determine whether animal faith is a belief or a set of beliefs shared by all animals, a set of truths implied by or implicated in action, or simply the manner in which certain (or all?) animal actions are performed. There is some evidence for each of these alternatives in Santayana's works. It is, of course, unlikely that Santayana held all three positions, even though he would not be guilty of a contradiction if he did. From the standpoint of the defensibility of his opinion, it is of central importance to determine which of these alternatives comes closest to his deliberate view.

The first point that must be made is that when Santayana speaks of belief or faith, he does not mean a consciously entertained conviction. To be sure, I may grow conscious of having such beliefs, but neither knowledge of holding them nor immediate awareness of the propositions I supposedly hold is a condition necessary to justify ascribing them to me. Santayana makes this point by saying that animal faith is "a sort of expectation and open-mouthedness"[6]—more nearly a behavioral attitude than an entertained position. As such, it is "prior to intuition" and thus to

6 *SAF*, 107.

all consciousness. This immediately identifies it as operating on the physical level, probably as an active attitude of the psyche.

We could affect great difficulties here, for on occasion Santayana writes as if animal faith operated on the conscious or mental level. He says, for example, that he includes belief under the category of spirit,[7] that animal faith is central to signification and without it "all would be intuition of data,"[8] and also that animal faith is the name he gives to principles of the interpretation of data.[9] Such statements seem to tie faith to mind, and not altogether inaccurately. There is a real connection between them, but it is not as direct as one might be tempted to suppose: animal faith, while not mental, has both effects and a counterpart in the realm of consciousness. Santayana is clear that belief is, first and foremost, physical: the animal may enact true beliefs even if it "does not realise them spiritually," viz., consciously.[10] Now animal faith is involved or precipitated in action,[11] and in directing her action on remote events, the psyche creates intent.[12] Intent is, roughly, the mental counterpart of animal faith. The active thrust of the animal on the hunt bursting beyond the confines of its present is matched by the transcendent force that carries the mind beyond the flat immediacy of the presented. Moreover, if Santayana is right, the active attitude or what underlies it is actually the cause of the urge we feel to take sense qualities (and other essences) as signs, or even parts, of physical objects. At any rate, if animal faith were to be experienced, it would surely report itself as a blind and imperious urge to hurtle beyond the facts.

The second point that needs to be made follows naturally from my discussion of the first. If animal faith on the deepest level is a physical force or attitude involved in action, we can speak of its "tenets" only tenuously. In an important sense it has no tenets, since it is, primordially at least, nonpropositional. When we think of "the original articles of the animal creed," we formulate and

[7] *Ibid.*, 272.
[8] *Philosophy*, 587.
[9] *SAF*, 299.
[10] *Ibid.*, 264.
[11] *Ibid.*, 106.
[12] *Ibid.*, 166.

give conceptual expression to an initially definite but unarticulated intensity. This is carefully recorded by Santayana, who calls such "tenets" of animal faith as that there is a world and that things sought can be found "the initial expression of animal vitality *in the sphere of mind*."[13]

It is more profitable to speak of the objects of animal faith than of its dogmas. In places Santayana writes as if there were only one object of the faith involved in action, viz., substance or the moving, changing world.[14] While no doubt accurate, this is not a complete description. In order for substance to constitute a field of action, it must be unevenly distributed in space and time. This crystallizes substance into things, modes of substance or, in another of Santayana's usages, substances. The objects of animal faith, then, are "alien self-developing beings" that are "capable of being affected by action"[15] or (what comes to the same thing) "the modes of matter which actually confront the human race in action."[16]

The central emphasis here and throughout Santayana's discussion of the starting point for his own philosophy is on the preconscious reality of action. Like Lucretius and other naturalists, he thinks we must begin with the birth and death, the dark natural struggle of the threatened animal. But unlike Lucretius and most materialists, he refuses to accept any graphic symbol as adequate or even privileged in revealing the inner nature of the world we meet in action. This is why his materialism appears so curiously vacuous. His interest is not in the nature of the stuff of the world but in its behavior. The primary objects of human knowledge are "things on the scale of the human senses,"[17] and the senses are in the service of action and survival. The ultimate test of our knowledge must always be "encounter in action";[18] we can never, in fact, go far beyond action or the physical probing that nature rewards with a yea or a nay. It may even be appropri-

---

[13] *Ibid.*, 180. My italics.
[14] *Ibid.*, 221.
[15] *Ibid.*, 214.
[16] *Ibid.*, 218.
[17] *Ibid.*, 175.
[18] *Ibid.*, 178.

ate to say, and if labels mattered much it might be worth arguing, that Santayana is not a materialist at all. Matter is neither the first nor a central idea of his philosophy; in fact, in the strictest sense, as the dynamic counterpart of essence, he does not have a concept of matter at all. The material world is for him, epistemologically no less than practically, a field of action. What makes it material is simply that it consists of actual, viz., contingent spatio–temporal–causal relations.

It is only this perspective that can explain Santayana's difficult but haunting idea of the latent materialism of idealists. For we can turn the matter around and say that perhaps all Santayana's materialism amounts to is the assertion that the natural world of action deployed in space and time is the only actual one or, at any rate, the only one of significance to us. This insistence on the centrality of action or, on its traditional counterpart, the primacy of practical reason, invites comparison of Santayana's views with venerable philosophical traditions and in particular with such so-called idealists as Fichte. Santayana and Fichte find themselves in agreement that the primordial reality with which we must begin is the deed. Their descriptions of the world that makes deeds possible and of the deed that in turn makes the world will, if accurate, not differ much from each other. The differences will be those of perspective and emphasis—subjective and largely verbal contributions to what we face in fact. An honest philosophy, viewing action with a minimum of assumptions and directed to disentangling the tacit commitments of ongoing life, should cut across the verbiage that separates idealist from materialist. In doing this, we should liberate philosophy from the controversies of the schools and return it to the service of sound practice and sane thought. This is the point of the philosophy of animal faith.

Let me take time for two brief remarks. First of all, there is an interesting similarity of this criterion for judging philosophies to the test Santayana set for religion and literature in such an early work as *Interpretations of Poetry and Religion*. The key throughout is how imaginative works serve, enhance, and express the quality and needs of human life. Second, one may note an obvious problem of terminology here. Materialism is no less a theory than is idealism; if the philosophy of animal faith cuts through the verbal differences between them, it cannot be identical with either. I pass by this issue without comment in the sure conviction that however wrong Santayana may be on other counts, he is certainly right that in such matters a purely verbal difference makes no difference at all.

Let me conclude this discussion of the primary object of animal faith as the thing encountered in action with a remark about Santayana's conception of action. It would be a grave mistake to look in Santayana for an idea of action as it may be conceived by contemporary action theorists. The latter typically collapse or collate ideas proper to matter and spirit, two realms Santayana is particularly careful to distinguish. He is unequivocal in asserting that an account of the actions of animals belongs in the sphere of scientific psychology. The method of such a psychology must be behavioristic,[19] and as a science, it is simply a part of "physics, or the study of nature."[20] Which movements constitute actions and which do not, then, is a problem for psychology and not philosophy. The philosopher must simply keep in mind that there is no radical break between the motions of matter, the movements of animals, and the behavior of men. This evidently does not commit Santayana to accepting any given proposed scientific account of the nature and limits of human action: it is only to remind oneself of the unity of nature and to identify the quarter from which accounts of natural fact are to be expected.

A more complete discussion of this issue would gain much by taking into account Santayana's treatment of teleology and the psyche in *The Realm of Matter*. But my present concern allows no such digression. For our purposes, it may suffice to say that although Santayana has not (and if we take him at face value, he should not have) worked out a concept of action in detail, he is very clear in designating the sorts of movements he considers actions. In speaking of the tacit commitments involved in action, he always chooses the basic animal acts of seeking, dodging, fighting, breeding, and eating to make his points. His paradigm, I believe, is eating. Animal faith is "an expression of hunger,"[21] he

[19] *Ibid.*, 219.
[20] *Ibid.*, 252.
[21] *Ibid.*, 214.

says, or "a conviction native" to it.[22] He bills the belief that "things seen can be eaten" as one of the "original articles" of animal creed.[23] He goes so far as to say that one assures oneself of the existence of the object of animal faith by devouring it[24] and caps it all by the staggering assertion (shades of Lucretius!) that substance is universal food.[25]

The third point I wish to make about animal faith is the generality of its initial tenets. The conviction native to action cannot be present in some actions and not in others. Only those beliefs universally present in all action can, therefore, be "tenets" of animal faith; the conviction that there is a desk in front of me now, though in some sense a manifestation of animal faith, is not one of its original articles. The distinction to draw perhaps is that between the beliefs one has in living by animal faith and the beliefs that may be justified by reference to the faith implicated in all action. The latter constitutes the general convictions that the philosophy of animal faith will view as justified; their identification is the task of the philosopher.

What Santayana has in mind is in some respects similar to a Kantian transcendental deduction. Kant's project is to identify the structures invariably present in all experience. Similarly, Santayana wants to pick out the convictions tacit in every animal act. Just as Kant designates these structures as necessary conditions of the possibility of experience, Santayana is prepared to say that instinctive faith as a physical impulse or attitude is indispensable even for "our simplest acts."[26] And just as Kant's transcendental deduction yields universal propositions of a very high level of abstraction, so the conceptual formulation of animal faith can give us beliefs or judgments of a very high generality only. A good way to test this similarity may be to compare Kant's categories of the understanding and his pure forms of intuition with Santayana's indispensable and presumable properties of substance. Since the issue of the transcendental method is an important one, it may be

22 *Ibid.*, 198.

23 *Ibid.*, 180.

24 *Philosophy*, 19.

25 George Santayana, *The Realm of Matter* (New York: Scribner's, 1930), 100.

26 *Philosophy*, 581.

appropriate for me to introduce a brief disclaimer. There are obvious and immense differences in intent and starting point between Santayana and Kant. I have no interest in a full exploration of their relation here. My sole present concern is to call attention to a similarity of their methods and the similar generality of their results.

Enough has been said, I believe, for us to begin to piece together the outlines of Santayana's philosophy of animal faith. In particular, it should be clear that when we speak of animal faith we do not mean to refer to actions performed in a certain fashion. To be sure, some of our actions may be characterized as confident, and perhaps there is an unwarranted boldness in the performance of all of them. But animal faith itself is more nearly something that is expressed or manifested in action and makes it possible than something that merely qualifies it. It is an attitude or a moving force or a living thrust within the animal; perhaps it is the counterpart in an organic being to the forward tension Santayana claims to detect in the natural moments that, he thinks, constitute the ultimate units of matter.

How does the philosophy of animal faith proceed? It must, of course, begin by accepting the reality of action. From there we have two alternatives. We may simply ask for the necessary conditions of the possibility of action, viz., for what must exist if action does or what must be true if it is true that animals act. Alternatively, we must explore the beliefs to which the animal is committed by virtue of its action in the world.

One's initial inclination is to think that Santayana would opt for the first of these alternatives. If he did, the method of proof in the philosophy of animal faith would be virtually identical with the transcendental method we associate with Kant. We could quickly proceed from the granted actuality of action to the reality of space, time, causation, and the uneven distribution of existents, among others. The advantage of this procedure is that it is straightforward. Moreover, that it yields existents or facts about existents makes it particularly harmonious with Santayana's interest in ontology and his desire to grow beyond all philosophy in which the focus is on consciousness and the problem of knowledge is central. Finally, it accords well with his language in those statements in which he places heavy emphasis on the logical relations (implies, presupposes, is implicated in) that supposedly obtain between action and the objects of animal faith.

In spite of these considerations, I think it likely that Santayana's method is closer to the second alternative than to the first. For one, his avowed aim is to isolate the *beliefs* that may be justified by the method of animal faith. Moreover, his interest is focused on the natural history of living animals, and that history is more directly a matter of convictions and involvements than of presuppositions and implications. He makes this point in two ways. Viewing his philosophy as the thought of one man, he says, "My criticism is criticism of myself: I am talking of what I believe in my active moments, as a living animal."[27] More generally, he announces at the beginning of *Scepticism and Animal Faith* that his aim is simply to give "accurate and circumspect form" to the "workaday opinions" and "everyday beliefs" of mankind.[28] Finally, we must take Santayana at his word: he calls his philosophy that of animal *faith*. If he had wanted to use human action as a jumping-off point for exploring its conditions, he would surely have said so. He could then have called his opinions "the philosophy of animal action" and his procedure "the method of deducing the conditions of behavior." In fact, however, it is clear that his interest is ultimately practical and moral. He wants to study the psyche's convictions and clean "the windows of the soul."[29] Honest study of the self may lead to self-knowledge, and self-knowledge promotes a better life.

How can one argue from action to belief? With caution. I see no serious problem with this. As I have already indicated, we deal here for the most part with beliefs we are not aware of having. There are at least two perfectly good ways of supporting the ascription of unconscious beliefs. On the one hand, we may find that some conviction we have commits us to certain others of which we were not initially aware. My belief that I talked with you last week, for instance, commits me to the belief that I was alive

27 *SAF*, 305.
28 *Ibid.*, v.
29 *Ibid.*, vi–vii.

then, even though I may never have focused on the latter proposition. In this vein, Santayana could argue that every action, at any rate every human action, involves some specific belief and that every such specific belief commits the agent to some or all of a set of general persuasions. My belief that I am looking for a lost manuscript, for example, commits me to a host of beliefs about the reality of space and time and the behavior of physical objects. A clever dialectician could spin a picture of the world right out of this.

On the other hand, we may take action as direct evidence of belief. It is a platitude that a person's thoughts are reflected in his actions; mercifully, we are less frequently reminded that we have to look to our actions to find out what we think. In fact, however, what we do is frequently the most reliable and, on occasion, perhaps the only guide to our convictions. The special condescension with which a man may speak to a woman or a black reveals beliefs and attitudes that, if they were stated for him, would cause him pained surprise. And no one has to be a Freudian to find a thousand instances of human beings earnestly reporting one belief while acting out another. Could Spinoza really have believed that he was an eternal, changeless mode when hunger made him wind his way to lunch? In this vein, Santayana could argue that what we do and how we act each day unveils a host of views, unspoken and unknown, that shape our lives and guide us in our ways. There might be some question here of how far in a sequence of beliefs the evidence of action will take us. Our actions certainly disclose that we believe in the reality of space, for example, but that we have a tacit commitment to the unity of nature is more dubious. These, however, are problems of detail that leave the principle of the philosophy of animal faith untouched.

The reader patient enough to have followed me this far is, I am sure, perceptive enough to have noticed that there are at least three major, distinct uses to which Santayana puts the phrase "animal faith." The first is to refer to a dynamic directional *force* in animals, a physical impulse that undergirds their agency. The second is to call attention to a new *method* of justifying beliefs in philosophy, viz., the method of attempting to give conceptual formulation to this force or to develop the tacit beliefs involved in or warranted by our actions. The third is to pick out the *beliefs* that can be justified through the judicious use of this method.

It is not unusual to find this sort of ambiguity in Santayana. Nor is there anything wrong with ambiguity; the mouse can avoid the trap if he knows it is one. If this paper has succeeded in clarifying some of the issues in Santayana's philosophy of animal faith, it will have gone a little way toward eliminating misconceptions and warning of the most blatant ambiguities. An incidental benefit may be the renewed attention it invites to one of Santayana's positive, neglected and, I believe, important philosophical contributions.

CHAPTER 10

Peirce, Santayana, and the Large Facts

S OME EARNEST SCHOLAR will someday produce a study of the remarkable similarities between the thought of Santayana and of Peirce. This is a rich lode to mine. Imagine demonstrating that two major philosophers, frequently supposed as distant from each other as Ryle from relevance, share assumptions, theories, and approaches! The topic does not lend itself to an easy dissertation: any adequate treatment would require mastery of the material and the keen skill of dissecting to find matching parts. Perhaps some analytic philosopher who has tired of "could have done otherwise" and turned to the subtleties of the ontological argument will now move past God and reach Peirce and Santayana. The training and temperament of such a person would enable him to do an excellent job: scholarship is scholarship whether you deal with the dead or the nonexistent.

I shall not undertake the full task of showing that in spite of obvious differences Santayana and Peirce are astoundingly similar. I should like simply to assume that they are, as if the work of careful and piecemeal comparison were already complete. But I find that I cannot. For the task of showing that Peirce and Santayana hail from the same family has not even begun. If I fail to make that claim at least plausible first, it will not be surprising that on the things that matter our two philosophers do not see eye to eye.

Let me, therefore, give a few pointers that might help to pick out similarities of pattern. I shall focus briefly on seven issues. There are many more, of course, that a full treatment would disclose. But these should be enough to make the claim of family resemblance thoroughly plausible. The only other comment I must make is that similarity is a complex relation that always involves difference. So we should never be surprised if my love, revealingly like a red, red rose, nevertheless needs no water and has no thorns. Even the finest picture of Dolly Parton leaves something to be desired or, shall I say, fails the original in a number of respects. So let us think of similarities as embedded in a context of differences and making those differences more important and more interesting.

1. Both Peirce and Santayana are realists. They maintain that the object of perception exists independently of the perceptual relation into which it may, on occasion, enter. They are deeply committed to the idea that the world is real in an irreducible way, that it is not the figment of some mind. Though each in his own way has a deep respect for the work of mind, neither thinks that the intellect through its cognitive act creates reality.

2. Both Peirce and Santayana are naturalists. It is not altogether easy to express what this means; the idea of naturalism is as elusive as it is important. They agree that the world, with whatever magnitude of order it displays, is a single system that articulates itself in space and time. This system is governed by its own laws, which diligent inquiry may disclose. Man is in some fashion continuous with the natural world and may find his fulfillment within it.

3. We find in both Santayana and Peirce a remarkable and central stress on action. One could put this aggressively and maintain that both of them are pragmatists. But this label is not very useful because it is not sufficiently specific. The similarity I have in mind is better conveyed by focusing on the intimate and intricate relation that Peirce thinks obtains between ideas and actions. Beliefs, for Peirce, are not primarily propositions entertained in consciousness. The element of awareness is clearly secondary; beliefs are constituted of habits of action. This line of reflection is nearly identical with Santayana's classical rejection of subjectivism in the early part of *Scepticism and Animal Faith* and the subsequent development of an entire philosophy based on animal action. For Santayana's point concerning animal belief is precisely that it is not an entertained essence or proposition but a habit of action as we work to pursue or avoid objects in our

environment. This habit may rise to consciousness. But what is then immediately present to us has a deeper source and reality in the life of action; and what confirms it is not propositional evidence but unhindered, successful operation. This philosophy of animal faith is the central reason for calling Santayana an American philosopher. It overshadows his Platonism, his commitment to spirituality, his arcane, Scholastic terminology. And it is, at once, a point of fundamental kinship with Peirce.

4. If one wanted to explore Santayana's indebtedness to Peirce, one would have to start with the theory of signs. I am not aware of any direct evidence that Santayana read Peirce. We know that he read Dewey and Husserl and Heidegger; there are copies of their works with extensive marginalia in Santayana's hand. No one has identified any copies of *The Monist* or *Popular Science Monthly* similarly marked up. Yet Santayana was well aware of Peirce's work. He followed the journals. He attended some of Peirce's lectures. He was in continued and intimate philosophical contact with James and others who corresponded with and/or were influenced by Peirce. Most important perhaps, the similarity of his ideas on the function of symbols in cognition to those of Peirce is too great to be coincidental if we take into account the surrounding context of indirect contacts.

But whether Santayana owes something to Peirce or not, the similarity of their ideas on sign cognition is remarkable. Both maintain that the very heart of intelligence consists in signification and that the mind's relation to its object is always mediated. Moreover, they share the insight that *symbolic* knowledge is no handicap; on the contrary, identity, resemblance, and inclusion yield no knowledge at all without the triadic relation that signification involves. The impact of this recognition is vast and tends to color one's entire epistemology. The fact that Santayana left the notion of symbolization half-developed and moved it in a literary direction while Peirce converted it into a romantic metaphysics in no way diminishes the substantial identity of their starting points.

5. Both Peirce and Santayana are committed to the independent reality of universals. To be sure, the world of universals is carved up in different ways by the two philosophers. Santayana

sees no essential distinction between qualities and general ideas, while Peirce is committed to distinguishing them as firsts and thirds, respectively. But this difference pales by comparison with the importance of agreeing that there are universals, that they are embodied in nature, and that their reality is in no way hostage to the whims of mind.

6. Both Peirce and Santayana reject the legitimacy of a universal sceptical reduction. Though Peirce does this by a theory of the nature and function of doubt while Santayana follows the sceptical enterprise to the point where it reduces itself to senseless irrelevance, they join in recognizing wholesale scepticism as an intellectual game unrelated to the business of serious inquiry. Universal scepticism proposes a standard, a rationalistic standard, that all knowledge worthy of the name must meet. The rejection of the sceptical enterprise is at once the rejection of this criterion of absolute certainty. The removal of this standard, however, amounts to the elimination of the possibility of what we nowadays call "foundationalism." For foundationalism requires that all knowledge rest on a bedrock of certainty: on intuitions or sensations or basic propositions by reference to which all other statements may be judged probable or true. Santayana and Peirce are unequivocal in stating their impatience with this view. The "myth of the given" is not exactly a recent discovery, nor was it Popper or some friend of his who first developed the notion that everything can be questioned in turn but not everything at once.

7. Last but not least, there are persuasive similarities between Peirce's and Santayana's fundamental categories. Once again, I am not inclined to deny that the resemblances provide a context for interesting differences; nothing is served by the futile attempt to show that everyone has the same ideas. But a close study reveals that what Peirce calls "firstness" is almost precisely what Santayana dubs "spirit": the stress on self-contained feeling makes the connection unmistakable. "Secondness" is what Santayana and Peirce both call matter, the realm of force and brute interaction.

"Thirdness" may be thought to present problems because it cuts across objective law and subjective thought, realms that Santayana takes special pains to distinguish. But in fact Santayana's realm of truth comes very near to capturing what Peirce had in mind. Truth encompasses both matter and mind, for it consists of all those orderly tropes that gain actualization in any medium. And by "trope," Santayana means the complex essence of a process, a notion closely akin to Peirce's general idea or law.

In focusing on these seven points of similarity, I do not wish to imply that there are no others. Quite the contrary. My purpose was only to render the claim of Santayana's similarity to Peirce plausible. The seven points should have accomplished this. If they did, I am free to go on to my main topic.

I find it remarkable that two philosophers who agree on so many important philosophical matters and on so many details should nevertheless hold such radically divergent views on the large facts. By "the large facts" (Santayana's phrase), I mean what he also calls "the moral truths" about the world. They are constituted by the alignment of circumstances of significance in the conduct of life. "The chief issue," Santayana staunchly maintains, "[is] the relation of man and his spirit to the universe."[1] The large facts are the ones truly important because of their bearing on this relation. They govern the role and prospects of the individual and the race. They determine the cost of happiness, the limits of existence, the forms of failure. They provide the necessary conditions of life and the possibility of the good life.

Philosophers rarely analyze these facts. Some consider them too cosmic to permit close examination. For the rest, they are situated near the outcome of philosophies as those final, unchallenged realities to which proper thought enables us to assume the correct attitude. What we think of these large or ultimate facts of life, therefore, is too frequently a function of temperament and prior commitments. Even though Socrates said that the purpose of philosophy is to prepare us for death, we often find that our attitude to death prepares our philosophy. I do not, of course, suggest that one's philosophy is but the mindless expression of one's sentiments. Least of all is this true of two such self-conscious and methodologically sophisticated philosophers as Peirce and Santayana. Yet one must be struck by the similarity of

---

[1] George Santayana, *Scepticism and Animal Faith* (New York: Dover, 1955), viii.

their technical philosophical premises and the divergence of their human conclusions, the consequences they draw for the large facts. Suffice it to say that we understand too little of the interplay of rational considerations with individual temperament and circumstances in the generation of philosophical views. Is it not astounding that an age as deeply devoted to metaphilosophical, methodological, and evidential questions as ours should have kept itself ignorant on this issue?

Peirce worked under difficult circumstances and was largely unappreciated while alive. Yet his philosophy exudes a cosmic optimism about the prospects of man in nature, even about the very structure, the growing rationality of nature itself. Santayana, on the other hand, was a successful professor, the darling of Cambridge society for a while. Yet in one of his notebooks he penned, "I have been called many names: sceptic, relativist, materialist, epiphenomenalist. But no one has ever called me an optimist." He made no secret of the fact that he thought the human spirit was an alien visitor in the tearing world, yet he held out no hope of another place from which we hail and to which we repair.

Peirce's optimism is not a dispensable afterthought of his system. Some might suppose that his discussion of creative love or agapasm is an unneeded and best-forgotten indiscretion. But in fact his entire philosophy is permeated with the cheerfulness of nineteenth-century evolutionary thought. This is reflected even in the way the categories are related to one another. Although firstness, secondness, and thirdness are in one sense independent, separate, and irreducible conceptions, they are hierarchically arranged in the direction of enrichment and order. Peirce indicates this with extraordinary eloquence in one place where he temporalizes the interrelation of the categories. In describing the sort of metaphysics his ideas adumbrate, he writes,

> In the beginning—infinitely remote—there was a chaos of unpersonalized feeling, which being without connection or regularity would properly be without existence. This feeling, sporting here and there in pure

arbitrariness, would have started the germ of a generalizing tendency. Its other sportings would be evanescent, but this would have a growing virtue. Thus, the tendency to habit would be started; and from this, with the other principles of evolution, all the regularities of the universe would be evolved. At any time, however, an element of pure chance survives and will remain until the world becomes an absolutely perfect, rational, and symmetrical system, in which mind is at last crystallized in the infinitely distant future.[2]

I chose to quote this passage at length because it displays, better perhaps than any other, the two great sources of optimism whose confluence shaped Peirce's philosophy. One is the empirically based theory of evolution, which promised to render the self-improvement of nature a matter of scientific fact. The disorder of spontaneous variation is harnessed—in a fashion that would make Royce proud—to provide enriching multiplicity for higher unities. The second source is romantic German metaphysics, which sees the actualization of mind as the ultimate motive force of all reality. Peirce knew this perfectly well, for he said "my philosophy resuscitates Hegel."[3] It is just that he should not have neglected to add that his insistence on the infinity that must pass before the self-perfection of the world is complete also resuscitates that most bittersweet of German romantics, Fichte.

Peirce thus thinks that we live in a universe that is upward bound. It is purposive to its core and naturally tends to impose order on its multiplicity. The order is referred to variously as law and mind, habit and general idea. Man belongs in the higher reaches of this self-perfecting cosmos. For man is a sign,[4] and signs are thirds. Our beliefs and behaviors are habits. All of life is but a train of thought, and all thought, in fact all mental action,

---

[2] Charles S. Peirce, *Collected Papers*, 8 vols. (Cambridge, Mass.: Harvard University Press, 1931–58), 6:33.

[3] *Ibid*. 1:42.

[4] *Ibid*. 5:314.

can in the end be reduced to the formula or law of valid reasoning.[5] Persons themselves are but general ideas[6] in no essential way different from the universals that structure the apparently nonhuman parts of the world.

There is, then, a cozy identity between man and the intelligible structure of the world. The identity is not only that of kind, however. For the principle of continuity makes the genuine isolation of any individual item impossible. We thus find ourselves fading into our neighbors on all sides; we are continuous with the cosmic stream of thought. Peirce expresses this idea in a variety of ways. In one place, he says that being "welded into the universal continuum" is "what true reasoning consists in."[7] In another passage nearby, he speaks of duty completing our "personality by melting it into the neighboring parts of the universal cosmos."[8] The unity of man and nature is rendered complete when we learn that "physical events are but degraded or undeveloped forms of psychical events."[9] We are in this way not only at one with the world but also represent its highest, most nearly perfect form of manifestation.

I need to add only one more factor to complete this sketch of Peirce's optimism. Just as individuals belong in the bosom of nature, so they are inseparable from the community. The development of truth and reality and the development of the community of investigators proceed isomorphically. Peirce says: "Every species of reality . . . is essentially a social, a public affair,"[10] and the very "conception of reality . . . involves the notion of a COMMUNITY, without definite limits, and capable of a definite increase of knowledge."[11] The community to which we belong has no definite spatial limits, and it stretches infinitely into the future. "Now you and I—what are we?" he asks. "Mere cells of the social organism," he answers without the least hesita-

5 *Ibid.*, 267.
6 *Ibid.* 6:270.
7 *Ibid.* 1:673.
8 *Ibid.*
9 *Ibid.* 6:264.
10 *Ibid.*, 429.
11 *Ibid.* 5:311.

tion. [12] We can be and be fulfilled only as integrated members of the cosmopolitan, nay the cosmic, community of inquiring minds. But since we naturally belong there, we have reason to be of good cheer. The community of investigators is as secure as order in nature, as emerging reality itself. The fate of the individual is of no significance so long as the scientific community marches on.

It is interesting to compare this glowing description of the glory of rational man with Santayana's more sober assessment of the realities. It is best to begin by calling attention to Santayana's much-neglected positivistic tendencies. His firm commitment to ontology and to scholastic language tends to obscure the fact that Santayana is a firm advocate of the fact-value distinction and a vigorous opponent of speculative metaphysics. The latter is amply demonstrated in the depth of his disdain for German idealism. Much of the moralizing metaphysics of that tradition comes under what Santayana calls "dreaming in words." The fact-value distinction, on the other hand, occasioned him to look particularly closely at the moral or perfection claims frequently made on behalf of the theory of evolution. He quickly decided that no description of natural developments is by itself adequate to support value judgments concerning what emerges. That more complex unities emerge in the course of natural evolution may well be a fact; that order is more nearly perfect than chance or that complex unity is better than diffused flashes of protoplasmic feeling are judgments expressing the less-than-cosmic preferences of animals.

Neither one of the great nineteenth-century sources of optimism is thus available to Santayana. He starts his philosophy, therefore, the way his admired Lucretius did, building on his observation of "the stars, the seasons, the swarm of animals, the spectacle of birth and death, of cities and wars."[13] There is little outside the sphere of human, or at most animate, life to suggest purposiveness. Values are irreducibly relative; comparative judgments presuppose a private imagination with all the private value

[12] *Ibid.* 1:673.
[13] *SAF*, x.

commitments that that involves. There is no reason to suppose that social organisms exist in any sense resembling the very real existence of individuals. Individuals enjoy, in Santayana's view, a reality that is—if not physically then at least morally—ultimate. States and societies derive their legitimacy from the way they express and satisfy the needs and values of individuals.

The philosophical paradigm here is the single animal making its way in a treacherous environment. The source of life, value, and preference is the psyche, the tenuous material organization of the animal body. The life of the psyche itself is finite and precarious. Nature, indifferent to our good, permits us to flourish for a day and then with equal indifference cuts us down. The universe is too vast for us to count for much; since everything passes, even those to whom we mattered are soon gone. To be sure, man's spirit can transcend this flux and contemplate the eternity of essence for the nonce. But spirit or consciousness itself is but a momentary achievement of its material organ. Like the mayfly, it, too, disappears, and there is nothing to show for it but the cold, impersonal stretches of the realm of truth that is a complete record of everything that was.

Of course, I do not want to say that in Santayana's view we can never rise above the mindless necessity of nature. On the contrary, a life of reason, a temporary reversal of the forces of death and decay, is often possible. But there is nothing in the very structure of nature that especially promotes it, just as there is nothing in iron ore that especially invites or promotes the manufacture of cars. A clever animal or group may avail itself of existing opportunities; when the vessel runs dry, the good life, and the bad life, all life simply ceases. Order holds sway contingently. And all the evidence points to the fact that soon this order will be replaced by another, perhaps without continuity and almost certainly without advance.

Santayana is no pessimist in the sense of thinking that everything is in vain. It is only the dispassionate mind viewing the world under the form of eternity, as "the chronicles of ancient wars," that sees the futility of everything. The heat of life is rarely affected. But the wise man's perspective on it all is framed in sadness. This surely is in sharp contrast to Peirce, who maintains that the wise man or the scientific investigator is precisely the individual who understands how logic and ethics hang together, how signification and reality constitute a seamless, structured web.

When I reflect on the immensity of the difference between Peirce and Santayana in these all-important matters, I find it hard to resist the thought that technical philosophical agreements do not matter much. I am then tempted to view philosophical theses as but support for what the heart desires. They certainly do not determine what we think of matters of great importance, or else Peirce and Santayana would be in far closer agreement on the large facts. But temptations are there to be resisted. Attractive as it may be, it is surely simplistic to see philosophies as but rationalizations of private hopes and feelings. So I am impelled to look for philosophical reasons for the divergences. And I think I can find two.

There are two sets of divergent generative images from which Peirce's and Santayana's differences flow. The first set relates to the individual. I hinted at this before and now want to make it fully explicit. Santayana has no sympathy with the Cartesian view that the individual or the mind is an independently existing substance. As to existence, both body and mind are conditioned, finite, tenuous beings. The body is a mode of material substance. The mind is a fruit of physical organs; its content is culturally determined. But morally, the individual psyche is a substance indeed: it is a self-contained arbiter of values. Santayana is committed to an isolationist individualism: there is an absolute gulf between persons, and within each of us privacy is absolute. This view of essential loneliness is what Peirce rejects by means of his principle of continuity. Moral and personal privacy become matters of choice, not of fundamental principle, the moment we view the individual as constituted by others, as continually touching everything around it. Santayana thinks we are inescapably unto ourselves; Peirce retorts that we belong in and to the community.

The second set of formative images involves the community. Santayana is unequivocal in his realism about the world: he thinks that physical reality exists in absolute independence from knowers and their knowledge. The world is fully determinate, the job of knowledge is to recapture in mind as many embodied essences as may be possible or necessary. To be sure, Santayana runs into problems here. The idea that to know is to capture the truth commits Santayana to the ideal of literal knowledge, to something resembling the old and discredited correspondence view. Yet he also insists that knowledge is probably never literal, nor does it need to be. And if knowledge is symbolic, then to some extent at least we create a reality for ourselves, a world articulated in our language, expressed in our native medium.

But Santayana disregards this implication of his notion that knowledge is symbolic. For he is deeply convinced that reality and knowledge are separate affairs and that no private image of the world can add anything to its structure or determinacy. Peirce, by contrast, is firmly committed to the notion that reality is always a social affair. The progressive self-determination of the world cannot occur without the stream of signification of which knowledge consists. In fact, Peirce's famous description of truth as that which the community of scientific investigators will in the end accept must not be taken merely as a statement extolling epistemic method. For the object of these future true opinions will be the real and thus the development of true opinions and of reality largely coincide. The real emerges as we get to know it and achieves full determinacy only as our beliefs come at last to rest in absolute truth. For Peirce, then, the social epistemic and the ultimate ontological mature together. We thus find the world, partly at least, a social product and ourselves the divine co-makers of reality.

These two sets of generative images should make it clear that the difference between Peirce and Santayana concerning the large facts is of vastly more than historical interest. For the first, the contrast between isolationist individualism and absorption of the self in the social fabric is a continuing problem of paramount importance in our society. And the second, the clash between the physical science view of an independent reality and the historicist idea of social world-creation, is but a cosmologizing version of the battle of individualism. Renewed interest in Marx and attention to such recent philosophers as Habermas have once again placed this issue at the center of intellectual controversy.

This is obviously not the occasion to adjudicate these matters. I want to make only one closing comment. It is immensely tempting to join Peirce and adopt his optimistic vision. The sense of belonging to a community of rational inquirers is exhilarating. The notions that we are integral parts of a self-improving nature and that our individuality is of no account because the community will accomplish everything we may have left undone provide infinite comfort. The thought of being partners in world-creation is ennobling to the point of exaltation.

Yet I cannot help noting that most of those whose optimistic comments I read are now dead. I cannot think that that is a matter of indifference. It is, of course, nothing to them; but then that is the very point. They are gone irremediably, as we will be. And there is genuine loss in that, not only to those about to go but cosmically. Individuality is a genuine value, and it is simply false that values are preserved. Whatever happens to the world and to our community, our own prospects are dim. So for you and me at least, cosmic optimism yields little consolation and will always sound hollow. And that is a fact unchanged by the consideration that in the short run we may be drunk with life and have a marvelous time.

CHAPTER 11

Hume on Belief

(with Michael P. Hodges)

T HE CONCEPT of belief is of central significance in Hume's philosophy. Accordingly, commentators have given it considerable attention. Issues related to it have been of interest to creative philosophers no less than to philosophical historians. Articles and books have addressed the subject for over two hundred years, with controversies flaring up like outbreaks of malaria.

In the light of this attention, it is surprising that we are unable to find a single writer who has noted an obvious contradiction between the *Treatise of Human Nature* and the *Enquiry Concerning Human Understanding* on the subject of belief. In the *Treatise* Hume explicitly proposes a definition of belief. He says,

> An opinion, therefore, or belief, may be most accurately defined, a lively idea related to or associated with a present impression.[1]

It is clear that Hume's use of the word "defined" is no accident or unintentional slip. Twice in the passages immediately following, he refers again to the account offered as a "definition." After a brief discussion of the previous quotation, he concludes that "it follows upon the whole that belief is a lively idea produced by a relation to a present impression, according to the foregoing definition."[2] A little later on, he says, "This definition will also be

---

[1] David Hume, *A Treatise of Human Nature*, ed. L.A. Selby-Bigge (Oxford: Clarendon Press, 1958), 96. (All further references to the *Treatise* are to this edition.)
[2] *Ibid.*, 97.

found to be entirely conformable to everyone's feeling and experience."[3] Hume is clearly of the opinion that a definition of belief is not only possible, but that he has actually offered one.

By contrast, in the *Enquiry* we find him denying the very possibility of what we have just seen him do. There he says,

> Were we to attempt a definition of this sentiment we should, perhaps, find it a very difficult, if not impossible, task; in the same manner as if we should endeavour to define the feeling of cold or passion of anger, to a creature who never had any experience of these sentiments. Belief is the true and proper name of this feeling.[4]

It now appears that the concept of belief cannot be defined. What, then, of the definition he offers in his earlier work? There is no indication that Hume thinks the substance of his view about belief has changed from the *Treatise* to the *Enquiry*. In fact, crucial passages on the subject in the later work are lifted verbatim from the earlier. Nor is there any reason to believe that Hume offers in the *Treatise* a definition of belief in one sense of "definition," while in the *Enquiry* he denies the possibility of definition in another sense of that word.

The plain and apparently unnoticed fact is that Hume contradicts himself. Also obvious, once one looks closely at Hume's account of belief, is the baffling array of terminology he uses. He speaks of belief as

1. a manner of conception (*Treatise*, 96, 629, Appendix; *Enquiry*, 63)
2. an act of the mind (*Treatise*, 629, footnote 96–97)
3. an operation of the mind (*Treatise*, 628)
4. a feeling (*Treatise* 621, 623, 624, 629; *Enquiry*, 62)
5. a sentiment (*Treatise*, 624; *Enquiry*, 61)

The difficulties for the student of Hume do not end here. Perhaps one could excuse this terminological diversity as due

---

[3] *Ibid.*

[4] David Hume, *An Enquiry Concerning Human Understanding*, Library of Liberal Arts (New York, 1955), 62. (All further references to the *Enquiry* are to this edition.)

simply to a lack of attention to detail if it concealed no fundamental differences. But, in fact, it hides some serious problems. For example, Hume asserts in the Appendix to the *Treatise* that belief, which is there referred to as a feeling, is not merely "annexed" to "the simple conception." By contrast, in the *Enquiry* he expressly maintains that belief is a "sentiment or feeling, which is annexed" to an idea.

Another important internal divergence in Hume's treatments of belief emerges when we consider the "related to or associated with a present impression" clause of his definition of belief. By building this into his definition, Hume seems to be claiming that belief differs from "simple conception" in two ways. First, it differs in its "manner of conception" or the way it is experienced or felt. Second, he appears to claim that its origin is essential to belief. It must be "produced by a relation to a present impression."[5] Now, whatever the merits of this view, Hume abandons it in the *Enquiry*. There he speaks of belief for which no such association can be found as belief "entirely without foundation,"[6] but as belief nonetheless.

Perhaps only one thing is more obvious than the tangled mass of terms and views that is "Hume's account of belief." That, we think, is the signal failure of commentators on Hume to note or to disentangle it. Antony Flew in his *Hume's Philosophy of Belief* spends only a few pages on the account of belief itself. Although he explicitly compares the *Treatise* and the *Enquiry*, amazingly enough he gives no indication of having noticed the obvious contradiction with which we began.[7] Nor does he comment on the multiplicity of the views of belief that can be found in the text. Flew seems to be too much interested in grinding his axe against privacy to pay attention to what Hume actually said. John Laird in his *Hume's Philosophy of Human Nature* is so impressed with Hume's denial of the possibility of a definition of belief in the *Enquiry* that he altogether overlooks the definition offered in the

5 *Treatise*, 96.

6 *Enquiry*, 612.

7 Antony Flew, *Hume's Philosophy of Belief* (New York: Humanities Press, 1961), 99–102.

Treatise.[8] While he is far more sensitive to nuances in the text, even Norman Kemp Smith fails to comment on the contradiction.

A careful examination of the relevant passages reveals at least four major views of belief in Hume.

1. *The liveliness-per-se view.* In Section V of Part III of the *Treatise*, Hume identifies belief with the liveliness that sometimes attaches to our perceptions. *"Belief* or *assent,"* he says, "is nothing but the vivacity of those perceptions they [the memory and senses] present."[9] Hume refers to this liveliness sometimes as a feeling, sometimes as a sentiment, and not infrequently as a manner of conception. "I confess that it is impossible to explain perfectly this feeling or manner of conception. We may make use of words that express something near it. But its true and proper name is belief," he says.[10] Statements of this sort abound also in the *Enquiry*.

2. *The lively idea view.* In a variety of places both in the *Treatise* and in the *Enquiry*, Hume identifies belief not generally with the liveliness of any perception, but specifically with lively ideas. Thus in Section II of Part IV of the *Treatise*, he says, "Belief in general consists in nothing, but the vivacity of an idea."[11] In several of the passages where this view is propounded, it is followed by reference to the relation of the lively idea to a present impression. That relation, however, is not conceived as of the essence of belief. Instead, it is viewed as but a source of beliefs in general and possibly as the source of all justified beliefs in particular. The passage we have just quoted, for example, is followed by the modest claim that "an idea may acquire this vivacity by its relation to some present impression."[12]

3. *The explicit definition view.* This is the position Hume endorses in his official treatment of the nature of belief in Section VII of Part III of the *Treatise*. There he says, "An opinion, therefore, or belief, may be most accurately defined, a lively idea related to or

---

[8] John Laird, *Hume's Philosophy of Human Nature* (New York: Anchor Books, 1976), 109–16
[9] *Treatise*, 86.
[10] *Ibid.*, 629.
[11] *Ibid.*, 208.
[12] *Ibid.*

associated with a present impression."[13] Here belief is viewed as a species of idea, namely, the sort that is "produced by a relation to a present impression." It is unclear whether Hume thinks there might be some lively ideas that are not produced by such a relation. But if there were any such, on this view they would not be beliefs.

4. *The enlivening view.* In a variety of places Hume speaks as though belief were something different from any experienced feeling, from liveliness, and even from lively idea. Instead, he appears to think of it as that which brings about differences in the "feeling" or "manner of conception" of ideas. Thus, belief is supposed to enliven our ideas in a way nothing else can. In one place, Hume remarks that "belief . . . modifies the idea or conception, and renders it different to the feeling."[14] Here belief appears to function as a dynamic agency, instead of an experienced vivacity. Of all four views of belief, this is the only one that is consistent with the way "belief" is used in the phrase "natural belief," made famous by Norman Kemp Smith. We shall have more to say on this matter later.

Once we isolate these four views of belief in Hume, it becomes easy to see the source of the contradiction with which we began. If belief is simply the experienced liveliness of a perception, it is evident that there can be no definition of it. It is something we experience, something to which one's attention can be drawn, but being a simple, it is not subject to the analysis or conceptual subdividing a definition requires. When Hume stresses the liveliness-per-se view of belief, therefore, he is quite properly inclined to say that belief is indefinable.

However, on at least two of the four views we have noted, belief is clearly definable. It is definable, first of all, as an idea of a special sort, viz., a lively one. Although the concept of liveliness is not definable and the concept of idea may not be, these two notions in turn suffice to define belief. And, second, belief is also definable in the view we have designated as (3). For there it is

13 *Ibid.*, 96.
14 *Ibid.*, 627.

defined as a lively idea of a certain sort, viz., one related in a special sort of way to some present impression.

If no further consequences followed from this contradiction and the diversity of views it reveals, we might simply note it and go on our way. We could then say that Hume at least consistently maintains that liveliness or vivacity is *in some way* centrally connected with belief and that this liveliness is something we experience, though we cannot define it.

Unfortunately, however, we cannot do this. For on reflection, it turns out that these divergent views of belief are mutually inconsistent, yet each is essential for the development of at least one central Humean doctrine. At the same time, none of them is compatible with all of Hume's philosophy. Accordingly, we shall try to show that Hume cannot hold all the views he wants to, views that we have come to associate with his thought, without commitment to each of his four ideas of belief. Yet each of the four views makes it impossible for him to maintain at least one of the important tenets of his philosophy. In short, we shall try to show that Hume *must* maintain all four of his views of belief and also that he *cannot* maintain them all.

The claim that Hume's four views of belief are inconsistent with each other is perhaps the easiest to show. Let us begin by considering the relation between the liveliness-per-se view (1) and the lively idea view (2). Clearly, if each is offered as a complete account of belief, then they are incompatible. For in the second view, belief is restricted to ideas, and thus no impression is ever a belief. In the first view, however, impressions can be beliefs no less than ideas. The same problem occurs if we compare (1) with the explicit definition view (3). Again, (3) restricts belief to ideas only. The enlivening view (4) is incompatible with each of the other views simply because, in each of the latter, belief is identified with some item or feature of experience. By contrast, in the enlivening view, belief is not an identifiable characteristic of our conscious life at all but an agency posited to account for certain features of experience. This leaves only the combination of (2) and (3) as possibly compatible. But the incompatibility is, alas, no less obvious in this case. In (2) all lively ideas are beliefs while in (3) some are not; in the latter view, only those lively ideas "related to or associated with a present impression" qualify.

It may be thought that the claim of inconsistency is too strong. For a closer look at (1) and (2) and (3) indicates a logical interconnection between them. Whatever is a belief in sense (3) is also a belief in senses (1) and (2). While this is true, it misses the point. As we understand Hume's views, he is not saying that since belief is liveliness per se (1), lively ideas (2) and lively ideas related to present impressions (3) will naturally also be beliefs. This would simply be to adopt (1) as Hume's official account of belief and to relegate (2) and (3) to the level of identifying particular species of belief. But this is incompatible with what Hume actually says. He thinks of each of the four views as his account of belief. And even if a Humean revisionist wanted to opt for this alternative, his course would be blocked. For, as we have already suggested, if any one of the four views is adopted as the "official view," fundamental elements in Hume's position have to be abandoned.

In order to bring this out, let us begin with the first of the views of belief we have distinguished. According to this, belief is liveliness of perception, wherever it is found. Impressions are our most lively perceptions; as such, they function as the paradigms of belief. To the extent that ideas come close to the vivacity of impressions they, too, constitute beliefs. Belief, Hume says, "always attends the memory and the senses" and consists in "nothing but the vivacity of those perceptions they present."[15]

A central part of Hume's philosophical program is the critique of certain beliefs. In the *Dialogues Concerning Natural Religion* and elsewhere in his works, he turns again and again to the vigorous criticism of a wide variety of religious commitments. His doing so raises the question almost immediately of the basis on which some beliefs are singled out for criticism and others are considered immune.

Essentially, Hume's view appears to be that beliefs of maximal vivacity are uncriticizable. Consider the following case. Suppose we disagree about whether or not there is a distinguishable shade of the color red between two shades that differ very little from

15 *Ibid.*, 86.

each other. If we managed to mix a shade that fits in between the original two, being slightly but distinguishably different from each, the matter is settled. Once we have an impression of that shade of red, there can be no further argument. Impressions are of such a degree of force and vivacity that they simply cannot be called into question. As Hume put it, "To believe is in this case to feel an immediate impression of the senses," and once such an impression is felt, it is simply not possible to raise any meaningful doubts about it.

But suppose, now, that someone claims to have a very lively perception of God. Suppose, moreover, that we are dealing with a reincarnation of St. Teresa and that she claims her perception of the Deity is as lively as, or more lively than, her firmest impressions. What would make the belief this perception carries criticizable? If this belief is not criticizable, she can proceed to construct an edifice of natural theology on the basis of her experience of the Deity, and Hume's fondest hopes for controlling the excesses of religious fervor are inevitably dashed.

How can Hume avoid this unpleasant consequence of the view that liveliness, wherever that liveliness may be found, is belief? Two alternatives appear open. The first is to abandon this view of belief immediately and proceed to the view that restricts belief to ideas. If Hume did that, St. Teresa could not claim the status of uncriticizable belief for her actual or virtual impression of God. The second is to find some independent principle that would help Hume in distinguishing between lively perceptions that are criticizable and others that are not.

There are two possible ways in which Hume might try to accomplish this. In our opinion both of them are condemned to fail.

1. If Hume could provide an account of the distinction between impressions and ideas on grounds independent of liveliness, he might be able to answer St. Teresa's challenge. For if impressions are uncriticizable, Hume must deny her the possibility of having an impression of God. This may be done by arguing that she may well have an immensely intense conscious experience of perception, but since what differentiates impressions from ideas is not merely vivacity, she does not in fact have an impression. Since

vivacious ideas are always criticizable, the sure foundation of her theology is destroyed.

In order to accomplish this, Hume has to give a reasonably adequate account of the distinction between impressions and ideas without reference to vivacity. There is some textual evidence that he was on the brink of seeing the need for such an account. For example, after his claim that the difference between impressions and ideas "consists in the degree of force and liveliness, with which they strike upon the mind,"[16] he goes on to say that "it is not impossible but in particular instances, they may very nearly approach to each other."[17] He follows this by the remarkable admission that "it sometimes happens that our impressions are so faint and low, that we cannot distinguish them from our ideas,"[18] clearly implying that the lack of distinction in terms of vivacity does not obliterate the difference between what is in fact an impression and what is an equally lively idea.

There are places where the text suggests that Hume might have had in mind some independent distinction between impressions and ideas and that he might have thought of force or vivacity as a good but not completely reliable mark of this distinction. Unfortunately, however, this is about all we can say. In fact, as we shall show later, this difficulty concerning the distinction between impressions and ideas is itself indicative of a fundamental rift in Hume's philosophical thought. There is no worked-out, deeper doctrine in Hume on this matter. There is only his apparently considered and much-reiterated view that the distinction is one of vivacity, after all. Moreover, even if one could find in him or invent for him the needed other view, it would be clearly inconsistent with Hume's evident commitment to the theory that impressions and ideas are distinguished by their liveliness. And even if we were to overlook *this* inconsistency, Hume would not be altogether out of the woods. For the question would have to be asked whether St. Teresa's perceptions of God were in fact im-

---

[16] *Ibid.*, 1.
[17] *Ibid.*, 2.
[18] *Ibid.*

pressions or ideas. Simply to classify them as ideas (supposing that we could distinguish very lively ideas from impressions in a way other than by reference to their vivacity) is to beg the question in the eyes of the religious believer.

And if Hume chose this way out, which is implausible enough already, he would run into yet other difficulties. Suppose that impressions and ideas may be of equal vivacity and yet retain different status. Why should impressions then be given a privileged position? Why should they and only they be considered uncriticizable and self-warranting, while ideas are denied this compliment? The principle that seems to underlie Hume's view here is clear. It is that somehow impressions put us in touch with "reality" in a way nothing else does. The historical source and the generating image of this principle go back at least to Hobbes. He maintained that thought was "decaying sense," meaning by this that the vivid perceptions that come to us through the senses are retained in the brain and are used for purposes of thinking as they lose their lively immediacy by slow degrees. The image is that of the native realism of common sense: we think of our natural senses as physical structures stimulated by independently existing external objects.

Yet this view is not one to which Hume can appeal. He himself says that if anything may be appropriately called "innate," it is our impressions.[19] As far as he is concerned, therefore, it is clearly impossible to justify according epistemological privileges to impressions that other perceptions of equal vivacity would not enjoy.

2. The second line for Hume is more straightforward. He might argue against St. Teresa that although her perceptions are very lively, they cannot be impressions for the simple reason that they are not perceptions of anything sensible. This requires an account of the proper objects of sensation. If Hume were to endorse some view of proper sensibles, viz., of the limits our senses set to the sorts of things we may experience by means of them, he could readily dispose of St. Teresa's claim. For God, supposedly, is not a

---

[19] *Enquiry,* 30–31.

being that can be characterized as red or blue, hard or soft, hot or cold, tasty or unappetizing.

The problem here is that Hume simply cannot adopt this sort of view. A theory of proper sensibles presupposes some prior knowledge of the nature, scope, and diversity of our natural senses. If we start from a conscious manifold of impressions and ideas, all distinctions must be derived from this experienced diversity. We cannot have prejudices as to what can and what cannot be perceived. The lumping of perceptions into the six broad categories of the five "external" senses and the "internal" sense is then but a loose and abstract grouping. It has no restrictive force and cannot function as a criterion of the genuineness of any perception. In brief, then, Hume cannot exclude St. Teresa's claim on the basis of the prior conviction that there can be no impressions other than those of colors, tactile qualities, smells, and the other proper objects of our senses.

Our conclusion is that if Hume maintains that belief consists of liveliness alone, he has to give up his critique of religious beliefs. We now proceed to the second view of belief we have identified, according to which beliefs are simply lively ideas.

If Hume accepts this view, he is immediately faced with a contradiction. For he also says that belief attends the operation of the senses, viz., each case of having an impression is at once a case of believing. This contradiction could be construed as a simple slip, were it not that Hume *needs* to maintain that impressions carry belief.

To make this point clear, let us begin by distinguishing two kinds of belief connected with sense perception. The first is the sort involved in the immediate presence of impressions. This is concerning the existence of some, possibly complex, item present to sense. The item is presumably believed to exist, even though no claim is made concerning its history before or endurance beyond the present perception. Such beliefs are limited to what is present to sense as and when it is perceived. The second sort of belief is that involved in our native conviction that there are enduring physical objects with histories of their own. This latter belief does not carry the uncriticizability of an immediate sensory claim. But without it, we could never significantly speak of physical objects.[20]

Hume clearly wants and needs to account for belief in enduring physical objects. He cannot do so without construing impressions as carrying immediate existential claims, that is, beliefs in the first of the above two senses. The reason for this is that any belief in an enduring object must have as its foundation existential claims about the occasional presence of parts, surfaces, or cross sections of the life history of the object. The belief in continued existence is simply the belief in the identity of the object through time. The impressions we have of it are then believed to be parts of a life history that typically stretches beyond them in both directions in time. If the impressions did not carry belief in existence, Hume would find himself in the anomalous position of attempting to justify a belief in enduring existence without either belief in or evidence for any existence out of which the enduring existent could be constructed.

Since Hume must maintain that impressions carry belief, perhaps he could avoid the contradiction with which he is faced by taking the following line. He might plead that only his terminology is sloppy and proceed to revise it at once. He could say that belief is not so much a lively idea as a lively perception, where "perception" is the generic word for any item that appears in consciousness. This revision would make it possible for Hume to consider both lively ideas and impressions as beliefs and thereby to avoid the problem at hand.

Unfortunately, however, this is in clear conflict with relevant passages in the *Treatise*. In most of those, Hume trades specifically on the distinction between impressions and ideas. But in any case, the current proposal reduces the second view of belief to the first. For here we no longer suppose that belief is to be analyzed as

[20] Some philosophers distinguish an even more basic level of belief involved in perception, viz., that of belief in immediately presented sense qualities such as red patches and squeaky sounds. Such beliefs, however, are not the starting point of Hume's account of perception. For him, the problem of perception is not one of how we construct objects out of sense data, but of how we can construct enduring physical existents out of our fragmented experience of momentary objects.

lively *idea*. Instead, it has become liveliness pure and simple, once again. As such, it is open to all the difficulties of that view.

So far we have shown that Hume's first view of belief makes criticism of religious beliefs impossible, while his second view effectively destroys his account of perceptual belief. At the same time, something like the second view is necessary if criticism of belief is to be possible, while the first view is essential to Hume's theory of perception.

A moment's further reflection should be enough to convince us that Hume's third view fails along with the second. For if belief is identified with "a lively idea related to or associated with a present impression," it is still restricted to the sphere of ideas alone. On this analysis, impressions cannot be or carry beliefs. This is in clear contradiction to what Hume says; it also leaves his theory of perception in serious trouble.

This leads us directly to the fourth view of belief. According to this conception, belief is an agency that renders our ideas more lively. Admittedly, this is the view for which there is the least evidence in the text, though it is the only one, as we noted above, compatible with the notion of natural belief stressed by Norman Kemp Smith.

It is obvious that if Hume were to hold this view, he would find himself in direct contradiction with the claim that belief is experienced liveliness or a lively idea, or a lively idea associated with a present impression. But more important, in having to reject the other three views, he would also have to reject his empiricist commitment to tie belief to some observable feature or quality of our experience.

For what is it that enlivens our ideas? It is either some unobservable disposition or the present impression combined with past conjunctions suggested in Hume's third view. We might suppose on Hume's behalf either that every belief is an unobservable power or that there are but two or three basic dispositions residing in "the frame of our being" that render some of our ideas vivid. The second alternative may be a little less difficult to believe, but even this lacks much initial probability. In any case, both are in direct conflict with Hume's empiricist intentions. For this reason, the current reading of the fourth view lacks plausibility altogether. If, on the other hand, that which enlivens belief is simply the present impression with some past conjunctions, we are back to Hume's third view, with all the difficulties that involves.

We conclude that each of Hume's four views of belief is at odds not only with the other three but also with substantial segments of his considered philosophy. He clearly wanted to say all those things concerning belief that he said in the context of the four contradictory views. Yet he seemed not to realize that he could not say them all and that, whatever he said, something else important to him would have to go.

The confusions in Hume's theory of belief to which we have called attention are symptomatic of a deep tension in his philosophy. The fact that Hume advanced a number of distinct and even contradictory views of belief is not an accident due to sloppy work or inattention. On the contrary, each view is the natural expression of underlying philosophical perspectives that are at odds throughout Hume's philosophical work and that, as Hume's theories of belief clearly show, are never brought to full resolution.

The view that belief is simply the liveliness with which impressions or ideas are entertained has its source in a latent naturalistic realism. The guiding intuition behind the claim appears to be that maximal vivacity somehow puts us in touch with reality. But if this is to be anything more than an unsupported dogma, it presupposes a naturalism with respect to the body and its surroundings and a realism with regard to sense-experience. The maximally vivacious perceptions are, then, those stimulated by the action of independently real objects on our physical organs. We are supposed to be natural creatures in a world of real objects, some of which impinge on us through our sense organs. Such sensory experience is epistemologically privileged because it typically results from direct contact between object and organ.

As we indicated above, Hobbes holds a position very much like this, and it is in this context of naturalistic realism that Hume's view is best understood. For Hobbes, sensations are exceptionally lively; this liveliness derives from the immediacy of the impact of physical objects on our senses. Thought is "decaying sense," where this decay shows itself in the diminution of the vivacity of our sense contents. The paradigm of contact with reality, and hence of natural conviction about existence, is sensory experiences of external objects. This is indicated by the liveliness of our sense-experience; everything less lively is by its nature less indicative of natural existence.

This sort of image is tacitly present in Hume's critique of religious belief as well. For, as we have shown, mere vivacity will not permit him to criticize the beliefs of someone whose religious claims are based on "religious experience." The criticism of St. Teresa presupposes a view of what one can conceivably sense and that, in turn, requires prior knowledge of the nature and limits of our natural senses. Without such information, the claim that divine or quasi-divine things cannot be sensed will remain an unsupportable dogma.

The tacit presence in Hume of this naturalistic metaphysics may go some distance toward explaining why he does not take seriously his own counterexample concerning the priority of impressions over ideas. In a celebrated passage about the unsensed shade of blue at the beginning of the *Treatise*, Hume admits an exception to what is often taken as his most important epistemological weapon.[21] But he immediately adds, "'Tis scarce worth our observing, and does not merit that for it alone we should alter our general maxim."

The phenomenon of having an idea of a color of which we have never had an impression is indeed scarce worth observing if we view the matter from the perspective we have been developing. The idea of blue poses no special problem for an empiricism connected to a straightforward realism about perception. For we already know that sight acquaints us with colors of this sort. Although the case of the unsensed blue is an interesting one and the mechanism by which we generate the idea may be obscure, there is no fundamental principle at stake. Therefore, it certainly "does not merit that for it alone we should alter our general maxim." Nor does this sort of exception open the door to those who would argue for such an idea as that of unsensed substance

21 *Treatise*, 6.

by analogy with the idea of the unsensed blue. Given the realist background, we know that blue is a possible object of sensation, while substance is not and cannot be. In fact, Hume begins his attack on the idea of substance precisely by calling attention to this, by asking from which of our senses it may be derived.

> If it be conveyed to us by our senses, I ask which of them; and after what manner? If it be perceived by the eyes, it must be a colour; if by the ears, a sound; if by the palate, a taste; and so for the other senses.[22]

Hume knows in advance what the objects and materials of experience will be because he knows in advance its source and medium.

The same naturalistic realism is expressed in Hume's fourth view, which identifies belief as a mechanism of enlivening ideas. There is simply no place for a view like this in an empiricism that approaches experience without realist assumptions. For here belief is not any item in or quality of experience; rather, it is an unexperienced mechanism that is supposed to account for certain features of our conscious life. The human body is provided with sense organs that determine the character and range of possible experience. Similarly, our constitution involves certain dispositions (no doubt rooted in our physiology) that condition the complex system of beliefs we tend to form. On this view, experienced liveliness is only an identifying condition of beliefs: whenever it comes to enhance an idea, we have a sign that some subterranean belief, which is a mechanism of enlivening, is present and at work.

The tacit naturalist-realist ontology just identified is but one side of Hume. On the other side, we have in him a deep commitment to phenomenalist empiricism. This finds clear expression in the central theme of Hume's account of belief, the phenomenologically identifiable quality he calls "liveliness." In one form or another, Hume always comes back to the experienced vivacity that, he is convinced, is centrally tied to belief. His project itself is a phenomenological one: he wants to focus on the experienced difference between cases when ideas are merely enter-

---

[22] *Ibid.*, 16.

tained and cases when they are actually believed. He is convinced that the difference will not only show up in experience; he thinks that it *consists* precisely in our different ways of experiencing.

This view is most clearly expressed in what we have called Hume's second view, viz., that beliefs are lively ideas. His attempt here is to focus the reader's attention on the distinctive experiential quality that distinguishes belief from other "manners of conception." It is perhaps significant to note the word "conception" here. Hume's intention is to distinguish those modes of experience in which we believe something from those in which we merely entertain it. No such distinction is present in sense-experience. There mere entertainment is impossible; we have a natural conviction of the existence of what we see. This is perhaps why Hume does not say that he wishes to distinguish belief from other "manners of perception"; it is in the sphere of ideas that he thinks belief has to be identified and understood.

It is a natural temptation for the phenomenologically inclined philosopher to move from the view that belief is lively idea to the view that it is really the indefinable phenomenal quality of liveliness itself. What Hume the phenomenologist searches for is the distinguishing mark of belief. Once vivacity is identified as that, it becomes impossible to confine it to the vivacity of ideas only; on this way, Hume's second view naturally turns into the first.

Throughout much of Hume's philosophy, there is a persistent tension between this phenomenological empiricism and the empiricism grounded in realistic assumptions. The tension is present as early as the first page of the *Treatise*, where Hume distinguishes between impressions and ideas. For he wants to ground that distinction on the phenomenological difference between them in liveliness or vivacity. But at the same time, he presupposes another difference as well. This difference remains even when impressions "are so faint and low, that we cannot distinguish them from our ideas."[23] Given the realist assumption, the difference between impressions and ideas, between those moments of consciousness derived directly from contact with the external world and those indirectly derived, is marked more or

[23] *Ibid.*, 2.

less reliably by the phenomenal quality of vivacity. On the phenomenological view, their difference is *constituted* by the phenomenal quality of vivacity; on the realist view, the phenomenal quality only *marks* a deeper, nonphenomenal distinction.

A thorough study of Hume's statements on belief reveals the same underlying tension between a hardheaded phenomenalism and a congenial but perhaps epistemologically loose naturalism. In the end, this tension accounts for the incoherence of Hume's ideas on belief. Hume himself never became fully aware of these two divergent motive forces that shape and undergird his thought. Perhaps for this very reason, he never fully realized the contradictions in which these incompatible commitments involved him. The weakness of Hume's theory of belief is a function not only of trying to generate a novel conception in a difficult field. It is also the direct result of irreconcilable projects, the unavoidable movement of his thought in opposite directions.

CHAPTER 12

Fichte's Idealism

FICHTE IS USUALLY classified as an idealist, yet the precise nature of his idealism is rarely examined. Idealism is frequently taken as the view that only minds and their states are real, and the temper of our times is such that this theory appears to need no refutation at all. The suggestion that the Ohio Turnpike is nothing but a state of your mind or mine, or even of some supermind, and the Leibnizian view that it consists of an infinite collection of harmonized souls seem to us to be manifestly absurd and to warrant serious examination only of the persons who are so deluded as to suppose them true.

It would, of course, be wrong to classify Fichte as an idealist in any such popular or easy sense. He does maintain that there is a watershed question for all of philosophy: the answer to this determines the total complexion of one's philosophical thought. The question is whether or not objects exist independently of the self. There are only two possible answers to this question, and of the two, only one is right. The dogmatist, incorrectly, asserts the absolute and independent existence of the world of objects. The idealist, by contrast, maintains that no object can exist independently of some self.

It is important to keep in mind, of course, that Fichte does not think that the world of objects, what we are inclined to call "the physical world," is in any sense the creature of some finite individual self, group of selves, or the infinite individual we call "God." Such might be the view of "dogmatic" or absolute idealism that, by Fichte's own profession, is in sharp contrast with what he refers to as his "critical idealism." According to the critical idealist, both finite individual selves and the correlative world of physical objects are the resultants of a single, unconditioned self. Much of the interest of Fichte's metaphysics derives from his fundamental claim that the undifferentiated primordial being that is the source of all is actually a self. The plausibility of his idealism hinges entirely on his ability to subtantiate this claim.

The central concept in Fichte's thought, then, is that of the self. What does he conceive to be the nature of selfhood? Without a reasonable account of this, his idealism is certain to remain vacuous. In attempting to determine his position on this and a variety of other issues, I shall be relying heavily on the 1794 version of the *Wissenschaftslehre*, the first complete English translation of which was published in 1970.[1]

The most convenient and most obvious starting point in developing Fichte's thoughts on the self may well be his famous aphorism in the early part of the *Wissenschaftslehre* of 1794: "Was für sich nicht ist ist kein ich"—what is not conscious of itself is no self. Self-consciousness is a necessary condition of selfhood: nothing that lacks the ability to reflect on itself can qualify as a self. Fichte affirms in a variety of places and in a variety of ways his conviction that self-consciousness presupposes consciousness of objects. This view may well be open to argument, but it is not my present purpose to dispute it. I shall merely note that a self must be, or at least have the ability to be, conscious both of objects and of itself. But even this is not enough for full-fledged selfhood: the intellectual, attenuated property of consciousness can never be enough to constitute the essence of a real being.

What, then, are the conditions both necessary and sufficient for a given existent's being a self? Are they to be consciousness and creativity? Or cognition along with a certain organization or structure of the elements of the being? Or the presentational and reflective activity of consciousness in conjunction with the purposiveness of all the activities of the being and the purposiveness of their union? Characteristically, Fichte has given ample thought to the problem, and equally characteristically, he infuriates his readers by never disclosing his answer in any systematic or straightforward manner.

The magnitude of the reader's frustration will be evident from

[1] J.G. Fichte, *The Science of Knowledge,* ed. and trans. Peter Heath and John Lachs (Cambridge: Cambridge University Press, 1982), is a reprint of this edition.

the fact that perhaps the best place for relevant hints on the nature of the self is in the chronically obscure practical part of the *Wissenschaftslehre* of 1794. There Fichte discusses the activities of the absolute self in their purity; and the activities and features that pertain to this primordial ego must be reflected, to a greater or lesser degree, in all finite individuals. The absolute self, Fichte maintains, has two divergent but interdependent fundamental drives. The two drives give rise to two divergent lines of activity; and since it is impossible to distinguish agent from activity on this level, the self is properly said to be constituted of these two sets of nontemporal acts.

The first activity of the self is its striving to fill out infinity. The practical drive urges the self on to infinite self-expansion, to an affirmation of itself and its own law without limit. The second activity is that of reflection or self-consciousness. The theoretical drive urges the self on to know itself as a unitary, self-expansive being. Using Fichte's physical model, we could conceive the practical activity of the self as a line stretching outward from a center to infinity. By contrast, theoretical activity may be conceived as a line reverting back to the center; but throughout, it is important to remember that the center is not to be thought of as any substantial or substantive being. The two activities are interdependent: reflection presupposes the outgoing activity that it restricts and turns back upon the self, while the effusive activity of self-assertion relies on the other to define its direction and to present it with the obstacles it must overcome. .

These two closely interrelated activities define the nature of the self. Anything that is both self-assertive and reflective must be a self; nothing that lacks these characters can qualify as one. Reflectiveness is nothing but what I have previously referred to as self-consciousness and identified as a necessary condition of selfhood. If we combine it with expansive or assertive activity, we have the necessary and sufficient conditions of selfhood as Fichte conceives it. And this, incidentally, also gives us the clue to why Fichte thinks that, at least primordially, self-consciousness and the consciousness of objects are necessarily connected. The explanation is simple if we bear in mind that he thinks of reflection as an activity that restricts the infinite outgoing act of the self and drives it back upon itself. Since both activities are primordial, neither can overwhelm the other; no sooner is the assertive activity restricted than it renews itself, and the ensuing oscillation (Schweben), in a manner of speaking outside the self, yet totally dependent on it, is what Fichte calls "the imagination." It is in this field of imagination that the presentations of which the empirical world consists are generated. The unavoidable conflict of the primordial activities manifests itself to the self in the form of the feeling of frustration and inability. This, in turn, is the source of the feeling of necessity or constraint that accompanies, in our experience, the presentation of external objects. In this way, the self's consciousness of itself is inseparable from the consciousness of external objects: the very activity of reflection is the cause, or at least a part of the cause, of the generation of objects.

What I have laboriously disentangled from the obscure parts of Fichte's work can also be found stated by him with the greatest clarity. Unfortunately, however, even the clearest and most elegant Latin is lost on the man who never learned the language. The meaning of some of Fichte's plainest statements becomes evident only after one has gone through some of his obscurest deductions; their clarity after one has understood them is often no less annoying than their vagueness had been before the light dawned. In a variety of places, Fichte reminds us that the self is what it does, that it consists of nothing beyond its activities in their dialectical relation. If we add to this his oft-repeated statement that the self posits itself and posits itself as positing, we have in an embryonic form everything I have said so far. For positing is nothing but the self-assertive activity of the self; and to posit the self as positing is to think it, to reflect on it, to know it as engaged in characteristic activity. The very essence of the self, therefore, is summed up by saying that it is something that both posits and knows that it does.

But have we helped clarity by introducing the concept of positing? Not if we can give no better account of the mysterious activity it stands for than the few commentators who have written on Fichte in English. Possibly the problem is one of translation: no English word captures the richness of the German original. The German word "setzen" is ordinarily translated as "to set," "to place," or "to establish." Its root significance is creative activity, an activity that can show itself in various modalities. It may be the simple physical act of placing an object in some location, the biological activity of bringing children into the world (Kinder in die Welt zu setzen), or the exceptionally complex sociopolitical action of raising some person to the throne (auf den Thron setzen). What we have in each case is practical activity that is productive or creative; it is always purposive and often voluntary.

The activity "setzen" denotes, however, is not only practical. The word may be used to express agreement and opposition (sich auf etwas, wider etwas setzen), as well as the propositional attitudes of supposing and affirming. Its connection with the intellectual and the intelligible is further confirmed by the overtone we find of it in the German word for law, "Gesetz." The richness of "setzen" is due precisely to this amphibious character: it is equally at home in the realms of theory and practice. Fichte takes advantage of the ambiguity: he uses the word to denote an activity that is both cognitive and creative and represents the unity of reason and will, the theoretical and the practical.

The word "positing" is, therefore, at once revealed as inadequate to express what is conveyed by the word "setzen." "Affirmation" and "assertion" come close to capturing the volitional element in the activity Fichte refers to, and "self-affirmation" is certainly a central part of what he means when he says that the self "setzt" itself. But both the creativity and the cognitive action implied or suggested by "setzen" is lost in the word "affirmation," and we can safely say that there is no word in ordinary or, for that matter, in extraordinary English that comes any closer. What Fichte designates by this untranslatable word, then, is a fundamental cognitive-conative activity. It is a purposive and productive act, an act whose creativity is the source of all that is real. If we keep this in mind, it comes as no surprise that Fichte thinks the organ of positing is reason itself. Reason in its primordial unity is thus conceived as the infinite and intelligent source of all, totally absorbed in its creative, all-encompassing act. For lack of a better substitute, I shall continue to use the word "posit" to stand for Fichte's "setzen." But it is important to remember that

I shall refer by this word to the cognitive-conative activity whose nature I have briefly indicated.

Positing is a nontemporal act. Its model no doubt is the Aristotelian concept of activity or "energeia" in which process and product, agent, act, and deed indistinguishably coincide. This concept of activity appears in Spinoza, whom Fichte frequently praises as the greatest and most consistent of dogmatists, as the infinite potency-in-act that is his all-creative Substance. Viewed dynamically, from the standpoint of the act, Substance or God is *Natura naturans*, an indeterminately infinite creative agency. Viewed statically, from the point of view of the deed, Substance or God is *Natura naturata*, an infinitely determinate, eternal modal order. Since productive act and completed deed are indistinguishable in the primordial, infinite potency-in-act and since no temporal lag separates activity from its end, creative energy and created world are inseparably one.[2]

I do not wish to minimize the differences between Fichte and Spinoza. But I also do not wish to overlook or underplay instructive similarities. Positing, as the absolute ego's primordial activity, is clearly analogous to what in Spinoza I have called "potency-in-act." And the relation of Spinoza's God as creative act to God as created modal order has a clear analogue in the relation in Fichte of the absolute ego to the empirical world of subjects and objects. The progression from indeterminate infinity to infinite determinateness is present in both systems: it is by this gradual determination that, in both, finite, fragmented beings are generated. And there is agreement that the progressive self-determination of the absolute is a necessary consequence of its nature. The two thinkers are in consonance even on the fundamental neo-Platonic dictum that determination is negation: the self-determination of the absolute, by its application to itself of ever more specific predicates, is at once a self-negation and self-limitation.

We may view Fichte's interesting theory of thetic judgments in the light of its relation to the emanation scheme that is one of his

---

[2] I acknowledge my indebtedness for this interpretation of Spinoza to E. F. Hallett's excellent *Benedict de Spinoza* (London: Athlone Press, 1957).

neglected, or at least little understood, versions of the generation of the finite from the infinite ego. A thetic judgment, according to him, is one that consists of the affirmation of the existence of a subject without any reference to a predicate. The prime example he gives is the judgment "I am." Now it is clear that the being of the absolute self would have to be affirmed in a thetic judgment, and the peculiarity of such a judgment is that it leaves the concept of its subject unrelated to any other concept, and thus totally indeterminate. This is the infinite indeterminacy of the absolute ego; yet no sooner is the indeterminacy ascribed to the self than it becomes inapplicable. Even as general a predicate as indeterminateness limits and determines: the very indeterminateness of the primordial self constitutes the first step toward its inevitable total determination. The finite world of empirical selves and physical objects naturally flows from the necessary self-determination of the absolute ego, and in the theoretical part of the *Wissenschaftslehre* of 1794, Fichte displays considerable ingenuity in tracing this dialectical development.

An obvious dissimilarity between Fichte and Spinoza, of course, is due to the historical fact of the presence of Kant between them. Spinoza strove to deduce the eternal modal order from the activity of his primordial Substance. By contrast, Fichte no longer wishes to deduce an infinity of beings, but only the structures and categories of experience. I shall not stop to explore this interesting point; it is peripheral to my main interest here. I have set out to examine the nature and to determine the tenability of Fichte's critical idealism, and I have now managed to reach a stage where his terms have been, I hope, adequately clarified and where we can set him a fundamental and, I think, disastrously destructive question.

Fichte spends considerable effort in deducing the categories, conceived as principles of unity in experience, from the self-postulation of the absolute self. It should be evident, therefore, that the primordial self itself is subcategoreal or precategoreal. We cannot say of it, for example, that it is a substance, even though we must think of it as, in a sense, nontemporally enduring. No predicate applicable in the world of experience is applicable to it univocally, and in its primordial being, which may be affirmed in a thetic judgment, no predicate is applicable to it at all. I shall not discuss here Fichte's apparent violation of this principle in conceiving of the absolute self as the cause of the world of objects. Instead, let me remark that Spinoza realized at least a part of the limitation of what we may predicate of the primordial being and conceived of his infinite potency-in-act as neither mental nor physical, although in a sense the source of both. The question fundamental for Fichte's idealism that thus arises is the following: What conceivable reason can we offer for thinking of the primordial agency-activity as a self? If there is good reason for thinking of it that way, it may be difficult to escape Fichte's critical idealism; if there is none, his central views will surely appear as unwarranted dogmas.

To say, as Fichte does repeatedly, that the absolute ego is not in any sense an individual person does not eliminate the question. On the contrary, it only raises the additional problem of how anything could be a self without displaying at least some of the determinate tendencies, attitudes, and intentions that are the hallmarks of individual personality. Now I think I can detect in Fichte three major lines of argument for his idealistic conclusion. Nowhere does he develop these arguments in detail. Their outlines, however, are clear enough, and he hints at them in a variety of places. I shall consider them in turn.

The first argument starts from the premise that the task of philosophy is to give an account of the origin and nature of experience. Fichte appears to be of the opinion that this can be attempted in only two ways. In the first attempt, we proceed from the side of the object or unthinking thing; in the second, from the side of the subject or self. Accordingly, as he insists in the *First Introduction* to the *Wissenschaftslehre*, there are only two possible philosophical positions: dogmatism, which attempts to deduce experience from a world of independently existing things or things-in-themselves, and idealism, which attempts to display experience as the result of the operation of an active self. The two theories are contradictory: at most one of them can be true, and at least one of them must be. Fichte makes no secret of the fact that he thinks we can never account for lived experience by reference to things or objects alone. In some places he goes so far as to assert that a dogmatism that attempts such an account is demonstrably false. If only two attempts at explanation are possible, the two are contradictory, and one of them is demonstrably inadequate, the other must clearly be correct. For this reason, idealism is the only tenable philosophy, and the primordial existent must be a self.

This argument appears to me to have no merit. First of all, even if we grant that one of the tasks of philosophy is the relatively vague one of explaining the nature and origin of experience, we have reason to doubt the remarkable claim that this can be done in only two ways: either by sole reference to things and their laws or by reducing all to selves and their operations. This is surely a gross simplification and excludes by edict far more philosophical views than it permits. It is this oversimplified picture that leads Fichte to the mistaken thoughts that idealism and dogmatism are true contradictories and that therefore by disproving the latter we can incontrovertibly establish the former. The contradictory of the proposition that in explaining the source and structure of experience we need have no reference to anything beyond things and the laws that govern their behavior is the proposition that such reference is necessary, and not the proposition that we need have reference to selves only. Even if we were to stay within Fichte's unreasonable thing-self dichotomy, the most that the refutation of dogmatism could show is that some concepts or laws other than those relating exclusively to things are necessary to give an adequate account of human experience. This would leave the door wide open to a variety of dualisms, among them the highly critical and attenuated sort held by Kant, who viewed experience as a unity of elements derived from self and thing.[3]

Let me wipe the slate clean, however, and permit the entire matter to be decided by an adequate refutation of dogmatism. On Fichte's own interpretation, such a demonstration of the inadequacy of dogmatism would be tantamount to a proof of his idealism, and even on a less charitable rendering, it would tend to increase substantially the probable truth of his position. Unfor-

[3] Fichte devotes considerable effort and ingenuity to the attempt to show that Kant held no such view.

tunately, however, one looks in vain through Fichte's works for the demonstration. It is, in fact, not even seriously attempted, much less accomplished. And in a bold about-face in the work in which he claims the demonstrable falsity of dogmatism, Fichte asserts that ultimate philosophical positions are susceptible of neither proof nor disproof; the view we adopt, without evidence and as a starting point, is a function of personal interest, commitment, and disposition.[4] I shall come back to this point later, but I now proceed to Fichte's second argument.

Here his reasoning amounts perhaps to no more than a version of the previous argument stated in the material mode. Whatever else there may be in the world, it is generally agreed that there are at least some selves. Now Fichte thinks it evident that no self can ever come from an unfeeling, unthinking not-self. If all is to have a single, unitary source and the only conceivable source of an ego is another one, it clearly follows that the primordial reality must be a self. We can view Fichte's attempt to deduce finite objects and subjects from an absolute self as giving added point and poignancy to this argument. Since nothing that lacks self-consciousness and self-affirmation can be the ground of a self, nothing that is bereft of these features of selfhood can qualify as an ultimate principle. His deduction aims at establishing that an ego, by contrast, is able to generate both selves and things and thus amply qualifies as the ultimate source of all.

I cannot make myself believe that this argument has anything to recommend it. First and foremost, I am entirely at a loss as to why anyone should think it evident that a self cannot have its source in the not-self. I do not propose to argue here that it can or does, even though the entire weight of evolutionary thought supports this hypothesis. I shall content myself with the comment that if no good reasons are presented for accepting it, Fichte's putatively self-evident premise is simply an arbitrary dogma. The issue of whether or not things can function as the source of selves is at the very heart of the problem of idealism; the bold claim that they cannot serves only to start the controversy, not to resolve it.

[4] *Science of Knowledge,* 16.

Fichte is no less vocal in avowing the belief that things cannot give rise to selves than he is silent about his reasons. Although it is idle to speculate on what these might have been, it is appropriate to make two brief remarks. The first is that his reasons could not have been of the sort that supported Berkeley's conviction that objects cannot generate spirits. For Berkeley thought of causation as the exclusive property of minds; for him, physical objects were impotent. By contrast, Fichte in no way restricts causal activity to selves: following Kant, he thinks of causation and of reciprocity as universally applicable. My second and more positive comment is that what might be behind Fichte's conviction that the not-self can generate no self is simply the time-honored causal maxim that decrees the impossibility of the like coming from the unlike. The putative emergence of mind, consciousness, or selfhood from the thoughtless and inanimate may appear to be a paradigm not only of the generation of the like from the unlike, but also of the absurdity of any such supposed generation. But in reality there is nothing absurd about it, and if Fichte's argument is to be grounded in this maxim of causation, we are perfectly justified in asking for the grounds for it. The blow of the hammer does not resemble the pain it causes, nor the brain of Shakespeare a page of manuscript. The vast majority of the causal sequences we know involve the creation of like by unlike; what are we to do with a maxim that decrees all this impossible?

Let us, however, forget all that has been said: let me suppose that Fichte has proved, as he has not, that the source of every self is itself or another. Would this be adequate to show that the ultimate existent must be an ego? Clearly not. This by itself leaves the door wide open, once again, to dualism: it is perfectly compatible with the view that there are two ultimate existents, say, a transcendental ego and a transcendental object. Fichte thus needs an additional principle, viz., the one that maintains that all is to have a single source. Yet why should we accept this principle? Surely not because unity is boldly asserted to be a demand of reason. This may well be the demand of reason in a tight little man perpetually at work imposing discipline on his children or the world, but it is surely no demand of universal reason. And even if it were, would it not be a begging of the question, an unwarranted assumption of the idealist principle that reason shapes the world—the very principle under examination—if we were to say that its demands are invariably met?

I now come to Fichte's third argument. This is never explicitly stated by him, but it appears to me to be behind what he says in a number of passages. We start with the assertion that the primordial being must engage in creative activity. Such an activity, since it is essentially self-assertive and expansive, resembles far more closely the activity of a self than that of some thing or not-self; self-assertiveness is in fact, as we noted, one of the marks of the ego. If the argument were correct, it would not, of course, prove that the ultimate source of all is actually a self. It would, however, show that such an unconditioned being must resemble selves far more closely than it resembles unconscious or inactive things—and this may conceivably be all that Fichte needs to establish his idealism.

This argument hinges on a fundamental unjustified assumption, namely, that the activities of the self are the paradigm of creative activity. Fichte clearly wants to stop short of the extreme position of asserting that only selves can engage in causally creative endeavor; since he does, he has to justify his taking the dialectical self-expansive/self-limiting activity of the self as the model of all creative agency. Why should we say that the primordial creative act is more like the self-expansiveness of a self than like the self-expansiveness of a gas or of a healthy tree? We search in vain for Fichte's answer to this question. It is clear that reference to the self's voluntary or intelligent self-assertiveness is of no avail: the absolute ego's expansiveness is unavoidable, and the self-expansion of a tree is law-governed and purposive. Similarly, there is little merit in the approach that professes to see in each tree's growth a pale replica of the ego's actions. These activities are different, and either one can be considered a pale or imperfect version of the other, depending on what features we select for emphasis. Fichte loads the dice by using the word "setzen" for the primordial activity; this suggests, without being evidence for, the view that the activity properly belongs in the sphere of the self. But what reason have we to suppose that the activity is selflike or self-connected and that "setzen" is not merely a misleading or question-begging name for it? As best I can see, none at all.

I must conclude, therefore, that Fichte's arguments for the view that the primordial being is a self fall altogether short of establishing their conclusion. As we have seen, each suffers from a variety of faults, but most blatantly the first fails because it presupposes an unprovided demonstration, the second because it must rely on an unacceptable maxim of causation, and the third because it begs the question by a prejudiced selection of the paradigm of activity. Does this leave Fichte entirely without defense? I do not think so. It would be open to him to use a version of his third argument, if not to attempt to show that the ultimate being is a self, at least to justify supposing it to be that for the sake of increasing our knowledge. This regulative version of the argument is well known in the history of idealism, and the likely reason why Fichte made no reference to it is that he thought it both valid beyond all reasonable doubt and inextricably intertwined with the entire enterprise of Kantian and post-Kantian transcendental philosophy. The usual argument is that since we know the self and its structures and activities best of all, we must use them as our model for understanding everything else. Fichte, however, might subscribe to a somewhat stronger version. His acceptance of Kant's theory that all intelligible structure is due to mental activity might lead him to the view that all we ever know is the self, its structures, and its activities and therefore have in fact no choice but to use them as our models.

Now I can find nothing wrong with using the self as our model in the attempt to see how far it will take us and what important or unsuspected insights it might provide. One can have one's opinions about the ultimate value of this model, but when all is said and done, there is no substitute for the actual full-scale attempt to push the idealist program as far as it will go. Surely this is all the justification Fichte needs for having attempted a deduction of the finite world of subjects and objects from a primordial self. It is an interesting and important fact that such a deduction is possible, and his having managed to complete it is a tribute to his dialectical skill. But the possibility of the deduction is one thing, its truth or bearing on the real world another. It is well worth keeping in mind that the way we choose between two deductions, say those of Spinoza and Fichte, is normally not by finding logical or dialectical slips in the one and none or fewer in the other. Philosophers notoriously have more logical than good sense, and though an idealist deduction proceeding on the basis of the regulative principle under discussion is clearly possible, it may well be severely at odds with reality.

So much for the weaker version of the regulative principle. The stronger version, according to which our only models for understanding the world are the cognitive, conative, and affective activities of the self, appears by contrast excessive and question begging. It assumes, without good reason, that all forms, structures, and activities are mental. By according such preeminence to the self and thinking of it as the source of all order, if not of all reality, are we not tacitly affirming idealism? And if such tacit affirmation is disavowed, what reason could conceivably be proposed for saying that the activity of gravitation or the orderliness in the growth of poison ivy reveals somehow the marks of intellect?

Let me conclude with some remarks on one of Fichte's characteristic, and typically exaggerated, claims. Acceptance of ultimate philosophical positions is a matter of personal inclination or interest, he maintains. Now, his argument continues, the highest and most exalted interest of every ego is that of self-affirmation or the free exercise of the intelligent creative powers of the self. This activity of self-creation and self-development is the source of all morality and goodness. But an activity of this sort presupposes a free and independent ego. The highest interest of man, the very possibility of morality demands, therefore, the primacy of the ego and its total primordial independence of determination by objects. This makes idealism, and with it belief in the primacy of the self, a demand of morality, Fichte concludes. But he refuses to stop even here and indicates that whoever does not acknowledge and exercise his freedom does not truly or for long possess it. And not to possess freedom is not to be a self, but a mere thing. For this reason, failure to subscribe to idealism is not merely a theoretical error: it is a practical act that disqualifies one from membership in the kingdom of ends. The dogmatist is not a person who is simply wrong; he is simply not a person.

It is difficult to think that this argument is anything but non-sense. It is a peculiar sort of morality indeed that sees the greatest requirement imposed on every man as self-assertion or the exercise of his native powers. But this peculiarity is nothing when compared to the astounding claims that practical life determines or should determine one's beliefs about what is, and that a single wrong opinion can strip us of selfhood and turn us into things.

The ultimate problem here, however, is the easy confusion between the absolute ego and the finite selves of individuals. Fichte devotes considerable attention to the deduction of the world of objects, but almost none at all to the deduction of finite subjects. To establish his idealism, he would have to prove that the unconditioned being is a self. Showing, as he attempts to, that the demand of morality is to think of individual selves as unconditioned and free does not in the least contribute to proving this. Good sense impels us to believe in the existence of a variety of finite selves: but if there is more than one of them, none can serve as the primordial unity from which all flows. If, however, all individual selves are to share a single transcendental ego, the analogy, central to Fichte's entire enterprise, between our finite selves and this primordial ego inevitably collapses. And even if this near disaster could be averted, what account could we give of the relation, so peculiar in this view, of transcendental to individual self? To this question, though not to this alone, Fichte provides no answer.

CHAPTER 13

Pre-Socratic Categories
in Fichte

THE MOST ENDURING philosophical concepts are pre-reflective. They are firmly founded in primitive experience. By their use, the most improbable of our philosophical fancies acquires plausibility; for however much what we say might seem a free construction, do we not see the same features and the same process, attenuated perhaps but real, before our eyes?

It is clear that there are such enduring basic concepts. A sceptical soul may argue, in fact, that the glimmer of plausibility that sometimes plays on philosophical systems is due entirely to their presence in them. But we need not be so negative as that. For the recurrence of themes and ideas in Western thought may amount to the *philosophia perennis* that, we would all like to believe, transcends the petty squabble of the schools. There is no enduring philosophy, of course, if our interest is in uniformity of perspective or of theses affirmed. But it is not without justification perhaps that some concepts are supposed native to mankind.

This need not mean that the human mind would spin the same web in every possible world or form its thoughts without occasion and reference. What is native to us is native in a context: if the world were different, our ideas would not be the same. But in its basic aspects, human nature has remained relatively unchanged in the past few thousand years. The portion of nature that surrounds us has also stayed relatively stable. The most fundamental features of our experience, therefore, have not changed much since Homer or the first city of Ur.

It still seems to us that certain things move of their own accord, change themselves, or bring about changes. Others, in turn, appear merely affected by what goes on elsewhere: if left to their own devices, they are without motive or motion. Typically, such activity and passivity are phases of the same thing: after a vigorous day of argument, Socrates will seem passive when asleep. And even in his waking hours, he will seem alternately active and passive, as when in an argument about her allowance he and Xantippe come to trading blows.

There is not a great deal we can or need to do to define these concepts; they are common property. To the relief of those who derive what philosophical insight they have from a study of how we talk, the distinction is prominently enshrined in English and, to my knowledge, in every other language. It is not—God forbid!—a distinction invented by philosophers. Instead, it is one we all experience and rely on to determine our behavior. All philosophers did was to focus on these prereflective concepts: they raised their widespread use to explicit consciousness. From the earliest, the ubiquity of the active and the passive was a temptation budding thinkers found difficult to resist. By the fifth century B.C., we find notable use of them as cosmic categories.

When I call the idea of the active and the idea of the passive "categories," I obviously do not have in mind any technical use of that term. For our purposes, let "category" mean a fundamental or very general concept. And let me also add that I am not among those who maintain that all categories worth dealing with are pre-Socratic in origin. I admire the old sages, but I am not less willing to admit their limitations than my own. I note the fact that these concepts are pre-Socratic primarily because they are. I stress it because it is instructive to find the same rudimentary concepts playing a central role both in what we view as primitive thought and in immensely sophisticated philosophical systems.

Although active and passive are not categories that have the visibility of some of the other fundamental concepts of pre-Socratic thought, they are nonetheless ubiquitous. Such concepts as earth, air, fire, and water, condensation and rarefaction, love and hate, the one and the many are the ones that normally command our attention when we consider the pre-Socratics. But the notions of the active and the passive are always there in the shadows structuring the way these primitive world conceptions are developed.

The view of Anaximenes, according to which the universe is made of air with constituent objects coming into being and passing away by the condensation or rarefaction of the basic substance, clearly incorporates a rudimentary dialectic of the active and the passive. The primordial material, he seems to maintain, undergoes periodic alterations from activity to passivity and vice versa. Both condensation and rarefaction are forms of activity; passivity occurs when the one activity has ceased and the other has not yet begun. Fully condensed objects that we might call "enduring beings" and a stage of rarefaction we might think of as nothingness, therefore, are both probably passive.

The theory of Empedocles suggesting that all things are made of the four elements through the agency of love and hate presents a more complex and sophisticated dialectic. For here, love and hate are the indispensable active ingredients: the elements of earth, air, fire, and water are explicitly conceived as operated on and passive. But the matter is more complicated, because when love is active, hate seems to recede into a passive state, and when hate operates, love seems impotent.

As an added embellishment, we find in Empedocles, and also in others, that even the elements get into the act, for some are more inclined to activity and some seem relatively inert. Fire is more active than earth. In addition, it is more active when operating on air or earth than on water. What we have, then, even this early in the history of thought is a conception of the complex interaction of the active and the passive. Admittedly, these thinkers made no conscious attempt to develop a full account of the structure of this dialectic. But the basic ideas are present for it and have served as a perpetual invitation for later dialecticians to go to work.

Even though the active and the passive are correlatives, they have not always been treated with equal justice. The balance of sentiment has run heavily in favor of the active. As a minimum, the active has been considered as more primary, more real, or better than the passive. More extreme philosophers have identified activity with being, a move that has made them think of passivity not only as identical with nonexistence but also as actually nonexistent. The partiality to the active has been so great, in fact, that many philosophers who realized the need to make room for the passive would admit it into their systems only if they could think of it as performing some function, viz., if in some respect, at least, it was active.

Descartes serves as a good example of someone who wants to do justice to active and passive alike. At first sight, it might seem that they enjoy equal status in his system: the passive, as extended inert matter, is no less a substance than is any active, thinking mind. But on closer inspection, it is clear that the active has special prerogatives. As mind, it is intelligent, Godlike, creative, and free. In the form of absolute, self-structuring activity—namely, God—it is identified as the source of the passive. Inert matter, by contrast, is dependent, valueless, and infinitely dull.

As in everything else, in this, too, Spinoza goes a step beyond Descartes. His position is the extreme one of identifying activity and being. Accordingly, our passivity is the measure of our nonexistence. He affirms the inseparable connection between reality and vigorous operation in a variety of places but perhaps nowhere more poignantly than in a remarkable passage in Proposition XI of Book I of the *Ethics*. There he argues that there must be a cause not only for the existence of the things that exist, but also for the nonexistence of whatever fails to be. His thought is that even possibles are necessarily in act, unless prevented by some other force. If—as he says—inability to exist is impotence, existence must be self-actualizing potency-in-act or the active display of one's latent power.

Plato grudgingly acknowledges the reality of the passive, but then finds it overwhelmingly tempting to assign some activities to it. The Receptacle for him is chaos or the pure potentiality for order. It waits ready to be formed by some cosmic artisan. Yet we are told that when the Demiurge imposes form on this material, the Receptacle resists. But to say that the passive resists is to view it as engaged in action. For recalcitrance is not a mark of passivity: the fully passive is as indifferent to the presence of form as to its absence.

The clear favor in which most Western thinkers have held the active may have been partly responsible for the association it acquired with mind. Some think they know exactly what they mean when they contrast idealism and materialism. But normally these labels are baffling or quite empty. There are few ways of making them clear and concrete, and of these, the best perhaps is by reference to the active and the passive. Read in this way, the distinction between materialist and idealist is one of where creative activity is to reside. The idealist will maintain that in some salient way the active always resembles the mind. By contrast, the materialist will assert that creative force is native to the world continuous with our bodies.

If we take this view, Berkeley comes close to being a model idealist. For him, activity is confined to the operation of minds, and he is explicit in maintaining that ideas, of which he thinks the world of physical objects is composed, are altogether inert. Since they are inactive, they can neither bring themselves into nor keep themselves in being: they live out their existence in total dependence on a self.

This perspective may also shed some light on why Kant, quite appropriately, is viewed as an idealist. For he, too, locates all activity in the mind. Reason, for him, is a faculty of spontaneity, and there is no other creative agency whose existence or nature we can know. But someone might urge that this is not strictly so. For our spontaneity is balanced by our passive nature, and if there is something for this receptivity to receive, there must surely be action beyond the sphere of mind.

This objection is quite without foundation. First of all, Kant is explicit that we can *know* nothing of active or passive beyond the range of sense and understanding. And what activity we can *impute* to the supersensible, viz., the causality of freedom, assimilates that world far more closely to mind than to thoughtless motion.

Second, though it is clear that the receptivity of the senses is indeed the counterpart of the spontaneity of our understanding, there is nothing intrinsically passive about sense-openness. The senses *work*, for Kant, no less than does the understanding: in intuition the sensuous manifold is taken up and synthesized in a variety of ways. One might be tempted to think of sense as part of our animal nature—as its representative, perhaps, in the sphere of knowing. This view is not incorrect, but it needs interpretation. We must not suppose that human nature is a genuine compound of independent or separable elements. On the contrary, it is much nearer the truth to view it as an inseparable active unity.

In this light, sense and understanding are but diverse activities or diverse manners of operation of our single nature. Our receptivity, then, is not a genuinely passive part in our system, a hole through which impressions of the world-out-there may enter. It is simply our unitary active constitution in one of its operative modes. This, in turn, means that the purely passive manifold of sense recedes to an infinite distance on the horizon. In cutting through synthesis after synthesis, we approach it asymptotically: though a transcendental condition of constituting the world, it is a limit we never reach.

I think this is a reasonably accurate picture of Kant. This, at any rate, was the way Fichte perceived him. Moreover, since Fichte's desire, at least through the early versions of the *Wissenschaftslehre*, was to provide a development and elucidation of the critical philosophy, this conception of Kant sets the task and defines the problem for his thought.

On the level of experience, we can draw a clear enough distinction between the active and the passive. A transcendental analysis may reveal a variety of activities in perception. But in lived perceptual experience we *feel* passive and the world appears to impose itself on us. If we started with the independent existence of the physical world, an explanation of passivity in the face of it would be ready at hand. But Kant and Fichte agree that such a starting point is, for other reasons, altogether bankrupt. There is, admittedly, a residue in Kant of the conceptual scheme appropriate to viewing man and world as independent interacting agents. Some commentators have taken this vestige of earlier views and used it as evidence for ascribing to him a sort of correspondence theory in which representations match features of beings or beings in the noumenal world.

I think this interpretation is not faithful to the philosophical intent of Kant. At any rate, Fichte saw the model of man operating in an independent physical world as fundamentally alien to Kant. And the purely passive manifold of sense also can provide no explanation of our passivity; without an active, independent world as its ground, it is itself in need of explanation. The only conceivable source of the self's passivity, therefore, is the self itself. This conviction is bolstered by the consideration that since reason is the only active power, it must be the source even of its opposite. The current line of reasoning brings Fichte face to face with the issue that generates the entire *Wissenschaftslehre*. Put in a way that belies its difficulty, the problem is how the active can ground or even relate to passivity.

Fichte puts the problem he must resolve in a variety of ways. But in each form, it comes back to the same abstract and ageless task of reconciling the active and the passive. The perception of this single task structures all of the *Wissenschaftslehre* of 1794. Much, if not all, of that work is a result of developing Fichte's own version of the dialectic of the active and the passive.

The problem is defined in Part I of this first major version of the *Wissenschaftslehre*, entitled "Fundamental Principles of the Entire Science of Knowledge." Fichte's starting point is the postulating—in his terms "positing"—of an unconditioned, purely active self. We must not think of this self as the self of an individual; it is, instead, an undifferentiated pure act of the sort reason in its primordial form might perform. But it is worth remarking that at this stage reason as a faculty and self-positing as its act are indistinguishable. The absolute self has no predicates; all differentiation is a later product. As the poet said not many years after Fichte had thought it, "In the beginning was the act."

The character of this primordial act is such that it is "at once the agent and the product of action; the active, and what the activity brings about; action and deed."[1] It is also a self and as such a subject. But, Fichte argues, "What does not exist for itself is not a self,"[2] and for there to be such self-consciousness, there must first be consciousness of objects, and hence objects. The absolute self cannot be itself without also being its other.

The inner logic of its being thus requires the active to posit—and that means to generate—the passive. This primordial not-self, counterposited to the absolute self, functions as pure pas-

1. J. G. Fichte, *The Science of Knowledge*, ed. and trans. Peter Heath and John Lachs (Cambridge: Cambridge University Press, 1982), 97.
2. *Ibid.*, 98.

sivity, nonbeing, or negation.[3] Fichte's problem now looms up before us with sudden and alarming clarity. How can the active, while remaining active, generate the passive? And once the active has posited the passive, as it must, so to speak, in its own bosom, how can it remain active? Self and not-self, the active and the passive are opposed to each other; unless their primordial conflict is mediated, they will destroy each other without residue.

The principle Fichte proposes for mediating the struggle of passive and active is that of divisibility. Once the primordial self is opposed by the primordial not-self, it must surrender its infinity. The infinitely active and the indefinitely passive lose their infinity and indefiniteness. Self and not-self share the realm of being: they limit each other and in that process create finitude.

The synthesis through divisibility is the first and thus the generative one in the dialectic of the active and the passive. It is generative of the rest of Fichte's system, with all its subsidiary syntheses, because it is only partially successful in resolving the conflict of self and not-self. By partial success, I mean that it advances us in the direction of understanding how the active and the passive may coexist and how they are in fact related. But we are not advanced far enough. For this synthesis, no less than each succeeding one, creates at once a new contradiction. It happens in the following way. The mutual limitation of self and not-self, when we spell it out, implies that "the not-self (actively) determines the self."[4] This immediately suggests that the active self is passive when confronted by the activity of the passive. But there is a clear, and double, contradiction in thinking of the active as passive and of the passive as engaged in act. These two contradictions must next be reconciled and then the ones that arise out of the succeeding synthesis.

This process must go on until the last contradiction is resolved. Before long it turns out, of course, that all the contradictions cannot be reconciled. But by then, with consummate dialectical skill Fichte has spun intuition, imagination, the Kantian catego-

3. *Ibid.*, 108.
4. *Ibid.*, 123.

ries, and much else besides out of the original conflict of the active and the passive.

I shall not follow the dialectic through its every tortured phase. Instead, it may be more interesting to ask why the theoretical enterprise of reconciling the active and the passive fails and how, in the end, Fichte proposes to resolve his basic problem.

The theoretical enterprise must fail, for Fichte, simply because it is theoretical. For reason in its theoretical employment permits, in fact requires, determination from outside itself. Knowledge, therefore, demands an inverted world in which the passive (not-self) is active and the active (self) is passive. There can be no ultimate resolution of the conflict between self and not-self here, because the entire enterprise presupposes a contradiction, an abomination that in the end simply cannot be.

The resolution can come only in the practical sphere, a sphere where self-determining reason propels us not to know but to do. And here, amazingly, the dialectic of the active and the passive turns into a moral fable. In moral action, the self determines the not-self. The balance of the world is restored as the active regains its activity and the passive shrinks in its presence. The absolute decree of reason is that "since there is no way of reconciling the not-self with the self, *let there be* no not-self at all!"[5]

The decree imposes a moral task on us, and active and passive are reconciled in the end through the striving this demand or task engenders. The demand is simply to destroy the passive, to bring all objects under the sway of self. Since the objective world is a necessary condition of moral action and thus of the fulfillment of the self, the task can never be completed. What we can and ought to do is to push back the limits of natural necessity and to substitute for it the law of freedom. This we must do without an end. Our fulfillment is in the striving, for we move in the right direction: this way the active gets ever more active, and the passive tends to disappear. If we could complete the endless process, the self would be an actual infinite while the not-self would be infinitely passive and as such would simply cease to be.

The insight that comes of this striking dialectic is that what we

5. *Ibid.*, 137.

have in Fichte is not a struggle of two independent forces. There is only one agent in this drama of cosmic self-realization, and that is the self. The passive is never a real force that faces the active. It is simply the active facing itself, the self temporarily alienated or wearing a foreign mask, to facilitate a later union. The ultimate truth is that there is nothing but the self-determining self, but its self-determination is mediated through the world. The active needs its own passivity or else it would have naught to overcome.

The categories I have dealt with are pre-Socratic. But their dialectic is well known to many who may never have heard of Fichte. For the general pattern of the dialectic of the self-actualizing active is present in Christian theology no less than in Spinoza. We find it in Hegel, of course, and also—with a new and clever social twist—in Marx. It reappears in surprising contexts and in thinkers where one would least expect to find it. Seeing this remarkable repetition, one might pessimistically conclude that there is no progress in philosophy. Alternatively, we may come to think that no pattern recurs this repeatedly by accident. It is just possible that without anyone's fully knowing it the history of philosophy has managed to expose a basic pattern of deep human thought.

CHAPTER 14

The Omnicolored Sky: Baylis on Perception

C HARLES A. BAYLIS'S published work contains the outlines of a theory of perception. He never developed the
view in the detail it deserves and needs for a full defense.
His students report that his lectures contained elaborations of the
theory beyond anything he committed to print. Unfortunately,
however, I have no reliable access to those lectures. I must base
my reflections on what he has published.

What is available by Baylis on perception shares the crispness,
clarity, and charm of his other published work. In these essays, as
elsewhere, he shows himself as an honest, serious, and level-
headed thinker. He has a respect for the facts of experience
rivaling that of the most devoted phenomenologist. He is keenly
aware of the social or cooperative nature of philosophy: his own
ideas are developed with constant reference to what others have
thought, and he is glad to rely on whatever advances Price,
Broad, Lewis, or Chisholm may have made.

There are at least two reasons why his theory of perception was
never systematically developed. The first is this very reliance on
the work of others. He obviously feels that many important topics
have been discussed well enough by others; there is no need for
him to duplicate their work. The second is that much of his
writing in this area has polemical objectives. He launches repeated attacks on epistemological dualism, especially as it is found in
Lovejoy's work. His longest article in the field is a critical study of
Chisholm's *Perceiving*.[1] Another long and interesting piece is

---

[1]. C. A. Baylis, "Professor Chisholm on Perceiving," *The Journal of Philosophy* 56
(1959): 773–91.

largely reportive.[2] Even in his most recent paper on the subject, which bears the promising title "Foundations for a Presentative Theory of Perception and Sensation,"[3] he cannot resist the temptation to devote a few pages to attacking Lovejoy.

In terminology that undergoes some changes from article to article, Baylis maintains as his main thesis that for the most part we perceive physical objects "correctly and directly."[4] That physical objects exist independently of perceptions and perceivers and that veridical perception of them is possible are minimal tenets of realism. I accept them in philosophy as I accept them in daily life. To do otherwise would make philosophy contrived or an irrelevant intellectual exercise. This will immediately identify my disagreements with Baylis as a family quarrel. Both of us believe in the independent existence of the physical world, and both of us look to science for more information about the process that underlies perception. But family squabbles are notoriously vehement, even though it is often difficult to tell what precisely separates the parties.

How very difficult it is to identify the difference between Baylis and the critical realists he so vigorously attacks is best seen by examining what he calls the "basic theses" of his "epistemological monism."[5] Baylis notes nine such theses. The first three are simply an expanded statement of realism; the critical realist embraces them as readily as the "epistemological monist." They are:

(1) There is a real world of objects and events which exists independently of our knowledge of them.

(2) We can and often do perceive such objects and events.

---

[2] C. A. Baylis, "The Given and Perceptual Knowledge," in *Philosophic Thought in France and the United States*, ed. Marvin Farber (Buffalo: University of Buffalo Publications in Philosophy, 1950). Hereafter referred to as "Given."

[3] *Proceedings of the Aristotelian Society*, N.S. 66 (1965–66): 41–54. Hereafter referred to as "Foundations."

[4] *Ibid.*, 41.

[5] C. A. Baylis, "A Criticism of Lovejoy's Case for Epistemological Dualism," *Philosophy and Phenomenological Research* 23 (1962–63): 536. Hereafter referred to as "Criticism."

> (3) In the vast majority of cases we perceive them
> veridically, although of course this does not mean
> that we perceive everything about any of them.[6]

The next proposition Baylis wishes to affirm is completely
innocuous. To say that

> (4) Where we misperceive we can learn of our errors
> and their sources from scientists who study per-
> ception by attending to objects and events and
> people's reports about their experiences of such
> objects and events.[7]

is not to assert anything controversial. Even a man of Berkeley's
persuasion could subscribe to this view. And a proposition that is
inadequate to distinguish between idealists and realists can surely not be what differentiates one realist from another.

> (5) Sense-data can be observed when we are sensibly
> stimulated, but need not be and usually are not.
> They are of most use for artists, beauty-lovers, and
> psychologists and of very little use for perceptual
> knowledge.

> (6) Sense-data are usually coincident with the surfaces
> of objects.[8]

Here Baylis's position appears commonsensical. He thinks that
for the most part when we believe that we perceive a physical
object, we do in fact perceive one. In such cases we typically do
not observe sense-data, sensible qualities,[9] or *qualia*.[10] Such sensible qualities are, however, probably always involved in our
perception, and we tend to be "sensibly aware"[11] of them when
they are striking or unusual. Thus on seeing the victim of an
automobile accident, we may note the pallor of his face. Or if we

---

[6] *Ibid.*, 536.
[7] *Ibid.*, 537.
[8] *Ibid.*
[9] "Foundations," 47.
[10] "Given," 451.
[11] "Foundations," 47.

could touch Cleopatra's hand, we might well note with surprise that it is broken out.

Now these seem to me to be altogether harmless distinctions. There is no reason why a critical realist could not embrace them. One could, of course, say a number of things about sense-data, even in the sense in which Baylis uses the term, which would help to distinguish one sort of realist from another. But Baylis emphatically steers clear of any such statements. He says little about the precise relation of sensible qualities to physical objects and nothing of the role *qualia* play in perception or the recognition of objects. He does not discuss the ontological status of sense-data and the apparent particulars of immediate experience that he calls "sensa."[12] And he simply sidesteps the problem of the relation of such sensa to full-bodied physical objects.

Even the claim of (6) is too weak to be of value here. The "coincidence" of a sense-datum with the surface of a physical object leaves it possible for datum and surface to be numerically distinct. The slipcover designed to look exactly like the seat it hides is coincident without being identical with it. The epistemological monist must insist on the identity, and it is puzzling, to say the least, why Baylis does not.

The next two propositions are also perfectly acceptable to critical realists. (7) is a natural corollary of a realist and causal theory of perception, while (8) follows from (1) and (2).

> (7) Images, on the other hand, are bits of mental content which have been internally, not externally, aroused. They are the stuff of hallucinations.

> (8) The objects that one person perceives are often perceived and are almost always perceivable by others. They are public constituents of our common world.[13]

This leaves us with (9) as the only proposition to distinguish Baylis's view from the realism he criticizes.

---

[12] "Given," 451.
[13] "Criticism," 537.

(9) Perception is usually *direct*, not in the sense of having no necessary means but in the sense of not involving conscious inference.[14]

Baylis evidently considers the idea of the directness of perception very important. He returns to it again and again, and in each case he makes clear that by "direct" he means "without conscious inference."[15] And if this is what it means to perceive directly, Baylis is entirely right. Of course, there is no psychological sequence of receiving data, organizing them, and then consciously inferring the existence of external objects. The philosopher who held this view of simple perception, if indeed anyone ever held it, should no more be debated than the man who believes that a heap of cinder blocks is an amorous princess. He should be told to go look again and not to return until he learns to rule his fancy.

Why Baylis should suppose that critical realists are committed to belief in a *conscious inference* from datum to object I simply do not know. He is aware that the dualists he wishes to attack insist on the numerical (though not on the qualitative) diversity of what is immediately present in consciousness and the physical object we perceive. The datum, therefore, is in some way intermediary in perception: it is only by means of it, by using it somehow, that we can perceive the independently existing material world. Perhaps Baylis thinks that the necessary mediation can take only the form of inference. But there is little reason to suppose that data are used as premises, and none at all that that is the only way they can be used. There is no conscious inference even in the case of such simple sign-relations as my thinking that it will rain on seeing gray-black clouds. And in reading, we surely make no inferences, conscious or unconscious, from printed shapes to meanings. We deal there with a noninferential mediation, the sort that is typical of symbols. The same or almost the same is true of situations in which a casual gesture signifies rejection or a Rorschach blot is seen as an obscene scene.

I do not deny that if we were asked for a justification of what we think or see or understand in the above cases, we would attempt

14 *Ibid.*
15 "Foundations," 42, 47.

to infer the desired conclusions from some reasonably acceptable premises. But it would be a mistake to confuse the structure of justification with the processes of consciousness. I also admit that the critical realist's idea of the way the sensibly given stands for external objects needs to be developed in detail. Along with every other known philosophical theory, it suffers from difficulties and has to meet a variety of objections. But my present task is not that of elaborating and defending this view. I simply wish to establish that critical realism does not commit one to maintaining that there is a conscious inference from datum to physical object. It is far more plausible, in fact, to construe the relation of what is immediately present to what is perceived on the analogy or as a type of symbolic designation. At least one part of the reason for this is that viewing the datum as symbol does not go blatantly against the facts of experience. Viewing it as premise for inference in simple cases of perception clearly does. Baylis seems not to realize that no critical realist need be committed to the thesis that conscious inferences are inextricably involved in perception. As a result, he fails to consider alternative, and more plausible, critical realist accounts of the relation of datum to physical object. Even more distressingly, as I trust my argument so far has shown, he simply does not succeed in distinguishing his own brand of realism from the dualistic one.

This appears to me particularly surprising, since the distinction is readily at hand. Whatever else critical realists maintain, they insist on the numerical diversity of datum and physical object. Direct realists deny this, either because they think there is no special (for instance, private) given element in perception or because they feel confident that the given is actually a constituent of the physical object. Critical realists must explain how the datum can yield knowledge of the object. Direct realists face the opposite problem of how we can ever err if our contact with the object is immediate.

The initial tendency of the critical realist is to say that the datum and the physical object simply *cannot* be identical. There is a powerful spatial image behind this conviction. The object, we think, is *out there*. It sends reports of itself into my head, where the process or act of perception, or at least the processes necessary for perception, occurs. What is present in the brain can surely not be numerically one with what is at a distance from it and was its partial cause. This captivating picture is reinforced by what we know of the physical and physiological conditions of perception. When we reflect on these, we realize that the separation of the immediately presented from the presumably unpresented but perceived object is temporal as well as spatial. In the case of distant stars, the temporal lag may be so great that by the time their light reaches us, they no longer exist.

But neither this image nor these reflections suffice to show that direct realism is an absurd or blatantly false view. Baylis is entirely correct in arguing against Lovejoy that we must distinguish the processes of perception from its objects.[16] And if this distinction is made, Baylis can readily accept all the mediating organs and processes scientists will ever find, without having to yield the claim of direct cognitive contact. For, he argues, the spatiotemporal separation is between the act or process of perceiving and the object perceived.[17] The processes of perception are physical and mediated. At about the time of the last event of the physiological portion of these processes, an epistemic relation arises between the perceiver and the object that stimulated him. Even though the physical process is mediated, there is no requirement that the cognitive relation it makes possible shall share this property. What makes the critical realist position appear plausible here is the supposition that in addition to processes there are also some data or objects in the brain. That, however, is just a way of assuming what was to be proved, viz., the critical realist view of the duality of data and what they reveal.

This argument successfully shows that Baylis's view is entirely possible. But is it at all plausible? The first remark to make is that Baylis deftly sidesteps the difficult issue of accounting for perceptual error. He does this by simply not distinguishing between the question of what causes perceptual error and the analysis of what such error consists in. There is little doubt that misperception occurs as a result of something going wrong in the process or medium or organs involved.[18] But to say that fire is caused by

16 "Criticism," 530.
17 *Ibid.*, 531.
18 *Ibid.*, 534.

striking matches is not to give an account of what it is. Similarly, to identify the sources of perceptual error is not to explain its nature.

Actually, if Baylis had undertaken the task of dealing with the problem of error in earnest, he would have found it to be even more difficult than the previous comment suggests. He would have had to explain not only what error is but also how it is possible if his view is correct. Let us accept, for a moment, the claim that in perception we stand in direct cognitive relation to the surfaces of physical objects. Viewed internally, viz., from the standpoint of the experience itself, perceptions and misperceptions are notoriously indistinguishable. Among other similarities, each has a qualified thing, event, or fact as its object. How could Baylis draw the line between veridical perceptions, misperceptions, and hallucinations?

He appears to have four alternatives. (1) He could maintain that each putative case of perception is veridical. But this is clearly unacceptable and would signal the bankruptcy of his view. (2) He could modify this claim and hold that although each putative case of perception is veridical as and when undergone, we judge some to be erroneous in the light of other, and for the most part later, experiences. But this blurs the important distinction between the erroneousness of perceptions and the way this is determined. In addition, it is seriously at odds with Baylis's realistic idea that there are "hard," determinate, mind-independent facts.[19] If some of these at least can be perceived, they can also be misperceived, and that independently of what we judge of the matter later. (3) He could admit the distinction between perception and misperception and characterize the latter as consisting of (*a*) direct perceptual contact with the object and (*b*) perceptual acceptance of the object as exemplifying qualities or relations it does not possess. But this does not account for hallucinations. In addition, since the percipient is immediately acquainted with the quality that by (*b*) does not characterize the object, Baylis must concede a duality of datum and the qualities of the object in at least some cases. This occasional failure of identity, combined with the internal indistinguishability of perceptions and misperceptions, can

[19] C. A. Baylis, "Facts, Propositions, Exemplification and Truth," *Mind* N.S. 57 (1948): 459ff.

now be used by the critical realist to cast doubt on the numerical identity of experienced and embodied characters in any case. And if the general duality of presented and embodied characters is admitted, the thesis of direct contact with the object becomes untenable. (4) He could maintain that in veridical perception we are in direct cognitive contact with the object, but in misperceptions and hallucinations we are not. But this is an even easier target for the critical realist than (3). For here in all but veridical cases we have an admitted duality of datum and object. Given the internal indistinguishability of the cases, it is then extremely difficult to make selective identity plausible.

Baylis maintains that when there is nothing "odd"[20] in the physico-physiological process of perception, about the time of the last event of this process a cognitive relationship emerges. This relation is a direct and probably unique one between the percipient and the physical object that initiated the process. The characteristic claim of presentative realism is that the object in perceptual consciousness *is* the physical object: there is no immanent object of awareness by means of which the transcendent object is cognized. This simple view seems at first blush very attractive. But it has some strange consequences.

Suppose we perceive a distant star that, in the time it took for its light to reach our eyes, has ceased to exist. If what is present to consciousness is the star itself, then the star still exists. Again, if the star is identical with what is present to us and it is no more, we can have nothing present to consciousness. To say that we perceive the star as it *was*[21] seems little more than a verbal gloss. If what is present now is literally identical with the surface of the star, that heavenly body cannot be nonexistent. And, conversely, if the star is nonexistent, we cannot be in contact with its surface. This result can be generalized to apply to all cases of perception. Since the perceptual process invariably takes time, what we perceive on Baylis's view is always the object "as and where it . . . was"[22] at the time of the initiation of the process. In what sense can the currently observed state of an object be identical with a

[20] "Criticism," 534.
[21] *Ibid.*, 531.
[22] *Ibid.*

hitherto unobserved past state of it? There can, of course, be qualitative identity: the two can exhibit identical qualities and relations. But this is not the sort of identity Baylis seeks. And to get anything stronger, we would have to treat each surface as a quasi-substance that endures, retaining its identity through change and time.

There may, however, be another line Baylis can take at this point. He could redefine the boundaries of the object in such a way that a large number of diverse sensa could all be legitimately considered as constituents of it. Some of these constituents could well linger on long after the nuclear members of the collection that is the thing have ceased to exist.[23] If he held some such view, Baylis could maintain that what we perceive is very frequently or almost always the physical thing itself. For then the physical object would, in effect, consist only or largely of such perceived or perceptible sensa.

Such an account of the architecture of the thing is not easily compatible with commonsense realism. Moreover, Baylis neither considers nor adopts this view. But he does discuss Price's ideas, which make in this direction, in a complimentary fashion.[24] And he himself comes close to such a wide, if not loose, definition of the constituents of physical objects in what he says about their color *qualia*. It is to this issue that I now turn.

At first sight, Baylis's view of the color of objects is a fascinating mix of the charmingly simple and the infuriating. Any object, he says, "has all the colours it is . . . reported to have."[25] Thus, it seems, the sky is truly blue if it is perceived as manifesting that color. But it is also gray, yellow, purple, and middle brown if it is honestly reported to have those colors. Baylis even goes a step further. Physical objects have not only the colors they are actually observed as having. They are characterized by every one of the color qualities they *could* be seen to display if only lighting conditions and perceivers with the requisite (or requisitely strange)

---

[23] I use "nuclear members" in the sense Price gives the phrase. See H. H. Price, *Perception* (London: Methuen, 1954), 222.

[24] "Given," 454ff.

[25] "Foundations," 53.

perceptual faculties were at hand.[26] And supposedly, they are characterized by these vast numbers of colors simultaneously.

It is a generally accepted and hence infrequently uttered claim among painters, philosophers, and interior decorators, at least, that two colors cannot suffuse the same surface at the same time. Different observers may, of course, see the sky or a yard of cloth as of different colors, as may the same observer at different times. But this is not what Baylis has in mind. He seems to think that the sky *is in fact* characterized by all those colors, though it takes a different set of lighting conditions and a special sort of eyes to detect each. Surely, the principle of the incompatibility of colors could not have escaped as acute a logician as Baylis. One's first inclination, therefore, is to interpret this view as amounting to a bold challenge of that principle.

If this should propel one to examine the literature, one will soon find that very few reasons have ever been offered, and perhaps none should be accepted, for the supposition that two determinates of the same determinable cannot characterize a given item. For that matter, I cannot recall any reason, other than the general nominalist conviction that determinables should be run back to their determinates, that has ever been offered against the mad metaphysical possibility that determinables may be embodied without the concurrent embodiment of any of their determinates. One could spend interesting hours speculating on these matters, but it seems to me that in the current context this would be pointless. The reason is twofold. First of all, to embrace such a counterintuitive thesis as the compatibility of determinates is sheer bravado. A view of perception that implies or requires it is so much the worse off. Even if it could be shown that no contradiction is involved, the implausibility of the compatibility thesis is so great that it must carry over to the view that implies it. Second, it is not at all clear what Baylis's claim of omnicolored objects actually amounts to. There is, I want to argue, good reason to doubt (1) that his position commits him to omnicolored objects in the onerous sense, (2) that he has adequate reason for saying that objects are omnicolored in that sense, and (3) that when he says

26 "Criticism," 534.

that objects are omnicolored, he does so in full and clear consciousness of the alternatives and consequences.

Let me put my cards directly on the table. It seems to me that Baylis speaks of color in three different and inadequately distinguished ways. He begins by talking of color as a sensory property or power.[27] As such, any object has exactly as many "colors" as there are different color experiences it can evoke. There is nothing mysterious about this, nor anything objectionable. If the colors of things are merely the powers they have to cause specific sorts of sensations, each object can be, in fact probably is, omnicolored without incompatibility.

Now when "colors" in the sense of dispositions or sensory properties are brought in the proper conjunction with beings endowed with the requisite sense organs, they give rise to experienced colors. In the current sense, "colors" are sensible qualities of which we are conscious and which usually appear to characterize physical objects. On this view, color is relational. Though from the standpoint of direct experience colors are simple qualities, their apparent inherence in objects is the result of a relation. No object can, then, be said to be of any color in and of itself. It will have the color C on condition that it has the sensory property x, that the intervening medium is in state y, and that a percipient with sense organs of type z is present. A change in any of these conditions will involve a change in color or a change from perceiving an object as colored to perceiving nothing at all. Once again, objects can be—and probably are—omnicolored in this sense without any incompatibility.

What puzzles me is the move Baylis makes at this point. He notes that "different people or the same people in different circumstances report"[28] that a given object has many different colors. "Why not say," he boldly asks, "that its surface has all . . . [of these] color qualities . . . . "[29] This seems to be a perfectly acceptable way of speaking, so long as we remember that the object has these color qualities relationally. But here Baylis takes, or appears

---

[27] "Foundations," 48.
[28] "Criticism," 534.
[29] *Ibid.*

to take, a giant step. He continues the sentence I just noted as follows: " . . . its surface has all . . . [of these] color qualities, though for these to be seen requires special combinations of a light ray of a certain sort with a perceiver of a certain sort."

Here it no longer seems that the colors of objects are relational. Colors seem to inhere in objects as primaries, quite independently of whether there is anyone there to perceive them. Special lighting conditions and special sorts of eyes give us access to these objectively inherent colors. When red light is flashed on a go-go dancer's body, it reveals to us a color that has been there all along, instead of being one of the conditions without which the color would not exist.

This position seems to me excessively improbable. That objects are omnicolored in this sense does not follow from the fact that they are omnicolored in the other two senses I have distinguished. And such a view is, of course, not readily harmonized with common sense or the findings of science. Baylis could, here again, maintain that the object is but a large collection of sensa; this would leave ample room for every color quality to be a constituent of it. But as I suggested earlier, this view itself is difficult to reconcile with Baylis's commonsense realism.

Does Baylis really mean to hold the idea that things in the world are objectively omnicolored? The passages I quoted, from one of the two articles where he discusses the matter, suggest that he does. Yet there is room for doubt. Consider these statements from the other of the two papers.

> Suppose the lighting conditions, X, remain constant throughout. Why not assume that the object has the power or capacity or dispositional property under these conditions to cause all those with a-type eyes to see colour 1? Similarly, it has the power to cause all those with b-type eyes to see colour 2. Again it has the power or capacity to cause all those with c-type eyes to see colour 3. Why not assume that the object has *in this sense*, at least, all these colours, since it has all these powers?[30]

30 "Foundations," 53. My italics.

Objects are indeed omnicolored "in this sense": they do indeed have the power to cause different color-perceptions in different perceivers. An even more pointed statement comes from a letter to the author.

> And there is no need to insist on just one real color per surface. Why not say that every surface has all the colors it can be seen to have under all possible combinations of the variable conditions required? A is red under conditions abd . . . , gray under conditions ayc, blue under conditions acx, etc. etc. *To say that it is that color under those conditions is to say that the specified color will be seen under those conditions.*[31]

If he thinks that to say that a given object is a certain color is to say no more than that under specifiable conditions that color will be seen to suffuse it, Baylis is clearly not committed to objectively inherent colors. Yet immediately following the passage from "Foundations for a Presentative Theory of Perception and Sensation" I quoted above, he says, "Different people simply have different powers to discern the different colors the object exhibits." Discerning the colors of objects is a very different matter from experiencing objects as characterized by colors that vary with the conditions of perception. Whether these apparent differences in what Baylis maintains are due simply to careless phrasing, I cannot decide.

Is Baylis's presentative realism defensible? A full defense of it would presuppose its full development. But Baylis's position is neither fully developed nor unambiguous. For this reason, one can only guess at how probable it could be made and how its strengths and weaknesses would compare with those of rival theories. The fact that he starts from a realistic premise inclines me to think that he is near the truth. But the difficulties inherent in the idea that we are in direct cognitive contact with the physical world make me suspect that he is not near enough.

---

[31] Letter to the author, dated April 11, 1966. My italics.

CHAPTER 15

Self-Identity Without a Self

THERE IS A sense in which the maxim *entia non sunt multiplicanda praeter necessitatem* has probably never been violated. No philosopher would think of contributing to the population explosion by the postulation of what he thinks are unnecessary or dispensable entities. Kant thought that there *had to be* twelve categories, a transcendental object, and a transcendental ego. Spinoza thought it necessary to maintain that there were an infinity of finite modes as well as of divine attributes; Santayana managed to dispense with God, but felt compelled to acknowledge a plenitude of impotent essences. It is unlikely that Occam's "razor" has ever been or will ever be violated because necessity is the philosopher's bedfellow, and perhaps his lawful wife. Philosophical controversy continues to rage mainly because, as in societies not given to polyandry each man has his private wife, so among philosophers each has a different notion of what is necessary.

Paul Weiss thinks that nothing less than a complete explanation of all there is will do for a philosophy. This desire to be all-encompassing defines the kind of multiplication of entities he believes to be necessary. For him, the method of philosophy is dialectical, and dialectic is the recognition and provision of that which would complete the given.[1] The technique is similar to what some psychologists have called "eduction of the correlate"; it is similar also to Kant's transcendental method of proof, which proceeds from our actual experience to the conditions under which alone such experience is possible.

The method of postulating faculties and entities that appear to

---

[1] Paul Weiss, *Modes of Being* (Carbondale: Southern Illinois University Press, 1958), 83.

be necessary to complete what we now have or have accepted is not without its difficulties. My paper will, I hope, constitute a case study of the dangers of this way of doing philosophy. Before embarking on the examination of a particular instance of dialectical postulation, however, I wish to make a comment about the dialectical method in general. The central and pervasive weakness of this philosophical procedure is that there are alternative ways of completing any given theory or structure. This is true even of deductive inference: there is no set of premises that can be "completed" in only one way, viz., from which only one conclusion follows. It is worth remarking that this weakness cannot be avoided even if we take the otherwise improbable view that what we do in philosophical reasoning is analogous to what we do in supplying the missing premises of enthymemes; there are always several sets of propositions any one of which would adequately complete such an incomplete argument.

An advocate of Weiss's dialectical method may try to avoid my conclusion in two ways. First, he may argue that even though there may be many ways to complete the given, there is clearly a *best* way. But there are as many "best" ways of performing a task as there are values in terms of which that task may be assessed. Which action or strategy is best as a means is a function of what ends we wish to obtain, and which of our theoretical aims—the mathematical precision or the intuitive plausibility of our theories, for example—would best conduce to success in uncovering the complexities of things is always an open question. Second, the advocate of the dialectical method may maintain that the given contains ample and unambiguous instructions for its proper completion. But if the instructions are so plain, we may legitimately ask why so many philosophers have missed them. Clearly, this claim is simply false: no fact or theory wears a dog tag. In themselves, facts, experiences, and theories do not even demand completion, much less do they prescribe the way it should be done. It is the inveterate habit of the human mind that prompts us to "complete" them: we do this by selecting one of the large number of systems of which they could be parts and asserting that that alone is their natural habitat.

My specific topic in this paper is the dialectical postulation of a changeless and enduring self. Such a self is clearly not a datum, but many philosophers have supposed that its existence is entailed by the presence or the character of the given. The self, in this view, is a unitary, unduplicable, and indestructible entity; it is the source of a man's potentialities and the locus of his moral life. The view seems to have survived Hume's attack and is, in one form or another, widely held today. Professor Weiss is perhaps the most distinguished exponent of the theory. I propose, therefore, to examine one by one the arguments that make, in his opinion, the dialectical postulation of a private and changeless self necessary. The arguments he presents for the existence of the self constitute a particularly clear instance of the dialectical method, and the self he feels compelled to postulate is a representative example of the sort of entity that forms, in the opinion of some metaphysicians, the central core of every human being. My attempt to show that the postulation of this entity is in fact not necessary and thus not warranted has, therefore, a threefold aim. First of all, I hope to exhibit the weakness of the dialectical method in at least one significant instance by making it obvious that some of the things philosophers think are necessary only appear to be so, and that under certain circumstances the "given" is less mysterious if left alone than it becomes when various entities are invented to complete it. Second, I hope to show the implausibility of the theory that there are substantial entities called "selves" by knocking out some of the main arguments that have been offered in its favor. Finally, I hope to throw some doubt on the adequacy of Weiss's metaphysics by exposing its weakness in a central sphere.

Weiss is not entirely unequivocal on the question of whether or not we are to regard a human being as the self exclusively, or as a combination of the self and its body and mind. In one place he speaks of man as possessing a self:[2] the same view is taken in *Nature and Man*, where we are told that the self does not exhaust man's nature—a man is a man only so far as he has a body.[3] Elsewhere in the same book, however, a man is said *to be* and not

[2] *Ibid.*, 49.
[3] Paul Weiss, *Nature and Man* (New York: Henry Holt and Co., 1947), 253.

to possess his self.[4] We can reconcile these views along the following lines. A man is neither a self as separate from body and mind nor body and mind as separate from self. The body is a necessary part of man. The self is also a necessary part of man. The man himself is the self as a locus of power and a source of diverse capacities;[5] he is the body-sensitizing self, the self as it is expressed in mind, in body, and in will. The implication of this for Weiss's doctrine of immortality as presented in *Modes of Being* is that no man is immortal though every self is.

What are the reasons that make, in Weiss's opinion, the postulation of the self necessary? As far as I can see, there are four main reasons, and Weiss states them explicitly in two of his books that deal with the question.[6] He maintains that without a self a man (1) could not be self-identical over a period of time, (2) could not be or be held responsible for his acts, (3) could not discipline himself, and finally (4) could not evaluate and criticize himself.

It will be noticed that the three latter points are primarily of ethical interest. I fail to see their force on the basis of any but a hypostatic, absolutistic ethics. If Weiss holds that ethical qualities are primaries belonging to the object quite independently of any subjective contribution on our part and that of all animals man alone knows good and evil and is capable of moral action and restraint, then he is, by rough analogy, an ethical naive realist, and the issue of whether or not we have to postulate an unchanging locus of guilt and of power as the core of man is thoroughly prejudiced. Apart from such ethical considerations, responsibility, self-discipline, and self-criticism do not demand the postulation of an underlying self. Let me begin with self-criticism and work back to a discussion of self-identity.

A machine can "evaluate" its performance as much as a man can. Weiss admits this in a brief remark on negative feedback,[7] but claims that feedback can evaluate only the degree of completeness of an activity, never whether the activity is good or bad.

[4] *Ibid.*, 241.
[5] *Ibid.*, 127–28.
[6] *Modes*, 48–50; *Nature*, 243.
[7] *Modes*, 50.

This contention is altogether too weak. There is no reason to suppose that a machine cannot be programmed to report the "goodness" or "badness" as much as any other feature of an activity—if we have communicable standards of the good and the bad. The alternative to such statable standards is some form of ethical intuitionism in which good and bad are construed as qualities whose presence only conscious minds can detect. Apart from the inherent weakness of such intuitionism, it would not be a viable alternative for Weiss, for it would leave human self-evaluation variable and arbitrary.

By a self-disciplined act, Weiss means one in which body or mind is taken as object and subjected to conditions of an ideal nature. Thus ideals, he claims, are not operative in any animal other than man. Since it has no ideals, the body cannot impose any on its behavior nor can it oppose its inclinations and tendencies. For this reason, the argument runs, we must postulate an entity that is concerned with the ideal, the abstract, and the future, and that is powerful enough to oppose and relegate to the background the concern of the body.

Once again the argument is weak, for a number of animals appear to exhibit just such self-disciplined behavior. Machines could readily be designed to duplicate most such feats. Unquestioning self-subordination to the good of the whole certainly involves an operative ideal and effective resistance of the concern of the body (for it may lead to the body's dissolution): this is the way ants act. Shall we then maintain that ants as well as men have immortal and unchangeable private "insides"? To object that the behavior of the ant in sacrificing its life in the defense of its community is prompted by instinct is a desperate measure. We can know about operative ideals in other human beings or in ants only by observing their behavior. If this is deemed an insufficient method and we insist on finding out what an animal senses or thinks when it acts in what appears to be a self-disciplined manner, the argument from self-discipline will justify the postulation of at most one self, the investigator's own. For we know as little about what other humans have in mind as we know about what ants have in their minds, if indeed they have minds.

In general, I might remark, it is not clear to me why self-discipline and self-evaluation should be considered nonbodily powers. On the contrary, the views that unless a body restrained itself (or was restrained by some physical force), it would never be restrained, and that unless a body evaluated its own activity, it would never be evaluated, seem to have a greater initial probability. This is a difficult issue requiring thorough discussion, but Weiss takes the former, *prima facie* less probable, alternative for granted from the start.

The question as to the precise conditions under which we may hold a person responsible for his or her acts or guilty is one I do not propose to discuss in detail. I shall make only two remarks here. The first is that the mere fact that people are held responsible or guilty is obviously inadequate as a reason for postulating an unchanging self as the locus of guilt or the responsible agent. Second, self-identity in some sense is clearly one of the necessary conditions of holding a man guilty. If this man were not now the same man that beat his father and mother a short hour ago, we could not consistently say that *he* is guilty. We have to know that the person who is under lock and key at police headquarters on charges of murder will be the same person tomorrow when he signs the statement and six months from now when the jury hears his case. Important as this admission is, it will not prejudice our account of self-identity. Whatever view of self-identity should prove satisfactory from a purely theoretical point of view will equally well serve our practical needs. Even though self-identity is a necessary condition of attributing guilt to a person or holding him or her responsible, this does not impose any special requirements on the results of our analysis of its nature and criteria.

Let me add that a person convicted of some crime (or a person found guilty by his own conscience) is often no longer the same as he who committed the crime. "He changed overnight," we say of him, and as subsequent events may show, possibly for the better. Despite this fact, however, we have no qualms about punishing him; for our purposes, we find enough continuity or similarity between the man as he was when he committed the crime and as he is now after having changed. We blame and punish, although we know the person is, strictly speaking, no longer the *same* person. It would be strange to say here, with Weiss, that we blame and punish because though "externally" changed, the man is "internally" the very same being he was before. It would be strange to say this because we blame not a man's self but his actions and impulses and desires; and we punish not a man's self but his body or his mind. Would it not be a strange iniquity if that which is no longer the same, and which therefore did not commit the crime, should have to suffer on behalf of that which has remained the same and has all along been the locus of the guilt? This is a paradoxical result, and it is made possible by Weiss's view that the self in itself is nonspatial and nonconscious. Since it is nonspatial, it cannot be reached for punishment; and since it is nonconscious, the punishment inflicted on its body is endured by its mind. There are two possible answers Weiss can make to this charge. First, he can deny that the self is nonconscious. Second, he can claim that since both mind and body belong to the self, it is the self that suffers in and through its body and its mind.

The first contention goes counter to some of Weiss's explicit statements. The self cannot be conscious: if it were, it would be changeable, and the self of a man sleeping would be different from the self of that man awake. But Weiss believes that the self is unchanging and that man preserves his self-identity even in sleep. It is a little more difficult to make precise the meaning of the second objection. At first sight it seems hardly more than a figure of speech to say that the self suffers in and through the body and the mind. Is this more than an alternative way of saying that both body and mind can be adversely affected, resulting in a consciousness of pain, and that since in addition to body and mind a man also has a self, that self is *in some way* involved in the suffering of the man? Apparently it is, as one of the prime functions of the self, for Weiss, is the sensitization of the body, and the mind has neither being nor power without the self. Thus while being nonspatial,[8] the self is said to be in every place where its body is alive.[9] Unless Weiss is ready to acknowledge this as a flat contradiction, he will have to maintain that the claim that the self is in

[8] *Nature,* 241.
[9] *Modes,* 51.

the body vitalizing it is to be understood figuratively rather than literally. But this is not an adequate explanation of how the self can be both in itself and in its manifestations, both nonspatial and in space, both unchanging and active. The problem is a crucial one, and the question at the core of it is that of the nature of *expression* that, according to Weiss, is the relation that obtains between the self and the five aspects of human personality, viz., body, mind, emotion, desire, and will. The discussion of self-identity, Weiss's most important reason for postulating a self, will lead to a consideration of this problem.

Weiss believes that we have to postulate a self that stands behind mind and body as the unitary source of a man's manifold capacities. The self is a necessary condition of the possibility of human self-identity. This claim may be interpreted in two ways. It may mean (1) that if we did not posit such a self, we could not *know* that humans are self-identical, or (2) that without such a self, humans could not *be* self-identical. (1) is divisible into two sub-cases: without an underlying self, I could not know (*a*) the self-identity of others and (*b*) my own self-identity.

(1) It is easily seen that we have neither need nor use for an unchanging self in our recognition of the self-identity of humans over a period of time. The reasons for this are numerous. First of all, it is proposed that we postulate the self in order to account for our belief that humans are self-identical and not, conversely, that we recognize the self-identity of humans on account of a direct perception of the self. Such a self cannot at all be perceived: it is an invisible, intangible, private "inside." I know the self-identity of others from what I see of them—from the enduring perceptual features of their bodies, from relevant character traits and typical modes of action. I know my own self-identity (if indeed I do—in amnesia I may not) possibly by introspection, at least partly by the enduring mass of bodily feeling that seems to be an inseparable adjunct of my waking life, and certainly with the help of memory. But none of these three puts me directly in touch with the self: the objects of introspection are ideas and operations of the mind, bodily feelings cannot help us establish direct contact with a self that stands behind the body, and memory will at best present a de-existentialized past self. The view that there is no con-

sciousness of objects without concurrent consciousness of self boasts an exceptionally long and illustrious history. However, if Weiss were to adopt this view and claim that such "self"-consciousness puts us in direct contact with the self, his notion of the self would have to undergo radical revision. Just precisely what kind of "self" it is of which we are conscious in "self"-consciousness is not immediately evident: it is at best an emaciated, contentless "self"—a Pure Ego that has few (if any) features in common with the enduring self that Weiss wishes to postulate. If this be granted, I need not go on to repeat arguments that have been brought against the claim that there is even such a Pure Ego involved in our "self"-consciousness.[10]

Further, it is important to note that we do not impute self-identity to people because of a *belief* we have that there is an enduring self hidden behind the facade of body and mind. If such a belief were necessary for knowing that human beings remain self-identical, either everybody would have the belief or some people would act as if they did not acknowledge the self-identity of their fellows. These alternatives are exhaustive, and both of them are false. We do believe that human beings remain identical over periods of time, but this is not the consequence of a temporally or logically prior belief that they have enduring and unchanging selves. The point may be pressed by insisting that we have an analogous belief in the self-identity through time of other animals. I no less believe that this blind man is the same blind man I saw yesterday than that his Seeing Eye dog is the same dog I saw with him on that occasion.

The question of the denotation of proper names that are names of human beings is a complex and difficult problem. Whom or what do we call, say, B. B. Brown? It seems to me there is no reason to suppose that we call Brown's self "Brown." On seeing him, we never say, "There goes the body that belongs to Brown," but rather, "There goes Brown." Of course, few will go so far as to deny that there is more to Brown than his body. His typical gestures, jokes, and idiosyncrasies are all a part of him, and so are

[10] A good discussion of the issue is to be found in C. D. Broad, *The Mind and its Place in Nature* (New York: Harcourt, Brace, 1951), 556–606.

his thoughts, feelings, and perceptions. Of course, I am not arguing that these are facts Weiss could not accommodate if we grant him the privilege of positing a self. What I am arguing is, rather, that these generally acknowledged facts afford no good ground for the initial postulation of a self of the kind in which he is interested.

(2) Since neither our *knowledge* of the self-identity of others nor our *knowledge* of our own self-identity affords adequate grounds for postulating a self, I shall assume that Weiss's view is that human beings could not *be* self-identical from birth to death if each had not a constant, enduring self that underlies his changing body and mind.

Now it is at least dubious that a person remains self-identical from birth to death. It is advisable to distinguish between myself as I appear to myself, the me-for-me, and myself as I appear to another, the me-for-him. There is not the slightest reason for believing that the me-for-me remains self-identical from birth to death. Not only do I experience profound and constant changes in myself, but during about 30 percent of my biological life, the me-for-me does not even exist. It passes out of existence each night when I fall asleep (self-consciousness ceases); its faithful restoration in the morning should never serve to blind us to this fact.

In considering the me-for-him, we are confronted with the opposite difficulty. Here self-identity is acknowledged for too long. We say of a person indifferently, "There he is, talking," or "There she is, sleeping," but also, "There he is, dead." A dead person is a person changed in many respects, but he is also "identically the same person" as the one who died. Was Napoleon on his deathbed identical with the man who had been beaten at Waterloo? In certain respects, at least, he was, or else the statement "Napoleon died" would make no sense at all. Of course, there are essential differences between Napoleon alive and Napoleon dead. Something is lost in death, though that special something is neither simply the me-for-me, for that is lost many times in life, nor the identity or continuity of the body as extended, informed material. The lost factor may be the capacity of Napoleon's body to act in characteristically Napoleon-like ways. It may be the vital functioning of the total body—something along the lines of what Aristotle meant by the *psyche*. It is useless to look for self-identity in the material, the cells and tissues making up the man. Metabolism effects a regular and in the long run complete exchange of the matter of the body. Cells die and are replaced. Identity is due to the action patterns of the body and not to the stuff out of which it is built. All new material must be organized in the form of the body before it can become a part of it. It is only in virtue of such sustained and unified action patterns that the body (and the person) remains a stable vortex in the universal flux.

This view seems, *prima facie*, to be plausible. However, Weiss explicitly rejects such a way of tackling the problem of self-identity.[11] An organizing form has no power of its own, but Weiss believes that the self we have to postulate must be one that is both concerned and capable of controlling the activity of body and of mind.

Concern, according to Weiss, is a way of reaching from the concrete present to the abstract future or, alternatively, an agency by which the future is focused on in the shape of some relevant possibility.[12] The concern of the self is for the good as relevant to all there is, viz., for the embodiment of the Absolute Good.[13] It seems to me (though Weiss does not develop this point in any detail) that his distinction between continuity and self-identity is based on the notion of concern. Continuity means endurance of form: a river remains a *river*, even though it may change from light to dark, from sweet to saline, from east running to west running. In the case of the self, in addition to identity of form there is also identity of content, and I take this content to be the concern of the self that is constant and of which the perpetual self-renewal of the self is a partial realization. Weiss does not specify how we are to decide whether or not we have such a sensitive concern for the good as pertinent to all beings. On the basis of everyday experience, the view is clearly counterintuitive. Hume

---

[11] *Modes*, 49–50.
[12] *Nature*, 53.
[13] *Ibid.*, 239.

believed that a concern for the good of all mankind was ingredient in human nature. To make such an optimistic view at all plausible, he had to deny that malice was operative as a spring of human action; he disregarded the fact that at least some people some of the time *would* much rather tread on another's gouty toes than on the hard flint and pavement. Weiss's view seems to be more extreme even than Hume's. It is extreme to the point of being heroic in holding that we have a concern for the good not of human beings alone but, potentially at least, of all beings what-ever. Surely, such a concern for the universal good on the part of humans is itself only postulated. It cannot, therefore, be expected to yield any compelling reasons for the postulation of the self. To put this argument in a less unsatisfactory way: our grounds for positing an underlying self would be less than adequate if they were to consist only or mainly of the supposed necessity to account for the possibility of a similarly postulated universal human benevolence. While the postulation of such benevolence is itself in need of justification, it cannot serve as the justification of further postulations.

Power and control. "The 'mind-body' problem is permanent and insoluble if the mind be viewed in isolation from a wider self," Weiss states and goes on to add:

> It is easy to create insoluble problems of this kind. . . . there is no problem of how a mind can be distinct from and yet cooperate with, influence, be influenced by and act independently of the body at different times— once it be recognized that one being owns them both and connects the content of the one to the other in these different ways.[14]

Weiss gives what he considers an analogous contrived problem, the "finger-mouth" problem that results if we choose to disregard the fact that the mouth and the finger in it do not exist *in abstracto* but as parts and in virtue of specific acts of a child.

This analogy appears to me to be entirely fallacious. It contrib-utes nothing to the solution of the mind-body problem to say that

[14] *Nature,* 220–21.

both body and mind are owned by a single being. An important part of the problem is how two ostensibly different kinds of energy may be interrelated. Bodily energy produces motions, mental "energy" produces sensations and emotions and ideas. No sensation, emotion, or idea is a motion. The only significance I can attach to an entity that is said to provide an instant solution to the mind-body problem is that it must be a center in which bodily and mental energy may undergo mutual transformation. Descartes thought the pineal gland was such a center: in it motion could be transformed into sensation and volition into motion. Weiss has a different solution: his transformer is the self possessing a type of energy all its own. This energy can, of course, be neither mental nor physical, for then the mind-body problem would reappear on another level; it must, in effect, be a *tertia energia*. Mind and body are thus no longer considered separate substances, but different manifestations of a single underlying substance. Unfortunately, Weiss is not altogether unambiguous as to whether he considers the self a substance or not—much less does he tell us what we should understand him to mean by "substance." If the self existed before the body, "it would be a substance separate from the body," he says in one place,[15] implying that the self is not a substance, or though a substance, is not separate from the body. The former alternative is an explicit contradiction of statements made elsewhere in the same book.[16] The latter suggests that body and self form a single substantial whole. But since no substantial whole is separable into its components, this interpretation would be in clear conflict with Weiss's doctrine of the immortality of the self.

The doctrine of immortality introduced in *Modes of Being* is in any case not easily reconciled with some of Weiss's earlier statements regarding the necessity of each self being connected to a body. If the self can exist after the body has been destroyed, there seems to be little need of the body except, perhaps, in connection with the initial generation of the self. A reconciliation may be attempted on the basis of a statement once made to me by Weiss

---

[15] *Modes*, 51.
[16] *Ibid.*, 23, 30, 146, 190, 337.

to the effect that after death the self engages, in some way, the community as its "outside." The suggestion is either that the self never remains without a body or else that it never remains without a body for long. Since this point is unfortunately not discussed by Weiss, I will not attempt to make up his mind for him and decide which alternative is to be preferred. Instead, let me remark that even this statement by Weiss is insufficient to show that there is *personal* immortality. For if the factor that individuates the self is the objective of its outside, all the selves that use the same community as their outside must be the same self: a plurality of selves upon separation from their respective bodies, or at the time when they begin to use the body of the community, collapse into singular, undifferentiated existence. And since for a self to lose its differentiated existence—its self-identity—is to lose itself, the ultimate implication of this line of thought is that not only personal but any significant form of immortality is impossible. The only thing that survives dissolution is some amorphous and impersonal "general self."

This leads me to a point boldly taken for granted by Weiss, which to my mind has none of the marks of self-evident truth. Why should we suppose that there is a one-to-one correlation between self and body, and self and mind? Weiss persists in speaking of *the* body of the self, implying that there could not be two bodies to a self or two selves to a body. But on the one hand, if we take his account of immortality seriously, we shall have to acknowledge at least one instance in which the self assumes a "body" that is many bodies—one that includes the bodies of a whole society of human beings. On the other hand, might we not be forced to admit that in cases of multiple personality a single body serves as the channel for making manifest the activity of several selves? And if the uniqueness of the self is a resultant of the primary body-directedness of its concern, there would seem to be striking evidence in favor of the view that in cases of alternating personality the activity of a single body is governed by two or three different selves. For there is good reason to believe that in a case such as that of M. Janet's Lucie,[17] her body's

---

[17] William James, *The Principles of Psychology* (New York: Dover, 1950), 1: 385.

objective changed concomitantly with her personality alterna-
tions. Sights and sounds that left her unaffected at one time
made, at other times, a deep impression on her. What was at one
point beneficial to her body became, when another personality
was to the fore, both painful and injurious.

Quite apart from the previous considerations, unless he believes this to be an inexplicable contingency, Weiss should have
provided some explanation of why *normally* the self is expressed
in one body and in one mind only. Also, he should have given us
an effective criterion for determining whether in any particular
case we are confronted with one self or with several selves.
Consider the case of a person with three legs. Clearly, we have
little reason to postulate a second self here. But what about a
person with two heads, the two sets of vocal cords originating
conflicting reports as to whose orders the body obeys? We would
indubitably agree that Siamese twins with common ownership
and possession of only one finger on one hand have separate
selves. But once again, what should we say about a case in which
"twins" share precisely one-half of each of their organs and one of
each pair of organs?

I have strayed from the main topic under discussion to consider
some related issues. I shall now return to an examination of
Weiss's notion of the relation between the self and its body and
mind. One of my earlier conclusions was that Weiss believes the
self is necessary in order that there be self-identity. The burden of
my argument is that this postulated self involves us in difficulties
whose profusion and magnitude suggest that while Weiss thinks
there could be no self-identity without it, it is more plausible to
say that there can be no consistent philosophy with it.

Weiss distinguishes three modes of action: (1) self-adjustment,
(2) expression, and (3) compulsion.[18] For an account of expression, which alone is of interest to us here, we have to go once
again to *Nature and Man*. There *expression* is described as an act by
which a being attempts to infect its outside with the object of its
concern. Again, expression is the mode in which a being is
manifest outwardly. The following statement a few pages further

---

[18] *Nature,* 58ff.

on is more revealing: "To express is to create and control in the light of the good."[19] "Expression is an art," Weiss tells us, "*requiring a concentration of energy*";[20] the expression of the self is in some way the externalization of the self. But *esse est operari* does not hold of a human being, as Weiss believes it holds of sticks and stones: no particular expression or set of expressions can exhaust the self. The self is a locus of energy. Some of that energy is manifested to us in the self's five modes of expression: in body, mind, emotion, desire, and will.

There seems, however, to be a fundamental difference between the expression of the self as the life of a body and its other four modes of expression. Emotion, desire, will, and mind have no being apart from or over against the self. They exist by virtue of and to the extent that they are generated by the self. The body, on the other hand, has an existence of its own that stands over against the existence of the self. The self does not create the body by a self-expressive act: it only vitalizes the body and attempts to master it. A body with objectives and tendencies of its own, a body that possesses the power to counteract the expression of the self's concern is a necessary condition of the effective expression of that concern.[21]

It would thus seem that the life of the individual is one of conflict between the objective of his self and the objective of his body. The body resists complete mastery by the self and in virtue of its resistance sometimes occasions a shift in the self's concern. What Weiss assumes all along is the free interchange of bodily and nonbodily energy: without this, it would be meaningless to speak of the subjugation of the body or of a conflict of objectives. I have already noted that, as Weiss conceives it, in the self in some unexplained way physical energy may be converted into mental energy, and mental energy may be converted into physical. In the nonbodily center that is the self, astonishing transformations of energy are effected. Energy is an essential feature of existence, and existence is one of Weiss's four modes of being. Energy is

---

[19] *Ibid.*, 64.
[20] *Ibid.* My italics.
[21] *Nature*, 159.

sheer existence, an expanding, restless force. As such, it is end-lessly divided into parts and constitutes a primordial exten-sionality. Weiss would probably argue that energy in this form is totally undifferentiated and can be made into physical, mental, or "selfy" energy depending on the nature of the being that appro-priates it or on its use.

One gets a sense of elusive unreality just by stating this view. The reason, I suspect, is not that it is readily seen to be untenable or untrue, but that one feels that one is left holding a bag of abstract words. The theory is vague and unspecific—in its cur-rent form, it is unintelligible. The first step toward giving it intelligible content would be to explain how we are to think of the transformations constantly occurring between the undifferenti-ated energy and the three types of differentiated energy. More specifically, it should be explained how "selfy" energy can be converted into physical (and mental) energy. Here Weiss is con-fronted with a dilemma. "Selfy" energy may be totally different in kind from physical energy. If so, self and body cannot interact, and the body cannot be an expression of the self. Alternatively, "selfy" and physical energy are not totally different in kind, making the self to act on the body. This makes "selfy" energy identical or continuous with physical energy. Weiss must reject total difference since it would controvert his claim that a person's acts are ultimately the acts of his or her self. He explicitly rejects the identity of "selfy" and physical energy by asserting that the former is both nonbodily and nonspatial. This leaves only con-tinuity. But if "selfy" and physical energy are in some sense continuous, they must be traceable in their transformations. Now if Weiss is willing to stake his claim regarding the existence of a substantial self on a possible future tracing of energy transforma-tions, well and good. However, I suspect that this would not be a particularly satisfactory course to take, since any self that may be discovered in this way would in all probability lack most of the features—and particularly the ethical features—that Weiss as-cribes to the self whose postulation he champions. If, on the other hand, we choose to deny that these energy transformations are traceable, the relation of the self to its body and to its mind will at best be mysterious. At present, in the production of a sensation by a brain event we have just such a type of suspected but mysterious energy transformation. The peculiarity of this alleged generative relation has prompted some honest but impatient inquirers to take the heroic course of denying the existence of consciousness. Our evidence for the existence of consciousness, though ultimately indirect, is nevertheless convincing because experientially based. There seems to be, and on the last alternative there is allowed to be, no experiential evidence for the existence of the self that is a locus of nonbodily power. And the postulation of an entity that leaves the world more mysterious than it originally was should be considered neither necessary nor desirable.